Quantum Capitalism

The Virtuous Science of Money, Power, and Prosperity

Stef Delarge

Quantum Capitalism

The Virtuous Science of
Money, Power, and Prosperity

By Stef Delarge
www.QuantumCapitalism.com

ISBN-10: 0615691854
ISBN-13: 978-0-615-69185-5

Design, Layout, and Typesetting
by Alexander Becker
www.alexanderbecker.net

Contents

Quantum Capitalism

The Virtuous Science of
Money, Power, and Prosperity

Stef Delarge

Dedicated to Humanity

Introduction

We are not equal and never were, and that's how nature intended things. Einstein was no more likely to slam dunk a basketball regardless of his knowledge of gravity than Wilt Chamberlain was to determine the trajectory of photons. Bill Gates is no more likely to hit the highest octaves in music as Mariah Carey is to develop an advanced universal language for computers. We are all endowed by our creator with unique gifts and talents that are designed for the benefit of humanity in the universal pursuit of happiness. And although we are clearly not all equal in abilities, we should each be equally free to pursue and create opportunities to develop and contribute value to as many people as possible and to be compensated commensurately with the perceived value of any contribution as determined by the free market.

Yet most people do not enjoy such liberty under contemporary conditions because of cultural indoctrination, the false, infectious construct of political correctness, and the nature of most governmental systems. Most such systems were designed to avert the meritocracy of opportunity and achievement in order to provide unmerited power and freedom for a bureaucratic or autocratic "elite" at the expense of the rest of humanity. In Europe and several other parts of the world these systems are directed by bureaucrats who start out by going from school to school and then straight to nanny state government, where they plan and promise the impossible—free stuff for everyone from cradle to grave, essentially rendering their citizenry dependent junkies. In the Middle East (with the exception of the Republic of Israel, where they don't even have the death penalty), the elite preserve their power and freedom at the expense of their citizenry through religious indoctrination, torture, and death, while much of the rest of the world does so through similar and secular brutal repression.

None of these systems *equitably* promotes and prioritizes for their citizenry the two things that socially distinguish and advance humanity from the rest of the animal kingdom—*intelligence* and *property*. At the most primal level, intelligence has allowed humanity to develop innovations for survival against the natural elements and other physically stronger animals. It has always been the few intelligent innovators whose contributions of great value improve life for the rest of humanity, and those contributions come not only from logical, left-brain activities but from right-brain creativity, as well. In the most truly advanced societies, intelligence effectively applied and incentivized, results in the innovation and technology which raise standards of living through goods and services and the property ownership thereof. Instituted systemically, intelligent innovation and the resultant productivity of goods and services foster both prosperity and evolution. However, even the most "advanced" bureaucratic, centrally planned welfare systems of human governance marginalize the intelligent innovators, because they indoctrinate their citizenry to believe that the arduous mental effort, risk, and sacrifice to innovate new products and services are of no more value than the mental effort required to move one's arms and legs in the perfunctory hourly labor in which most of us began our entry into the division of labor. In fact, even though the masses are the beneficiaries of the goods and services contributed by the intelligent innovators (automobiles, airplanes, cars, cell phones, computers, iPods, fashion, the arts, etc.) and the productivity they foster, most of these advanced societies are instead further indoctrinated to believe that they have been exploited by them, requiring "social justice" to redistribute their property. No matter what artful language they appropriate for indoctrination, there can be no justice in stealing the fruit of one's labor and giving it disproportionately to another who has not earned it. To the contrary, taking the yield of their toil, as well as the inventions of the intelligent innovators, is clearly social *in*justice, which promotes thievery instead of virtue.

Those who have attained power without virtue usually envy the intelligent innovators for the power they have *earned* from their contributions, and the fact that as a result of this earned power, they cannot be easily controlled as the rest of the masses. Therefore, global alliances of unmerited power characterized by lack of virtue perpetually form to control freedom and the unlimited power, merit, and prosperity of natural capitalism. And history has revealed an effective formula for which the elite bureaucratic and autocratic planners of the world have consistently employed and for which *truth* shall hold no quarter. In order to effectively violate fundamental notions of fairness and justice with minimal resistance in a civil society, the populace must be indoctrinated through the appropriation and perversion of language coupled with the designation of an enemy, internal or external, to deflect the true cause of exploitation and oppression. That enemy is usually the intelligent innovators who find no sympathy in the envy of the masses, notwithstanding that the intelligent innovators most often come from and bring the greatest benefits to them.

And this presents the fundamental schism of paramount importance from which the world's populations ascend, stagnate, or descend: The justice of truth and the way it is held among each society. Much of the world believes that truth is relative and is important only as an effective tool to be manipulated for conjuring perceptions to further an agenda. For them, the agenda is more important than the truth, as their ends justify any means. The remaining exceptional minority of the world knows truth to be the immutable constant of no agenda for which humanity aspires to enlightenment. Truth is that which is actual and factual, as absolute as the knowledge that the sun will rise in the east. It is always the few who bring truth to the world, but not without the resistance of those whose perceived self-interests conflict with that truth. The intelligent innovator and genius Galileo exemplified this, imprisoned for divesting the Church authority of its doctrine, which maintained that the earth was the center of our solar system. But because the eternal truth ultimately prevailed, we of course now know that the sun is the center of our solar system. Without this truth, we could not have projected an accurate course to the moon or sent the satellites into space that our material comforts rely upon. When a patient is sick, we must diagnose the truth of the cause of illness if we are to restore health. If we are to progress to an enduring broad prosperity, the truth must be ascertained. Instead, most societies allow the envy inspired by the intelligent innovators to color the truth so that the few unmerited power-seeking elite achieve their ends. They believe they can advance their self-interests at the expense of truth without consequences. They do not realize that insofar as it conflicts with truth, self-interest is as ephemeral as our bodies, while truth is as eternal as our souls. Neither the national socialists of Nazi Germany, the socialists of the Soviet Union, the current redistributive socialist nation-states of Europe, and America nor the theocracies of the Middle East could sustain a broad national prosperity at the expense of the intelligent innovators, no matter what falsehoods they propagated.

Notwithstanding the differences in the world's governmental methods to preserve elite rule at the expense of the citizenry, they all have one common cause to rally against, the one threat that could undermine their power to control the masses—the meritocracy, freedom, and equitable prosperity of natural capitalism. When you put aside all the propaganda, indoctrination, and the resultant political correctness and simply *look at the evidence,* nature reveals through the rare convergence of genius in several deceased British expatriates a meritocracy of unparalleled success based upon a constitution of natural law, the preservation of human liberties, checks and balances on governmental power, and a free economy operating in accord with the laws of physics for prosperity, all while testing virtue.

That system was America's, and began its entropic dismantling in 1913 when the majority passed the 16th Amendment and a progressive income tax in order to loot the minority in contravention of the prescient warnings of the Founding Fathers. In that same year, an elite central planning institution was created to control human labor and employment when the money supply it was dependent upon was placed in the hands of a few men of the newly created Federal Reserve [Act of 1913]. In the typical fashion of elite central planners, the Federal Reserve caused a serious crisis, the Great Depression, shrinking the money supply by a third along with its attendant labor and employment. That crisis was used as a pretext to vilify capitalism and create the elite rule over a welfare state fueled through plunder legalized by the 16th Amendment and the progressive income tax code. The virtue of self-reliance yielded to dependence and theft thereon, and America lost the benefits of a greater sustained prosperity. Natural capitalism as it existed between 1865 and 1913 was the same as today's notion of conservative libertarianism. It provided that under a nation-state charter of natural law, whereby government is limited to the protection of life, liberty, and property, people are free to do as they please so long as they do not harm others and contribution of perceived value to others is incentivized—*the greater the contribution of perceived value to others, the more money, power, and freedom to the contributor.* There are obviously exceptions whereby people acquire money without contribution of perceived value to others, but those exceptions are of natural design to test virtue and therefore have consequences. The consequences of money without contribution include jail, the painful feelings of envy, lack of self-worth, guilt, unhappiness, and the attendant motivations to control through coercive redistribution those who earn meritoriously.

Natural capitalism is nature's system. Because the nature of money, nation-state systems and values are so integral to the prosperity of humans and their aggregate nation-states, they must be revealed at the quantum level but be simplistic enough to relate and understand in our daily life. Accordingly, as I will discuss in the chapter "Money," physicist Max Planck's Nobel Prize (scientific, not political) winning transformation of the study of physics with his discovery of the nature of energy as separate quantum packets or units, yields absolute proof of *exactly what money represents*—quantized units of human energy or labor. This important truth, as well as the first and second laws of energy, constitutes "the invisible hand" which facilitates nation-states' economies. Thus, the operation of the law of conservation of energy, along with the decay of entropy and its attendant antidote of virtue, will be discussed in detail in the chapter on "Energy."

But in what will be the most astonishing revelation is the explicit illustrative proof demonstrating that nation-states are not only organic open systems which exchange energy and matter, they fundamentally operate just as the human body does. As I will explain, each consumes energy when value is perceived and converts and channels it through its organs for expenditure to function. This is because everything naturally decays in accordance with the second law of energy (entropy), and thus energy must constantly be consumed and expended to resist such decay. It is the value of the energy consumed (GDP for nation-states) and the value of the method of energy expenditure (how money/energy is spent or directed for nation-states) that determines the health and prosperity of open systems. To optimize or improve open systems for health and prosperity against natural decay requires intelligent innovation or evolution so as to increase the efficiency and value of both the energy consumed and the method of its expenditure. *Virtue* is the antidote to the decay of entropy, as only certain cultural values can produce the evolutionary conditions to perpetuate intelligent innovation. There are consequences to what we consume individually in the energy of biomass/food *and the information of transmitted cultural values*, just as there is at the aggregate level as nation-state consumers of goods and services transmuted from human energy in thought and labor (first law of energy). Thus, the health and prosperity of both humans and nation-states are largely a measure of such individual choices in consumption, both qualitatively and quantitatively. When the consequences of such individual choices are shifted to others and institutionalized, neither prosperity nor its requisite values can be sustained.

Nation-states are fueled by the energy-labor of its individual cells, which produce goods and services. Goods and services perceived as value by others for consumption are converted into money ("liquid") and chan-neled through the organs of the nation-state known as the economy. A portion of that money is distributed to the organ of government at the top through taxation. Thus, the energy of the people fuels the government from bottom up, but only so that the government can protect the life, liberty, and property (minimal regulation) of its cells or citizens to maxi-mize intelligent innovations for constant growth or resistance against the decay of entropy. Yet most nation-state systems are designed the other way around, with outsized government attempting to fuel the citizenry from the top down and the citizenry promoting the opulent lifestyles, liberties, and properties of the unmerited elite central planners. This is inconsistent with the way open systems are to function for health and prosperity in accordance with the laws of energy. As Maimonides stated, "study astronomy *and physics* if you desire to comprehend the relation between the world and God's [nature's] management of it."[1] The more coherent with the laws of nature, the healthier and more prosperous the system will be. Of course the converse is also true, the evidence for which is scattered around the globe throughout history, from the destruction of the evil national socialists of Nazi Germany, the collapse of the murder-ous Union of Soviet Socialist's Republic, the European Union's socialist disaster, and America's socialist decline to the stagnation and oppression of Middle Eastern theocracy/mullahcracy. *These systems are the manifes-tations of values—the elements of social behavior.* Most strikingly illustra-tive is that even as the oil-rich monarchy of Dubai roiled in bankruptcy, the Middle East's most oil-*barren* nation-state—the world hated (envied) Republic of Israel—continues to enjoy great prosperity, with the second-highest technological innovations in the world, second only to the other world-hated (envied) Republic of the United States of America.[2]

The system which most parallels the process by which open sys-tems must operate to maximize health and prosperity is natural capital-ism. In general, natural capitalism equitably provides any individual or group with a level of power and freedom commensurate with the contri-bution of value that society perceives from such entity. This, combined with the ingenious U.S. Constitution's promise to protect life, liberty, and property, has resulted in the greatest freedom and prosperity in human history. Natural capitalism was successful because it was mostly consistent with the nature of humanity, the physical laws of the universe, and humanity's most virtuous aspirational values of self-reliance, responsibility, self-determination/liberty, contribution, and enlightenment. As a result, and despite the decay of such values, the United States of America has landed men on the moon, sent robots to Mars, saved billions of lives worldwide through medicine and the military, and has proliferated the highest tech communications tools, entertainment, and transportation throughout the world, making countless lives better while preserving liberty for humanity. It is impossible to rationally deny that the greatest achievements and opportunities in human history have come from the former values and primacy of the United States of America and its constitutional system of governance for its multicultural citizenry. Natural capitalism is nature's true system of empowerment, freedom, and opportunity, and it must be restored for an equitable prosperity. No amount of political correctness or indoctrination can change these truths. Again, *the evidence is in.* The ideological systems have been tried, and we have the results. The laws of nature are immutable. No matter how hard the power-seeking, envious, guilt-ridden or ignorant ideologues try to subvert and suppress humanity to parity with redistributive systems, they do not work, and in fact over the last one hundred years they have been perniciously destroying the world's last bastion of freedom—The United States of America.

And with the election of the most radical socialist president in American history, the sinful, murderous, and coercive history of socialism no longer carries shame or stigma, but is even in vogue. The coercive elite who would compel the labor of others have been so emboldened by those in power of the current Marxist U.S. administration that for the first time in American history, mainstream media television hosts openly and proudly proclaim to America that they are socialists calling for the *total* transformation of America.[3] Even one of America's most culturally recognized national magazines, *Newsweek*, boasted a cover distributed throughout the country's supermarkets, newsstands, and offices with the headline "We are All Socialists Now"—a line stolen from the 1930s, when socialism was also in vogue.[4] However, contrary to the fears of those with relatively virtuous values, President Obama and his corruptocratic administration were divinely sent to spotlight America's current values. Over the last one hundred years, Americans have tolerated, elevated, and now acutely exposed the unmerited, systemic theft from top to bottom— the U.S. president to the workers unions—of the hardworking taxpayers. They have fleeced America to decline in both values and prosperity. Americans were too socially conditioned, indoctrinated, and blind to see this before such values were celebrated and proliferated from its highest platforms—the White House leadership and their sycophants in the House and Senate. America has been rotting from the inside out through the pernicious decay of the values which previously promoted and protected freedom for humanity. To paraphrase President Ronald Reagan, if America does not protect humanity's freedom, who would?[5] We must acknowledge and cultivate the different talents we each possess instead of promoting envy and theft, so that we all mutually benefit from one another in a system of values and governance that elevates humanity in freedom.

SECTION I

LAWS OF NATURE

Chapter 1

TRUTH

Humanity is in a state of semiconsciousness; we are aware of our existence but are born without biological instructions about our source, purpose, and the immutable laws of nature which govern us. The answers lie latent in the deepest reaches of our universally tethered minds. As we evolve, we gradually gain further access. As polarized cells of awareness, we are to evolve to consciousness—as nature intended—experientially through self-reliance, discovery, social discourse, conflict, and trial and error. The answers would not simply be imposed upon us, or we would have no earthly purpose. The most effective means of learning is through experience and judgment—when we make, implement, and feel the repercussions of our own decisions for happiness and prosperity or misery and poverty. But we would need some type of guide to the natural world, and even that guide—the laws of nature—would have to be discovered.

And through self-reliance and trial and error, discover we did! Courageous individuals with a burning desire for enlightenment persisted in their quest for knowledge, yielding the discovery of many laws of nature in several fields and subfields of endeavor, including anthropology, astronomy, biology, chemistry, economics, Newtonian physics, sociology, thermodynamics, and quantum mechanics, among others. The application of natural laws has translated into great advances for humanity, as evidenced by the moon landings, the airplane, the automobile, nuclear energy, vaccines/medicines, the personal computer, the cell phone, and the Internet. The design of the natural world is such that it gradually leaks clues for our discovery and enlightenment with evidence from as simple as the fossils of our ancestors to the complexity of subatomic hadrons. Imagine the frame of an empty jigsaw puzzle; the emptiness represents unconsciousness, and with each discovery a piece of truth displaces that unconscious void as the big picture gradually emerges. Thus, as we evolve, we gain more and more pieces of truth in our ascent to consciousness. And with more truths came more technological advances to reveal that at least part of our purpose is to learn the laws of nature and apply them *for the benefit of humanity*. For those few who have gained access and peered into the picture of truth, an advanced level of consciousness attains and cannot be reversed, only ignored.

The Universal Constant

Truth is that which is *actual and factual*, the constant of the universe, and the sine qua non of enlightenment. Humanity has been endowed with the freedom of thought, resulting in a diversity of beliefs and opinions as to what is actual and factual in the natural world and what is right and wrong regarding human behavior and governance. This is the struggle for humanity—finding truth through discovery and experience among competing beliefs, ideologies, and the indoctrinated masses. Anyone may believe, advocate, and indoctrinate anything, rational or irrational. Many people believed that bleeding sick people would cure illness, that rain dancing would bring rain, that virgin sacrifice would bring a good harvest, and that the earth was flat, yet this did not make any of these things true. Ultimately, the natural world of which we are a part consists of universal truths and rules specific to human prosperity. Even if the natural world is an illusory construct of the human experience, as quantum physics indicates, *humanity is nevertheless governed by the immutable truths or laws of that natural world*. Truth is as absolute as the fact that you *comprehend these four words*. Truth is as absolute as two plus two equals four. Natural laws require that certain formulae consistently have the same results. The same is true with political and economic systems of the social sciences. Truth and logic dictate that humanity and its aggregate nation-states are part of nature—both are open systems which exchange energy and matter and act in accordance with applicable natural laws. These natural laws apply to human conduct, which includes human governance. At the elementary level, natural laws of human conduct are otherwise known as *values*. *Values determine prosperity and misery*. Certain values have certain results. There are truths as to why some cultures prosper while others do not.

No Truth?

Of course there are those who foolishly believe and advocate that truth is relative ("relativists"), yet this is merely the fallacious rationalizations of those who would abdicate responsibility for their life in order to justify any type of behavior or agenda. This is the great schism of humanity, between those who understand truth as the constant of enlightenment and those who believe there is no truth other than that which serves to indulge individual desires and agendas. Those embracing the latter can be readily identified by common statements such as "that's my truth," or "that's his truth," or "there is no objective reality." They conflate self-serving or self-indulgent *beliefs* with truth, including the notion that if one believes something, then "it is true for them." Such beliefs are generally espoused by the self-indulgent left. The right generally requires structure and order of the immutable truth. Both are hardwired biologically and affected culturally.[1] Relativists confuse *beliefs* with truth. But the two are distinct, and enlightenment cannot occur unless beliefs intersect with truth. No matter how much a person may believe in alchemy, gold is an element, and therefore alchemy cannot be true for *anyone*. It is simply a false belief.

And when the relativist finds it impossible to dispute the applications of truths in natural science from which intelligent innovations have served their material comforts, they foolishly retort that truth applies only to natural science, but that there is no truth in the *social* science of human behavior. However, humanity is part of the natural world, and the laws of nature cannot cease to apply just because they don't conform to indulgent desires or agendas. Just as there are elements in the natural sciences, there are also elements in the social sciences. *Values are the elements of human behavior.* Combining certain natural elements yields consistent results, and combining certain values will too. The terms *natural* and *social* serve only to distinguish categories of science, not applicability of the laws of nature. To say that truth applies to natural science but not social science is an affront to logic. So according to the relativist, the truth is that there is no truth. NO TRUTH IS THE TRUTH? Such an inherently contradictory proposition logically requires acknowledgment of absolute truth.

Just as there is truth and logic in natural science, there is truth and logic in social science. Relativists continually proclaim that all current social systems should yield to collectivist "open society" and world government as the correct system for humanity. But if there is no truth in social science and all cultures are equal, as the relativist would maintain, then all social systems of governance should be just fine the way they are without the need for their open society and world government. Most importantly, if there is no truth in the social sciences, then there can be no cause and effect *and no right and wrong when it comes to human conduct. This* is the whole strategy of the relativist—to establish that there is no right and wrong when it comes to human conduct, that all values are subjective, and that all cultures are equal. They deny that prosperity and misery are natural barometers of implemented values. However, under such reasoning, if there is no right and wrong when it comes to human conduct, it follows that it cannot be wrong for a relativist's most cherished loved one to be raped, slowly tortured in agonizing pain, and then beheaded. *It was the truth of the person who would commit such acts*—he has his reasons, and it is not for the relativist to judge. In fact, this scenario is consistent with the Islamic cultural practice known as "honor killing."[2] When the relativist admits that this conduct of barbaric values is wrong, he admits that there is truth in social science, as there is in natural science. Just as mixing the same recipe of ingredients or elements results in the same flavor, the same is true of ideological systems. The flavors of prosperity and misery each have a different recipe of different ingredients or elements. *Those elements are values.* Combining certain values yields certain results. The values of self-reliance, individualism, cooperation, respect for life, liberty, and property yield prosperity. The values of dependence, collectivism, coercion, tyranny, and envy yield misery.

Uncertainty of Truth

After thousands of years of discovery and experience, there is obviously still quite a degree of uncertainty as to the truth, but this does not mean there is no truth or that we are not certain of many truths. There must always be *degrees* of uncertainty on the earthly plane. Just as the Heisenberg *uncertainty principle* in the natural science of quantum physics tells us we cannot know both the location and destination of a subatomic particle simultaneously—only one or the other—nature allows us only *access* to certain truths, but not all truths at the same time.[3] If every truth was simultaneously accessible, there would be no self-determination, because every personal action and reaction could be mapped, and we would have no spontaneity or purpose here.

Political Correctness, Relativism, Substantivism

Political correctness (cultural Marxism), relativism, and substantivism are ingredients of the current prevailing elite world doctrines of tyranny. Their inherent nature is antithetical to truth, i.e., each is based on falsehoods. When deliberate subterfuge upon the populace is an integral ingredient of a governing system, it cannot be a healthy and prosperous one.

Political Correctness

Political correctness was surreptitiously developed in the 1930s and 1940s by the Institute for Social Research, a Marxist think tank founded in Frankfurt, Germany in 1923.[4] Known as the Frankfurt School, they fled to the United States when Hitler came to power, and found a home in New York and then California—today's epicenters of political correctness.[5] When World War II ended, they expected Russian communism to take hold in Western civilization but soon recognized the impediment: Western culture revolved around *individualism*, not collectivism. However, they determined that if the individualist impediment could be removed *culturally*, it would pave the way for a Marxist society. And the best way to accomplish this was to "change their speech and thought patterns by spreading the idea that vocalizing your beliefs is disrespectful to others and must be avoided to make up for past inequities and injustices."[6] Similar to "Mao's 'Sensitive training'. . . speech codes were born . . . a sophisticated and dangerous form of censorship and oppression, imposed upon the citizenry with the ultimate goal of manipulating, brainwashing, and destroying our society."[7]

And they did it! Western civilization would never be the same. Those expressing innocuous and obvious truisms about individual differences of race, creed, or values which conflicted with Marxist ideology of the collective would be labeled, vilified, and stigmatized. Everyone is the same, there are no differences in people, and if some are lazy, less productive, and contribute less value to others, then institute laws and codes to give them the income of those who contribute more value to others. Those who make the lives of others easier with goods and services are greedy, and the wealth earned makes people feel unequal and envious, and that's just unfair. So to solve that problem at the expense of virtue and a broad prosperity, penalize those who contribute the most value through confiscatory progressive taxation, and redistribute it to those who contribute the least value to others. And make sure the indulgent political class is the greatest beneficiary in the pay-to-play corruption inherent in the

redistribution process. To prevent achievement by the meritorious so as
not to hurt the feelings of the incompetent, institutionalize discrimination against those who demonstrate exceptional talent or qualifications by
lowering standards and creating a special priority in employment based
on anything but qualifications and character. To be consistent, compensation should also not be based on merit but on tenure or duration, and
no one should lose their employment or compensation for lack of performance or productivity. That's Marxist equality. Those who express dis-
agreement with the system are irresponsible, greedy racists, and "justice"
will be instituted through both the judicial system and the Marxist media
for sins against the collective.

Relativism

As for relativism, an avatar emerged as the late Saul Alinsky
(1909-1972), and his relativist ideology became incredibly influential
among progressive/socialist radicals.[8] The truth had revealed that in a
free society with a constitution designed to protect life, liberty, and property, the greatest concentration of money and power generally went to the
intelligent innovators who meritoriously gave the most perceived value to
others in goods and services. Such values of merit meant that the overwhelming majority of millionaires would be self-made to the exclusion
of the indolent, incompetent, and dependent. Alinsky sought to change
all that through the elimination of truth, and apropos of that endeavor he
dedicated his philosophy to "Lucifer" at the beginning of his famed book,
Rules for Radicals—the semi-official manual of the neo-radical progres-
sive/socialist left.[9] Rules for Radicals explicates the relativist philosophy
embraced and professed by the most powerful leaders of the most powerful country in the world—U.S. President Barack Obama and U.S. Secretary of State Hillary Clinton. Prior to becoming the current leaders of the
neo-radical progressive/socialist left, Obama was trained in and taught
Alinsky's ideology as a "community organizer," while Clinton was a close
friend and disciple of Alinsky.[10] In fact, Alinsky was the subject of Clinton's senior college thesis upon graduation from Wellesley—a ninety-two
page document titled There Is Only the Fight.*

In collaboration with the felonious international financier of ill
gains George Soros and his Open Society Institutes, both U.S. leaders

* While Hillary Clintons' husband, Bill Clinton, was the U.S. president, the White
House persuaded Wellesley to suppress the document from 1993 to 2001.[11]

Barack Obama and Hillary Clinton have implemented Alinsky's doctrine with great efficacy as written in *Rules for Radicals*:

> "An organizer working in and for an open society is in an ideological dilemma to begin with, he does NOT HAVE A FIXED TRUTH—TRUTH TO HIM IS RELATIVE AND CHANGING; EVERYTHING TO HIM IS RELATIVE AND CHANGING.... To the extent that he is FREE FROM THE SHACKLES OF DOGMA, he can respond to the realities of the widely different situations. . . ."[12] [emphasis added]

Alinsky primarily states that "all values and factors are relative," going so far as to announce that the laws of nature are made up by men "creating scientific systems like Newton's."[13] Of course the objective reality is that Newton did not create gravity or the laws of motion but instead gained special access to esoteric natural laws which he delivered to humanity as truth. The laws of motion accessed and delivered to us by Newton and memorialized as Newtonian physics are immutable truths, the foundations of which quantum mechanics developed. Without the discovery, delivery, and application of such truths, Alinsky and his followers would not have been able to travel by plane, train, or automobile to disseminate his falsehoods to the world. Again, if there is no truth, there can be no cause and effect and no right and wrong. If there is no right or wrong, there can be no morality. This is significant because values determine the prosperity or misery of societies, as evident in the decadence and decline of Roman and now American primacy, and in the perennial stagnation of nation-states which *never* had values consistent with truth for prosperity.

Substantivism

Similarly, from primary school through post-graduate "higher education," Western educational authorities (Marxist indoctrination camps) vehemently advocate and indoctrinate as social science the falsehoods of cultural relativism and political correctness. This logically requires moral relativism. They cloak this philosophy in the euphemistically palatable and scientific sounding term *substantivism*, referring to the substance of a culture.[14] Under this doctrine, most of Western civilization's educational authorities believe and indoctrinate unwitting students that we must not view the variability of behavior in any particular society as right or wrong, but we must "understand" them in the context of their culture and history—as if cultures were dealt like a hand of cards, with no responsibility assigned to those whose behaviors created them. Followed to its logical extent, all you have to do is create a culture and tradition and you can conduct any behavior desired. Truth and logic dictate that cultures are the result of the dominant behaviors of the individuals that collectively comprise a society. Political correctness, relativism, and substantivism excuse individual and cultural responsibility to humanity and science, especially those cultures that preach and practice sanctioned hate, murder of homosexuals, subjugation of women, barbaric torture, and amputation of limbs for no medical purpose. Under relativism, substantivism, and political correctness, such cultures are no worse than those that advocate liberty, good works, and contribution of value to humanity, even though they each have corresponding disparate empirical results. Yet political indoctrination and resultant political correctness perpetuate such affronts to humanity ultimately to preserve the statist rule of an elite few. Without the obstacles of right and wrong embodied within the enlightenment of truth, any self-interested, whimsical elite directive is solely authoritative and without constraint. Allegiance to any other authority, such as natural law or God, and any declarations of self-evident truths codified by charter or constitution to protect life, liberty, and property are an impediment to the directives of such elite tyrants.

Fortunately, what most people believe is irrelevant to truth. In fact, it is generally the righteous few who bring truth to the masses, violently shaking the foundation of those who have built their cosmological security on falsehoods. Truth to them is kryptonite, and they will therefore resort to physical contortions and name-calling before dealing with substance. Consequently, many have been tortured and murdered in the quest for truth by those seeking to preserve their own cosmological security or mental comfort. Even the revered genius of his time, referenced in the introduction, Galileo, was ridiculed and imprisoned for his heliocentric discovery. The geocentric believers could not accept a "lesser" role in the universe. Yet truth was unearthed, and we have since known that the sun is the center of our solar system, not the earth. Similarly, there are also truths as to how humanity is to govern itself in order to bring about the broadest prosperity. It is critical to understand, notwithstanding indoctrination and the resultant political correctness, that we are all at different levels of evolution toward the truth, both individually and collectively as societies, depending upon the particular beliefs and conduct.

This is but saying that we are all at different levels of evolution toward enlightenment, as individuals and indoctrinated nationals.

Beliefs Must Be Judged

Beliefs are either true or are in a certain proximity to the truth. Therefore, if we are to evolve to truth, *beliefs must be judged* by their proximity to it. Those who famously state "do not judge," disingenuously and perfunctorily perpetuate folly, or otherwise excuse responsibility for improper conduct and/or inaccurate beliefs. As human animals of the animal kingdom, we biologically judge others *autonomously* in order to determine any potential threats to what we believe are in our interests for survival and well being. This includes judging values and the conduct they spawn. We are to judge and be judged by our conduct and its consequences. The next time you hear someone misappropriate the phrase *do not judge*, look at the mental or physical condition of the person who makes such proclamations, and then you will understand why. Without judgment, accurately informed decisions could not be made, and mistakes could not be remedied and/or prevented for progress in our ascent to the enlightenment of truth. Individuals and societies are NOT equal. They are either closer or further away from truth. Those who are in harmony with truth are favored by nature with prosperity, while those who are in conflict with truth are disfavored by nature with misery. This can most readily be seen on a macro scale with nation-states and their resultant prosperity, or lack thereof, depending upon whether or not their values and ideological systems of governance are in harmony with truth. This is also why world government should not be considered at this stage of human evolution, because the minority and their values closest to truth or enlightenment would decay and dilute into the majority furthest away from it.

Ideological systems reveal values and elicit behavior. Some cultures advocate falsehoods, coercion, and suicide-homicide to achieve all their ends while others advocate truth, cooperation, life, love, liberty, and contribution to humanity. It is not a coincidence that the latter has resulted in prosperity while the former languishes in poverty. Thus, truth is the constant that we are all evolving toward and which we seek to live in harmony with. It is either true or untrue that certain foods will lead to health or disease. It is either true or untrue that $E=mc^2$. It is either true or untrue that certain systems of government comprised of certain values will result in prosperity or poverty. Thus, truth is not relative but absolute, and it governs all of humanity and the systems by which we govern ourselves.

So how do we know what is truth without absolute proof? Proof usually delays its arrival until after the intensity of the battle, and for good reason. If proof was evident to humanity from the start, there would be no purpose for our extant struggle of learning through conflict. In fact, there would be no struggle or conflict since everything would be laid out for us, and our role would be as meaningless automatons following a script. Moreover, the absence of proof develops and enhances the human qualities of self-reliance, hope, faith, and persistence while fostering the courage to confront and overcome the world's most common conflict catalysts—fear and envy.[15] The greatest discoveries by Newton, Edison, Marconi, and Einstein all lacked proof at the time of their initial claims, yet they had logical coherence based upon scientific methodology to advance science until proof arrived. In fact, most people at one point believed they were crazy or stupid. As Shopenhauer stated, "All truth passes through three stages; first, it is ridiculed, second, it is violently opposed, and third, it is accepted as being self-evident."[16] In the absence of proof, we must look to logical coherence in order to advance, as nature accommodates logic. "The universe rests on a logical coherence that cannot be proven but to which men must commit if they are to create."[17]

Chapter 2

HAPPINESS

Happiness is the ultimate desire of every person, whether in America or Afghanistan. If you ask a rational person what they want and *why* they want it, no matter what answer they provide, if you continue to press, their answer will ultimately *equate to* "because it will make me happy." Although happiness is humanity's paramount aspiration, it is the lessons learned in our pursuit of happiness that brings us closer to our unconscious purpose. That unconscious *purpose* is to attain the enlightenment of ethical virtue in the lessons learned through our relationships and treatment of other beings. Happiness is only the goal that keeps us striving forward, and it can be attained only through the conduct of our relationships, both as individuals and as aggregate groups of individuals.

Nature's design of humanity requires interdependence upon one another to insure that relationships are formed so that we hopefully learn through interactional conduct. These relationships begin at the family level with the individual infant who is dependent upon the relationship and nurture of the primary caretaker (usually the parent who also shapes the initial values of the dependent) for survival up to a certain age, requiring a minimum level of materialism/property such as food, shelter, and clothing. *This dependence upon materialism/property required for survival is nature's conduit to social relations*, as we generally become reliant upon the cooperation or coercion of others in seeking material things even at the subsistence level, and therefore must form some type of relationship requiring reciprocal conduct. It is this conduct toward one another that is the litmus in our evolution toward enlightenment to virtue. And it is not just the conduct of relationships at the individual level. The social structures graduate to the conduct of families, businesses/corporations, local communities, cities, counties, states, and nation-states' relationships to one another in the world community through both war and peace. These social structures are facilitated by the various world economies which channel the energy of human labor in the form of goods and services. And even though the people believe they are just creating goods and services, they are primarily establishing relationships[1] and interactive conduct through interfacing economies which serve as relational conduits on a macro scale. Thus, it is our relationships and our conduct toward one another that test our growth toward enlightenment to virtue, through lessons revealed of experience.

The Bait

The bait to test our virtue in such relationships is the gratification of our physical/material needs and desires. Humans instinctually *believe* this to be the path to happiness. This is by natural design, as the flesh is a surrogate of pleasure and pain to test how we treat other souls to gratify it. Such gratification, also by natural design, generally requires the *energy-labor* of others in goods and services. This may be attained by cooperation or coercion. Will we obtain the energy-labor of others by cooperation or coercion, and which will bring happiness? These decisions test and temper virtue. As I will discuss in subsequent chapters, they are also a part of the core distinctions between capitalism and socialism, wherein the former requires cooperation and the latter coercion.

As unique individuals, we all have different paths, different issues, and different lessons to learn through our relationships formed of individual pursuits of happiness. So it is not a coincidence that we are all born with different abilities along with different idiosyncrasies and predilections that we believe will make us happy. The best conditions to bring the fulfillment of happiness are those that provide the greatest freedom to develop our individual unique abilities and convert them into value for as many people as possible, while also pursuing our individual predilections or interests without violating the rights of others. Since we all have such divergent abilities and interests that we believe will bring happiness, freedom is the ideal condition for our varied talents and pursuits. Yet not everyone can share the same level of freedom, as true freedom is really a measure of our ability to do what we want when we want, and in a sedentary society with established divisions of labor, freedom is a measure of the amount of human energy-labor we have the authority or influence to direct. Thus, true human freedom is generally the ability to avail ourselves of the goods and services of others. With the authority to direct a sufficient amount of energy-labor from others, we may travel practically anywhere in the world or even into outer space at levels of comfort directly correlated to the amount of human energy-labor one commands. Unless we have the individual ability to solely build and power an aircraft or space shuttle, such travel requires the energy-labor of others. With the energy-labor of others, we may gratify our grandest physical/material needs and desires, from the finest cuisine of an elite chef to the luxury lodgings of a palatial estate. Even the right to be left alone is a measure of our authority to direct human energy-labor, for if we cannot prevent our own unjust persecution by the energy-labor of others, we are not really free.

Power

The authority or influence to direct the energy-labor of others, whether through cooperation or coercion, is called *power*—the more power, the more freedom. Therefore, we seek power in small or large measure, depending upon how much freedom or need for directing others which we believe we require to achieve happiness. And as any visit to a restaurant and encounter with a waiter/server indicates, there is nothing wrong per se with acquiring the power and freedom to direct others, as long as we do so through voluntary cooperation rather than coercion. Such power and freedom in small or large measure is sought and achieved in different ways but primarily through: 1. status-prestige; 2. money; and 3. political leadership. All three are frequently intertwined. Status-prestige brings political leadership and vice versa, and both can be monetized, while money in sufficient quantity also brings status-prestige that can be leveraged for political leadership. Thus, status-prestige, money, and political leadership all bring power and freedom, if not happiness. Self-worth is the sine qua non for sustained happiness, and this may be realized only when one feels they are of value to the world. Developing one's abilities and conferring them as value to others is the effectual route. *Effort is not enough*; value must be conferred. This is patently evident even at the simple physical level of athletics. The most gratified players are those who contributed the most value to achieving the prestige of victory. The greatest joy is felt by the most valuable players, not the benchwarmers, by the victors, not the losers. And of course those who contributed the most value are the most celebrated and rewarded with status-prestige that is usually monetized, and sometimes leveraged, for political leadership.

Cross-culturally, status-prestige is paramount in achieving power and freedom, regardless of whether political leadership or money is obtained. People generally desire to be associated with and to confer their energy or attention upon those with status-prestige, further perpetuating the status of the conferred. Status-prestige is nature's *incentive* for people to distinguish themselves from the masses for conduct perceived as value to society. The word *perceived* is operative, because certain conduct perceived as value by a culture may conflict with the truth, and it could actually be detrimental, e.g., cutting off or mutilating the limbs of children who steal. Conversely, certain conduct perceived as detrimental to a society may conflict with truth, and may in fact be of value, e.g., women's voting and driving. Societies don't always comprehend whether certain conduct is of value or detrimental until truth reveals the consequences of the conduct. This may be instantaneous or millennial. And even though it often seems to be the latter as history repeats its mistakes time and again, it is all part of the experiential learning process for each generation until we get it right.

Just as status-prestige brings power and freedom as nature's incentive, shame brings rebuke and condemnation, thereby repelling the energy-labor of others while also providing incentive to avoid conduct perceived as detrimental to society. Thus, status-prestige and shame, along with their associative concepts, generally serve as behavioral guidance. Of course each culture embraces and eschews different values and assigns status-prestige and shame accordingly. Those assignations determine each culture's prosperity or lack thereof, depending upon their proximity to truth. Generally, those cultures that have values of virtue, such as cooperation, self-reliance, contribution, and liberty, are prosperous, while those that embrace coercion, dependence, entitlement, and servitude are not prosperous.

Nature's Accountability—Unique Identities

We are held accountable for our values and conduct in this world; otherwise, nature would have designed us as nameless, faceless drones. Instead, upon our entrance into this world, nature assigns each person unique DNA, finger prints, irises, communication signatures in voice and writing, and identities apart from all others. This is to bring accountability for the conduct of the individual, good or bad, status-prestige, shame, and everything in between. Concepts and entities, including nation-states, are also accorded appellations for accountability, so that we may confer upon them the same varying degrees of status-prestige or shame, depending upon their perceived level of value or detriment to humanity. Again, the accuracy of such designations is dependent upon the designator's relationship to the concept of truth, whether they believe it is a relative term to serve an agenda or whether truth is the constant of the universe and ultimate enlightenment. Thus, our name and identity generally bring some modicum of accountability for our conduct, good and bad. We see the names of those who contribute great value recognized and celebrated, whether it is a "Ferrari" automobile, a "Lear" jet, an "Uzi" compact machine gun, a "Picasso" artwork, a "P.T. Anderson" movie, or a "Shakespeare" story. This is true for many who made valuable contributions in the many diverse fields of endeavor, both arts and sciences. Whether it is Newtonian physics or Orwellian literature, they gained access to natural concepts and delivered and pronounced them for us to relate through their works. Deliver, and you shall be delivered. Similarly, artists test the value of their artistic labor with accountability in the credits bearing their names on the movie screen, the pages of a book, or the label of a song. And then there are also distinctions of shame accorded to those who represent conduct such as coercion. Whether it is for persecution labeled "McArthyism" (named after Joseph McArthy) or the predatory practice labeled "Ponzi Scheme" (named after Charles Ponzi). Shame evokes rebuke and condemnation. Shame also brings unhappiness, nature's hint that we are to avoid conduct which produces such feelings, while status-prestige may bring fulfillment and happiness if achieved in a cooperative and contributive manner. BUT STATUS-PRESTIGE AND SHAME ARE MEANINGFUL ONLY IF THE CULTURE WHICH DESIGNATES THEM EMBRACES VALUES OF HUMAN CONDUCT GROUNDED IN TRUTH FOR HUMAN PROSPERITY AND ENLIGHTENMENT. A culture may bestow status-prestige in killing their own children and shame for assimilating with other cultures, even of the same nation-state (Islam in Europe). Truth is the ultimate foundation from which specific values reveal specific manifestations—happiness or misery.

Distinction among the Masses

Individuals and groups that sufficiently distinguish themselves graduate from individual entities to symbols or avatars of ideas and concepts. Beauty, intelligence, wealth, evil, and virtue are among such conceptual ideas and concepts, all represented by famous recognizable faces in each culture, or internationally, depending upon influence. Certainly a face comes to mind when processing a universal concept or idea. If we choose intelligence as humanity's most revered modern quality, what face comes to mind for the concept of genius? Most would see the face of Einstein. As a result of the tremendous value he contributed to our understanding of the universe, Einstein became the symbol of humanity's most revered quality of intelligence, and thus his face has become the most recognized and celebrated, from which great monetization continues to enter his estate.[2]

We are incentivized to distinguish ourselves, as this brings the power and freedom of access to the energy-labor of others and to the coveted love and adulation. As previously stated, the energy-labor of goods and services in the division of labor is designed to gratify physical/material needs and desires. Such gratification is the paramount ambition of most human beings, as most *believe* it will bring happiness. Nature has cloaked our purpose, testing our virtue in the instinctual pursuit of gratification and happiness. But this is nature's Grand Illusion, for sustained happiness cannot be attained by mere gratification of physical/material needs and desires. The method by which we obtain the energy-labor of others or *our relationships* determines the fulfillment of sustained happiness. We must contribute value to others in exchange for their energy-labor, through cooperation rather than coercion. These are not just platitudes, as there are no known happy dictators.

Although status-prestige and political leadership bring access to the energy-labor of others, nature has provided the masses with the broadest access to such energy-labor through the acquisition of money. As I will demonstrate through Max Planck's discovery of the quantum in the following chapter, money represents quantized units of energy in human labor. More practically, each denomination of money represents redeemable credits of human labor. This is also superficially evident by the energy-labor of goods and services which money yields in proportion to its quantity. So of course a vigorous universal pursuit of money rages to acquire the energy-labor of others in order to gratify physical/material needs and desires. The more money acquired, the more human energy-labor one commands. However, nature's test is HOW we acquire money, either through cooperative contribution of commensurate value or through coercion without contribution of commensurate value. *These determine the levels of fulfillment and enlightenment to virtue, or emptiness, guilt, and envy—factors that determine happiness.*

Since self-worth is a prerequisite for general sustained happiness, one must believe that he or she has at least some value to humanity. By developing our abilities and contributing them as value to others, we validate or prove that we have some degree of self-worth, enabling us to achieve the fulfillment of happiness. Only a free society where life, liberty, and property are protected can provide the conditions whereby everyone can find and develop their worth or value as they see fit. In such a society, one may contribute the value of their abilities to others and be compensated commensurately with the perceived value of such contributions. The more value perceived, the more money acquired, and more money means more power and freedom to direct the energy-labor of others in pursuit of happiness. However, perceived value is obviously not always real value. Nature is of such an intricate design that it provided for money to be traded for not just real value, but *perceived* value as well. This is because each person goes through their own evolution and growth toward enlightenment to virtue and must therefore learn on their own what is of real value in life. A person may at some point believe that heroin is of real value until they learn experientially that artificial "highs" bring commensurate destructive "lows" to destroy the mind and body. Such a person has not yet been enlightened to such truth (or achieved sufficient discipline), and if money was exchanged only for real value, truth would already be defined as to what is of real value in life, and no evolutionary individual experiential growth process would occur. Everyone would know by litmus what was good or bad simply by whether or not it was exchanged for money. Under such circumstances, the virtue of our conduct toward others also could not be tested. We would be compelled to convey real value in our pursuit of money, rendering us the previously mentioned automatons following a script with no mechanism for experiential growth or enlightenment to virtue. Money is simply the bait that determines how you will treat others in order to get it. Will you lie, steal, cheat, or kill or otherwise violate the natural rights of others to gain money, or will you make the reciprocal contribution of value? Nature's system of capitalism in a free society of protected natural rights provides freedom of choice, and humanity makes the decisions. And of course our decisions have consequences. We learn the best lessons when we make and implement our own decisions rather than when they are imposed upon us. Decisions on how we conduct ourselves toward others, especially with the lure of money, are the tests of the universe. Nature generally requires obliviousness to this fact, and even those who are aware would have to resist the natural power of physical/material gratification, which would subvert the conscience, for if you were always consciously aware, there would be no experiential evolution to the enlightenment of virtue. As the Russian author Aleksandr Solzhenitsyn stated:

"The meaning of earthly existence lies not, as we have grown used to thinking, in our prosperity but in the development of our souls."[3]

When one grasps this sublime profundity, it will become evident daily. Viewed through this paradigm, the obscure Grand Illusion will come into focus. Simply read or watch the news on any given day. The same underlying general patterns of conduct surface, only different details. Nature has even designed the arts to put this on display and into focus for us. Every movie, television program, musical, comedic performance, and lyrical song is generally about how we treat one another, and a consequent lesson or "moral of the story." These are only clues, for it must always be remembered that the broader patterns of nature are generally consistent with just enough aberrations to keep you mystified and searching so that your choices are not directed. If you have the choice to violate the rights of others for material gain but knew that doing so would bring the same misery upon yourself, you would probably choose not to do so, and thus you would not learn experientially. Knowing what each choice would ultimately bring predetermines your actions so that there is no real choice. Without choice you have limited opportunity to grow from decision-making. Without growth there would be no point to our earthly experiential evolution to the enlightenment of virtue. Many clues as well as many designed obfuscations reveal the truth that only contribution to humanity and our reciprocal benevolent relationships can bring sustained happiness. Yet, this will not suffice for most, as the lure of nature's Grand Illusion controls most conduct. Therefore, people will do almost anything for material gratification, in the belief that it will bring happiness. And there is no better mechanism to test and temper our virtue than dangling the gratification of our material needs and desires through quantized units of other people's energy-labor. This is money.

Chapter 3

MONEY

Amazingly, after thousands of years, money—one of the most important and discussed subjects in the world—remains so greatly misunderstood. Politicians, economists, "experts," and "professionals" pushing self-interested agendas routinely make foolish statements and policy regarding money, all to the great detriment of nation-states. If they fundamentally understood the simplicity of what money represents, the freedom of prosperity would not be so elusive. Paradoxically, the simplicity of money can be found in the abstract science of physics.

In 1900, the great physicist Maxwell Planck dramatically transformed the field of physics with his "discovery of energy quanta," for which he won the Nobel Prize in 1918.[1] *Quanta* is the plural of *quantum,* and in the context of physics, means an amount of energy regarded as a unit and/or the smallest amount of something. Although it may appear that energy is a continuous flow like a nonstop waterfall, Planck mathematically accessed the subatomic world, which we can't see, and revealed otherwise. Instead of a continuous flow, energy comes in discrete packets or units—like poker chips—with each unit containing a specific amount of energy or value that can manifest certain material results. To illustrate this concept, Planck conducted experiments by heating material called a "black body," which radiated the beautiful colors of the spectrum like a rainbow. The visible spectrum from the lowest-energy colors to the highest-energy colors include the following, respectively: red, orange, yellow, green, blue, and violet.*

Each color required a certain "denomination" or unit of energy to manifest itself, much like the different-colored poker chips of different values. To manifest red, which is the lowest value at the bottom of the spectrum, required the smallest denomination of an energy unit, e.g., a five-unit packet. Each ascending color of the spectrum required a larger denomination energy unit to manifest a higher energy color. Accordingly, to manifest violet, which is the highest value at the top of the spectrum,

---

* The lowest-energy, infrared, and the highest-energy, ultraviolet, are not visible.

required the highest denomination of an energy unit, e.g., a one hundred unit packet. Thus, energy comes in denominated or quantized units like poker chips of different values, each commanding a certain amount of power—just like *money*.

MONEY SIMPLY REPRESENTS QUANTUM UNITS OF ENERGY, SPECIFI- CALLY HUMAN ENERGY AS QUANTIZED LABOR. Each quantum unit of money represents a certain amount of energy in human labor. In America, units of human energy or labor are quantized or denominated by the dollar. The quantity of dollar units determines how much energy in human la- bor one may literally command for almost any purpose, depending upon how many units one controls. As stated previously, power in sedentary civilization is simply a measure of *authority or influence to direct the labor of others.* This is an immutable truth. Money is a medium of that power— THE QUANTIZATION OF HUMAN LABOR. Thus, both money and power are interchangeable in authority or influence to direct the energy-labor of oth- ers. And the more authority or influence a person has to direct the labor of others, the more freedom for that person. Therefore, in the simplest practical terms, money in a free capitalist society is freedom fuel. The more of it you have, the more freedom and power you enjoy.

Any free person in a free capitalist society possessing the mon- etary equivalent of $10 units of human energy can command the labor of others to dig a small hole; $10,000 can command the labor of others to build a modest-sized swimming pool; $100,000 can command the labor of others to build a large, luxurious heated spa; and $1,000,000 can com- mand the labor of others to build a luxury oasis that includes waterfalls and servants with hors d'oeuvres.

If someone breaks your window, they may be indebted to you for the monetary cost or replacement of the window. Since glass windows don't grow out of the ground, they owe you *the labor* required to manufac- ture glass from sand and to craft and install a window according to the proper specifications.

Thus, money represents quantities of energy in human labor. Money given to an entity which represents an idea or concept, whether it is an ideology, product, service, charity, or political candidate etc., *infuses those entities with energy in the form of human labor.* Money brings ideas and concepts to the masses and to the marketplace for judgment. The more money the entity representing the idea or concept receives, the more energy force of human labor available to expose and perpetuate it.

Medium of Exchange

Before the advent of money to quantize human labor with redeemable credits of such labor, goods and services were usually exchanged directly. In agrarian societies this may have caused a great waste of labor and produce. A person who labored for months to harvest corn may have needed some ceramic bowls. Therefore, corn could be directly traded for the ceramic bowls. However, even after acquiring the ceramic bowls, a surplus of corn may have remained. There may not have been much else that the corn grower needed after that harvest for which he could trade the surplus corn. And even if he did need another good or service, the person providing that particular good or service may not have needed or wanted corn, so he would not accept it as trade. Even the people who did need corn may not have had a good or service that the corn harvester needed for it to make sense to trade. Under such circumstances, unless all the surplus of corn could be eaten by the harvester, it could have either been given away or traded for something unneeded; otherwise, it would go to waste since it could not be stored for too long before it rotted. In that case, a portion of the corn harvester's months of labor would be wasted. However, with the development of a capital system of money in place to quantize the labor of the farmer with a medium of exchange, the labor which produced the surplus of corn could be exchanged even to someone with a good or service not needed, so long as that person wanted corn and had the medium of labor called money. Thus, the corn surplus could be sold for money, and the money/labor could be accumulated and "stored" by the corn harvester until a future need of labor arose. Money/labor does not rot like corn, so it would be accepted in exchange for a variety of goods and services (labor), whereas corn could be used only for payment to someone who wanted the corn before it rotted and who had something the corn harvester desired in exchange.

Money and Natural Resources

Money is often conflated with natural resources such as gold and land, and therefore must be distinguished from them. Although gold is currently worth more than $1,300 an ounce and land might be worth hundreds of dollars per square foot, BUYING GOLD OR LAND WITH MONEY IS SIMPLY TRADING *LABOR* FOR SCARCE *NATURAL RESOURCES*. While it is true that labor is required to locate, process, and facilitate transactions involving gold and land, that labor is factored into the total cost of the natural resources. Therefore, with such transactions a certain amount of human labor is traded for both a certain amount of limited natural resource and some human labor to find and bring the limited resource to market.

Value

Adam Smith, known as the father of capitalism, may have been ahead of his time, but when it came to understanding the critical issue of value, he was way off and *really wrong*.[2] He saw the value in things by the amount of labor it required.[3] Ironically, his position on value is consistent with the socialist/Marxist creed "each according to effort."[4] This position is logically untenable. Many people toil for years in an effort to provide resources and products that nobody wants and which hold no value. VALUE IS DETERMINED BY DEMAND/DESIRE, SCARCITY, AND MOST IMPORTANTLY BY WHAT ONE IS WILLING TO SACRIFICE.[5] This is impossible to logically dispute. A common natural resource such as water, is quite plentiful and easy to acquire. Therefore, it is inexpensive, so people don't have to sacrifice much for it. But if people want to acquire something that is limited in supply such as gold, it is expensive, so they are willing to trade many units of human energy-labor, which is represented by money. If the gold was finely crafted into jewelry of limited supply, where rare skilled human energy-labor was required, it would cost even more than just the value of the gold itself, e.g., a Fabergé egg. Similarly, a rare and unique prehistoric petrified flower may have been preserved and unearthed. If there are no more of these flowers known to humanity, people of means would sacrifice a large amount of human labor in the form of money to acquire this rarity, as it aesthetically inspires and provides prestige to the purchaser since no other human possesses the prehistoric flower. Scarcity is also critical to the value of labor, from the arts to medical and legal services. When a desired artist dies, the value of their original work or *labor* increases because they can no longer make original artwork, so their originals become limited in supply for acquisition. Since their labor is no longer available or is in limited supply, the value of that labor increased. Of course prints of their work are inexpensive because they can be mass-produced and are not scarce. Scarcity even belies the socialist propaganda of labor equality and compensation based upon effort rather than value. When a socialist or their closest loved one requires critical medical surgery or they are wrongly accused of a capital crime with their lives on the line, would they prefer the doctor or lawyer who gives the most effort even if it's ineffective or the one who is most effective and valuable at achieving the desired outcome? Truth dictates that nature provides a limited amount of such exceptional talent in labor, not enough to go around to all those who need it. That is why such qualities are by definition "exceptional." The most talented and effective are scarce, as nature's pyramid of excellence consistently proves. That scarcity makes the labor of the most talented the most valuable. Since money represents human labor, the more valuable the labor, the more money required. Hence the most talented are the most highly paid, from football players to food preparers. The test of value for a specific type of desired labor is the relative availability in replacement of that same labor. Replacing a top brain surgeon in contrast to a pizza delivery driver is illustrative.

Effort

When a person seeks a good or a service, they generally want to gratify a need or desire. They pay for results, not effort. Of course results cannot always be guaranteed when they depend on an act of nature or the decision of a judge or jury, but people can make choices based upon available information and a record of the effectiveness or value of a product or service. Prestige is conferred upon the most effective goods and services as an indicator of value and reputation. Shame is conferred upon the most ineffective goods and services, regardless of effort. Effort alone may not gratify a need or desire. Nature reserves its rewards of prestige, remuneration, fulfillment, and happiness to those who contribute value to others. Effort alone cannot yield those rewards. In fact, the more value, the more prestige, remuneration, and fulfillment. Training children to believe that effort alone warrants reward is foolish. Not everyone deserves a trophy. Nature does not endorse such a standard, as the child will find out later in the adult world. Nature has made its distinctions by the rewards it bestows. Challenging those distinctions is futile, as millions have learned through the failures of every effort-based socialist state in history. Basing reward or compensation upon effort is an attempt to artificially equalize individuals. But individuals cannot be equalized, only *equally treated* under the law so that everyone has the opportunity to develop and contribute the value of their talents to as many people as possible.

Monetary Standard of Exchange—Perceived Value

As unique individuals, we all naturally have different preferences, needs, and desires. People perceive different value in different goods and services. Moreover, some people may perceive value in a good or service that may actually turn out to be harmful, while a good or service that some might perceive as harmful may turn out to be of value. Certain goods and services need to be experienced over time in order to measure their impact. Sometimes even goods and services which we know are harmful, such as certain foods, cigarettes, and alcohol, may serve over time to test and temper virtue, discipline, and character. For at least all of the foregoing reasons, the standard of exchange for money must be based on *perceived* value as the free market determines.

Money (accumulated labor) Appreciates or Increases only when Lent as Value for the Use of Others—Bank Accounts, Interest, Loans

Bank accounts represent the storage of accumulated human labor available for use to others through lending. Interest on bank accounts is what a bank must pay to acquire and hold the power of other peoples' accumulated labor at the ready. But interest is also money, and by definition also represents human labor. Thus, when banks *pay* interest, they are paying a portion of their stored human labor to those who provide accumulated stores of human labor for the bank's inventory.

One of the most fascinating facts about money is that it appreciates or increases only when it is lent for the use of others. If money is buried in the ground or left in a mattress for many years, its value will decrease due to the normal course of inflation over time. Obviously, it costs much more to buy things today than it did a hundred years ago. However, when money is lent to help others with reasonable interest for the value it may provide, that same money increases as an earned return for assisting another, provided it was lent and collateralized to a creditworthy borrower. This is nature's hint that money must not be hoarded but must be circulated, contributed, and used to help others. As I will show in the following chapter, value must be created from energy, or else it will dissipate in accordance with the second law of energy/thermodynamics. Loans are simply a service that provides stores of accumulated energy in human labor, which may be used by the borrower for things that may have otherwise taken years of personal labor to accumulate. Instead, for an additional premium in extra labor paid over time (interest), the borrower can have immediate access to great stores of human labor which would be required to build or acquire things such as houses, office buildings, cars, trucks, and recreational vehicles. Unfortunately, however, the method for facilitating such loans with fractional reserve lending has been catastrophic for economies. Under fractional reserve lending, banks are permitted to loan many times what they actually have in assets. They are lending *productive* labor that does not exist (labor may be unlimited, but *productive* labor or labor of value is only *potentially* unlimited). Typically, labor perceived as value is exchanged for money, and this money may be stored in a bank account as productive labor for lending to others. Fractional reserve lending of money which was not actually acquired means that no labor of perceived value was actually exchanged. Since money represents quantized labor, lending money one does not actually have is tantamount to creating fictional productive labor. This practice has been the suspected cause of boom and bust cycles. It is unnatural for an entity to lend something it does not have.

In addition to loans for acquiring personal and real property, loans or venture capital are also obviously used to start companies that provide goods and services which improve standards of living. Venture capital has been called the most catalytic force in the world's economy.[6] Venture capitalists are generally experienced entities tasked with vetting and catalyzing the potential of goods and services that may benefit humanity. If they believe an idea or entity for a good or service may benefit humanity and therefore yield profit for them, they will back the good or service with the energy of human labor, or money, which is redeemable credits of same. Without venture capital, Microsoft, Apple, Google, and Facebook might not exist today.

Taxes

Finally, we come to one of the most important appropriations of human labor which affects the prosperity of societies—taxes. Since taxes are paid in money, taxes are obviously a transfer of a portion of human labor to the government. Unfortunately, most of our leaders making economic policy and the media have no understanding of the actual concept of taxes and money and their effect on security and freedom to pursue happiness and prosperity. Ridiculous statements by national leaders on television news interviews reflect such abject ignorance. On February 1, 2010, the Majority Whip of the U.S. House Democratic leadership, James Clyburn, appeared on the most watched televised news network in the country and sincerely declared to the nation in the midst of the deepest economic downturn since the Great Depression:

"WE'VE GOT TO SPEND OUR WAY OUT OF THIS RECESSION, AND I THINK MOST ECONOMISTS KNOW THAT."[7]

This is an astounding statement that explains why America is drowning, with no recovery in sight as of 2012. It also defies physics, as the next chapter demonstrates. It is easy for Mr. Clyburn to make such a statement while the taxpayers labor to pay for his salary and privileges, even as he inequitably redistributes their labor to his constituents. And this is a common call from leftists and progressives. Also, appearing on that same televised news network, in March of 2010, was a popular leftist L.A. radio talk show host, who responded to a question about how to pay for entitlements during the worst economic catastrophe since the Great Depression:

"ALL WE NEED TO DO IS WRITE A CHECK."[8]

As if it's merely just another piece of paper. If she understood what she was really saying, it would read as follows:

"Those who labor to pay the bills of this country in this most difficult time need to give even more of their labor or the labor of their progeny so that we can pay for the comforts of other able-bodied deadbeats who contribute nothing in labor but who will vote our party back into power for our resilient ability to steal the labor of others."

This is actually the position of the current administration, their acolytes in the progressive/liberal media, and even their appointee to the highest court in the United States of America, Supreme Court Justice Elena Kagan, who has said:

"Why is a big gift from the federal government a matter of coercion? In other words, the federal government is here saying: we're giving you a boatload of money. There are no, is no matching funds requirement. There are no extraneous conditions attached to it. It's just a boatload of federal money for you to take and spend on poor people's healthcare. It doesn't sound coercive to me, I have to tell you."[9]

A jurist of America's highest institution of justice, who attended Princeton, Oxford, and Harvard, and was tasked with teaching law students at both the University of Chicago and Harvard doesn't understand where "federal money" comes from? Both the government elite and the "elite" media pundits who spent most of their life in institutions of "higher education" do not feel the hours of labor which the public is required to sacrifice for taxes. They just see it as pieces of paper with pictures of deceased presidents and use it as if money was in unlimited supply. They don't understand that money represents labor, and with unemployment at such great levels, it is currently a limited pool of productive labor. Moreover, with America over sixteen trillion dollars in debt and over 130 trillion in liabilities, the citizens and their progeny are literally enslaved to labor for this incomprehensible sum. America currently does not have the productive labor pool to cover such deficits and debt, much less the financial consequences of the poor health decisions of others as the healthcare mandate requires. And unfortunately, overtaxing a society enervates the population, because it becomes excessive labor just to cover their own responsibilities in addition to those that the government leaders took on for the taxpayers in union vote-buying cycles. Outrageously, we see our leaders and mainstream media personalities, generally leftists and progressives, stating that in a deep economic crisis, we need to "spend our way out." As the next chapter explains, this is the same as telling an exhausted runner who is about to collapse that running harder will replenish his energy. More spending while in massive debt means enslavement to more labor in taxes to cover the bill. But a much more fundamental problem is *the immorality* of the current system of taxation, and Americans have been conditioned to accept it along with a substantially decayed level of virtue as a nation-state. All human beings should be treated equally, and any system which discriminates against those who contribute greater value to others is inherently inequitable and without virtue. As I will discuss in subsequent chapters, the indulgent nature of an unenlightened majority covets the fruits of the exceptional minority. But only depravity could institutionalize its implementation into the current U.S. tax code, while only virtue can mitigate it. To mitigate the ills of an abjectly corrupt political class and an overindulgent and obese society of unhealthy decay, taxation on consumption would probably be the best system, as existed during America's greatest prosperity of the Industrial Revolution. In fact, this is the only way the Founding Fathers would have it as they codified it so in the U.S. Constitution. (In 1913, when Woodrow Wilson became president and implemented his progressive agenda, the majority chose to loot the minority and corrupt the entire political process with the 16th Amendment and a progressive tax code. See Chapter 9, "America.") They didn't believe in an *income* tax, and now they are probably rolling over because of the notion and predictable effects of a progressive one. In the words of Founding Father Alexander Hamilton in Federalist 21:

> *The amount to be contributed by each citizen will in a degree be at his own option, and can be regulated by an attention to his resources. . . It is a signal advantage of taxes on articles of consumption, that they contain in their own nature a security against excess. They prescribe their own limit; which cannot be exceeded without defeating the end proposed, that is, an extension of the revenue. When applied to this object, the saying is as just as it is witty, that, 'in political arithmetic, two and two do not always make four.' If duties are too high, they lessen the consumption; the collection is eluded; and the product to the treasury is not so great as when they are confined within proper and moderate bounds. THIS FORMS A COMPLETE BARRIER AGAINST ANY MATERIAL OPPRESSION OF THE CITIZENS BY TAXES OF THIS CLASS, AND IS ITSELF A NATURAL LIMITATION OF THE POWER OF IMPOSING THEM.*[10] [emphasis added]

However, for today's socially conditioned society, a more palatable system of virtue is best expressed by the following illustration of two American brothers named Ray and John. Ray worked hard for years in a textile factory doing service labor. After observing the current manufacturing process and the products they yielded, he came up with an innovative idea for a new process and fabric for garments which would provide tremendous value to others. Since he didn't have the money for patents and a prototype, he not only scrimped and saved but he mortgaged the house where his two daughters slept every night. Failure would be devastating, but success would be liberating. Through hard work and sacrifice,

Ray pulled it off and amassed a ten million-dollar profit. His brother, John, was equally bright, but he was much younger and had a much different personality. John didn't believe in taking risks. He lived for the moment and liked to enjoy his youth as much as he could with his own car-detailing business. After spending most of what he earned on food and entertainment, John had only a one hundred-dollar profit left. Both Ray and John were happy to pay their fair share in taxes so as to protect the life, liberty, and property of the nation-state which they enjoyed as citizens. That year, Ray paid a million dollars, and John paid only ten dollars in taxes. Although Ray paid almost *one million dollars more than John,* this is absolutely fair because each paid *an equal percentage* of their profits. Unfortunately, this is fictional because America does not a have fair/flat tax system. Even though Ray and John are both human beings and should be treated equally, *under America's actual current progressive tax system, Ray paid over three million dollars, and John paid nothing.* That's what Ray gets for taking risks to contribute great value to others. This is unfair. Tax policy should not favor or disfavor any group, sociopolitical or economic. IT SHOULD BE NEUTRAL. Unfortunately, each generation of Americans is indoctrinated to believe that it's morally acceptable to have different laws for different groups in spite of the politicized equal protection clause of the U.S. Constitution.

Backed or Fiat Money

Many respected public personalities have for years stated in the public media that the United States prints money whenever needed and that it is not backed by anything, since President Nixon eliminated the gold standard in the 1970s. This has led the masses to believe that unlimited pieces of paper known as fiat money were printed from nothing. This was false until recently, when the Fed began its "quantitative easing" program, also known as "QE," as I will discuss later. Prior to this recent and foolishly desperate move, the concept of fiat money was a major misconception foisted upon the public even by the few well intentioned media personalities and conservatives who wanted to stop the reckless spending. Historically, the United States did not just print money without issuing corresponding debt that was to be repaid. Otherwise the dollar would have been so devalued by competing currencies that it would be rendered worthless. Thus, there was generally no fiat money.[11] The U.S. dollar is backed by American labor. Prior to "QE," when the United States printed

money, it had to borrow in order to spend. This was accomplished by issuing what is commonly referred to as bonds in exchange for the cash to
print money. Domestic and foreign entities enable the United States to
print more money when they purchase those bonds. Of course America
has to pay back not only that money but the interest on it, as well, in order
to pay off the bond holders. America repays this money by taxing its citizens. American taxpayers generally pay their taxes in dollars. The dollar,
or American money, represents quantized units of energy, specifically
American labor. Therefore, taxes remitted to the U.S. treasury by Americans taxpayers are paid with American labor. Hence, the dollar has generally been backed by American labor, as it should be.

The Gold Standard

Those pushing for a return to the gold standard to back the dollar are sorely misguided and/or have a financial interest in gold. If they
understood that money simply represents energy in the form of human
labor, they would not be conflating a scarce natural resource of value such
as gold with American labor. There is no connection between gold and
American labor, and thus there should not be one between gold and the
dollar other than that they both have separate and distinct values that can
be traded, and that when the value of the dollar goes down, gold goes up
because of its demand as a safe hedge in the security of a valuable metal.
Gold should not control American labor, for those who control the gold
would also control American labor. Unfortunately, American labor is enslaved to several lenders to pay for the seemingly insurmountable debt
incurred by American politicians, and backing money with gold won't
change that fact. In any event, this foolish argument would be put to an
end if people understood that gold is limited in supply, while productive
human labor potentially is not. There is not enough gold in the world to
back the growth of productive human labor.

Natural Backing—Productivity and GDP

Since the dollar represents American labor, the dollar should be
naturally backed by the value of the goods and services created by the
labor of the American people. In fact, the value of every nation-state's
currency should be determined by the value of their goods and services.
This is saying that productivity or GDP should determine the value of a

nation's currency. Productivity is the amount of output per hour of labor. Gross domestic product (GDP) is *the value* of the final goods and services produced within a nation's borders in a year. GDP and productivity have a positive relationship. Generally, the greater the productivity growth, the greater the per capita GDP.[12] Only productivity can fundamentally revitalize an economy. Therefore, the value of money should naturally be adjusted according to the productivity or GDP of human labor.

Money Supply and the Fed

One of the greatest slanders in world history says that capitalism caused the Great Depression. One of the most profound, suppressed, and *proven revelations* in American history is that the elite central planning institution, the Federal Reserve, caused the Great Depression by contracting the money supply *by a third, and along with it a third of the labor force* (see Chapter 9, "America"). Empirical proof revealed through data discovered in the 1960s unequivocally verified this, but it was suppressed in an era when America and the world became invested in centrally planned socialist societies.[13] Since money represents productive human labor, and productive human labor is *potentially* unlimited (depending upon conditions for intelligent innovation and industry), money cannot be limited like a pie, unless those who control its physical creation artificially dictate so. For labor to be productive in a free market economy, it must be perceived by others as value for conversion to money. And the money supply should expand or contract in correlation with such productivity values, or GDP. When productivity dictates, money circulates and should be expanded naturally for the benefit of all who would participate in contributing perceived value to society. Instead, the money supply and the corresponding supply of productive human labor remains concentrated in the hands of a few personalities of the Federal Reserve System:

> *"It is a bad system to believers in freedom just because it gives a few men such power without any effective check by the body politic—this is the key political argument against an 'independent' central bank.... To paraphrase Clemenceau, money is much too serious a matter to be left to the central bankers." —Milton Friedman*[14]

This is also why it is quite common to see the least virtuous involved in handling and controlling money and banking entities, as they may be interested first in the direct power of money to control others rather than earning that right through money's natural condition precedent—innovation and/or providing goods and services of perceived value to others.

As a result of the current Fed chairman's knowledge of the true cause of the Great Depression, he has greatly overcompensated in order to prevent a similar scenario today. His solution to the current American economic crisis was to *excessively* increase the money supply by creating money out of nothing and using it to buy debt, otherwise known as monetizing the debt or quantitative easing. Of course when you significantly increase the supply of money without a corresponding increase in productivity or at least the retirement of equivalent debt, the value becomes diluted. Therefore, the value of the dollar and of American labor decreased significantly. With a devalued dollar, inflation arrived, as more dollars are required to purchase the same goods and services, creating an indirect tax on the populace. The current Fed chairman apparently learned little from history. Quantitative easing or its equivalent of monetizing colossal debt is the last move of history's failed currencies. Neither the similar currency-breaking policies of the Nazis' precipitating Weimar Germany nor the lessons of Zimbabwe restrained today's Fed. They did not fundamentally understand that only *the energy of productive labor by individuals* can revitalize the economy, along with reducing unnecessary spending. All else is futile. Instead, the Fed has exacerbated the crisis, only delaying a more painful correction than if the natural course of free markets were permitted to cleanse the economy through the *creative destruction* of intelligent innovation.

America's history of intelligent innovations/innovators brought great prosperity in waves with each discovery of new technologies. Railroads from Vanderbilt, kerosene light from Rockefeller, electric light from Edison, steel from Carnegie, and conglomeration from Morgan all forged America's infrastructure and spawned many new industries. Computer technology came later, followed by software technology and then information technologies, with the Internet, cell phones, and touchpad computers. However, America is now in an unprecedented position where its debt is so great and unemployment is so high that it is difficult to imagine enough current productive labor to pay taxes to cover it. But again intelligent innovations are here for the rescue if government would get out of the way, as recent technologies have revealed processes to extract trillions of dollars of value in natural energy resources. This in addition to private-sector energy technology in battery power could be the partial solution to America's economic woes (values and virtue are the primary solution from which all else stems). But first Americans must recognize that self-serving political leadership has inhibited and continues to inhibit such solutions while spending citizens and their progeny into servitude just to preserve and increase their own power. A balanced budget amendment to the U.S. Constitution must be undertaken. Making the painful but necessary spending cuts may make the leadership unpopular to government-dependent junkies, but America's survival and prosperity is more important than preserving the political power of a few self-serving elite.

Chapter 4

THE LAWS OF ENERGY

The Invisible Hand

Energy is omnipresent, and thus the laws of energy are so important that they govern every aspect of our life. Energy transfer, often referred to by physicists as "work," is the area of science technically known as the laws of thermodynamics (hereinafter referred to as the laws of energy). These laws are the secret keys to the universe, from which the doors of perception reveal something of profound, magnanimous significance to the prosperity of human beings and nation-states. Scientists know that human beings are considered to be organic open systems since they exchange energy and matter. To function and resist decay they must consume energy, convert it to chemical and electrical form, channel it through the bodily organs, some of which is transmuted into mass, and expend it. Nation-states also exchange energy and matter. But to use the words of Einstein, "a somewhat unfamiliar conception for the average mind" is the fact that nation-states are organic open systems with processes like those of human beings. They are aggregate systems of human beings, complete with organs collectively referred to as the economy and fueled by the energy of human labor (modulated by information) in the form of goods and services, "the Invisible Hand." If we hovered above a nation-state or looked at a satellite photo, we would see the organs of the economy manifest with structures such as factories, office buildings, and storefronts, along with arteries of streets, highways, railways, subways, waterways, and airports, all containing human cells, often within cars, trucks, trains, ships, and even tubes called airplanes (fig. 1). "Neurotransmitters" such as cell phones, radio, television, and the Internet transmit information between the "cells." The parallels between humans and nation-states are significant. They both consume energy, convert it for use or expenditure, and channel it through their organs in order to perpetuate the life, health, and prosperity of their respective systems.

If we understand how the laws of energy operate through open systems and the conditions under which open systems prosper, we can determine which systems of nation-state governance are consistent with such conditions in order to foster prosperity. Although history has already made these determinations, most have failed to heed such lessons. Hopefully, the immutable truth of science will eventually awake humanity to the fact that the health and prosperity of open systems begins with the value of the energy consumed. For nation-state systems this is from the bottom up (GDP), from the energy labor of the individual citizens who impart values and create goods and services which are converted to money as it is channeled through the economy for consumers, a portion of which is distributed to the organ of government for taxation at the top. It is NOT the other way around.

Fig. 1: Downtown San Francisco, 2004 (Satellite image by GeoEye)

The First and Second Laws of Energy

Properly understood, the first law of energy may be utilized to manifest any dream one desires so long as the dream comports with the other laws of physics. The second law of energy tells us how we are to govern ourselves as open system individual human beings and nation-states. It says that open systems deteriorate and die unless energy is constantly consumed and expended. But it is both the value of the energy consumed and the value of the method by which that energy is expended that determines the health and prosperity of the system. *Effort,* or expending energy, means nothing or has no benefit unless it creates *value* to the system. Moreover, systems must constantly improve or evolve to prevent decay, because energy is constantly dispersing. There is only going forward or sliding backward but no standing still. Therefore, the efficiency or value of energy must be increased through intelligent innovation or evolution (this is also why when GDP is not growing for two quarters, it is called a "recession"—a recess or recession meaning a move backward). The greater the value created from energy consumption and expenditure, the greater the system. This applies to animate as well as inanimate systems.

As discussed in the chapter "Truth," at least part of our purpose is to discover the laws of nature and apply them for the benefit of humanity. Although the laws of energy were discovered a long time ago, they have been applied too infrequently when it comes to the way we govern ourselves both individually and as societies. This is because the laws of physics are relatively abstract or complex and not always easy to grasp. Thus, in this chapter I will attempt to simplify things. Accordingly, this chapter cannot be an exhaustive or detailed exposition on the laws of physics, for such complexity would require a literary volume of its own beyond the scope of this treatise. Therefore, the third law of energy which states that absolute zero cannot be achieved will not be discussed, nor will isolated or closed systems. Furthermore, I will generalize technical terminology in order to foster understanding of the fundamentals, and I will consider only the practical, real-world applications of the laws of energy and its effects upon humanity. The understanding, integration, and application of the essence of these laws would dramatically improve the quality of life and prosperity, both as individuals and as nation-states.

$E=mc^2$

The first law of energy is called the law of conservation of energy. This law says that there is a fixed or finite amount of energy in the universe and that it can neither be created nor destroyed, only transferred from one system to another in many different forms.* Energy transfer occurs all the time, whether it is the consumption of food or the creation of goods and services. But most of the energy transfer we see derives from the sun. The sun transfers its energy to plants, and plants transfer that energy to animals, including humans, and when animals and humans die, their remains likely become fossil fuels. Humans then transfer the energy of those fuels to power nation-states with electricity, transportation, and machinery, and as an ingredient in many of the products we

* It also states that upon transfer of energy, some energy is lost as heat in the initial process, but not destroyed.

consume, including plastics and clothing. *But the most important transfer of energy for prosperity is the energy of human thought in the transmission of information as values, because they produce the conditions for intelligent innovations of human labor, which are transmuted into the mass and matter of goods and services of value.*

Energy and mass are really the same thing, as expressed by Einstein's famous equation $E=mc^2$. Thus, the universe is made up of all the same stuff, which is generally interchangeable. In the words of Einstein himself:

> "...mass [matter is comprised of mass]* and energy are both but different manifestations of *the same thing*. A somewhat unfamiliar conception for the average mind. Furthermore, the equation E is equal m c squared, in which energy is put equal to mass, multiplied by the square of the velocity of light, showed that very small amounts of mass may be converted into a very large amount of energy and *vice versa. The mass and energy were in fact equivalent ...*" [emphasis added][1] [Also see how the calculation works!]†

As semiconscious, polarized cells of awareness, we are obviously transmuting the emanating energy of our thoughts into the mass and matter of goods and services all the time. We just can't see the mechanics at the cellular level because *we are the cells* transmuting energy into mass

---

* The difference between mass and matter: all matter consists of mass but not all mass has matter, e.g., a mouse trap spring that is wound back has mass that is not matter. The potential energy wound back from the spring doesn't display matter, but the potential energy that is released when it's tripped is equivalent to mass.

† Nothing can travel faster than the speed of light (approximately 186,000 miles per second). The speed of light squared in Einstein's equation, or multiplying the speed of light times itself, is used only for the purpose of determining the amount of energy in mass, and vice versa. "So why would you have to multiply the mass of that walnut by the speed of light to determine how much energy is bound up inside it? The reason is that whenever you convert part of a walnut or any other piece of matter to pure energy, the resulting energy is by definition moving at the speed of light. Pure energy is electromagnetic radiation—whether light or X-rays or whatever—and electromagnetic radiation travels at a constant speed of roughly 670,000,000 miles per hour. Why, then, do you have to square the speed of light? It has to do with the nature of energy. When something is moving four times as fast as something else, it doesn't have four times the energy but rather 16 times the energy—in other words, that figure is squared. So the speed of light squared is the conversion factor that decides just how much energy lies captured within a walnut or any other chunk of matter. And because the speed of light squared is a huge number—448,900,000,000,000,000 in units of mph—the amount of energy bound up into even the smallest mass is truly mind-boggling."[2]

and matter, which we channel through the nation-state organs/economy. Any individual with the thought of an idea is simply transmitting impulses of *energy* at the speed of light—the metaphorical light bulb in the brain—the ultimate speed attainable in the universe, at which point the perception of time stops.* You don't notice time at the same moment you have the energy impulse of an idea. OUR BRAIN AND BODY ARE BUT CELLULAR CONDUITS TRANSMUTING THE SPEED OF OUR THOUGHTS INTO MASS AND MATTER AS WE SIMULTANEOUSLY DIRECT OUR ENERGIES OF MENTAL AND PHYSICAL LABOR. For practical purposes of human prosperity, the frequency and value of ideas generally derive from the transmission of information into cultural values which provide conditions conducive to intelligent innovation. As long as the concept which the idea or impulse of energy expresses remains plausible and consistent with the laws of physics, it can be transmuted or manifested into the mass and matter of goods and services with the energy of persistent will or desire. And as discussed in the chapter "Money," any such idea backed by money or venture capital is simply adding additional energy-labor behind the idea to catalyze its manifestation to physical reality. As a lofty example, think about the concept of flight. Humanity has had the energy impulse thought of flying and desire to do so since time immemorial, yet we cannot just transmute that thought into manifestation, jump into the air and fly like Superman. In order to transmute the thought energy impulse of flying into manifestation, the manifestation must be consistent with the other laws of physics, such as the concept of lift, one of the critical laws of physics discovered to enable flight. But to get to the point where the laws of physics are understood well enough to discover the concept of lift, the conditions of cultural values consumed from transmitted energy of proper nurture must be conducive; freedom, education, discipline, and the desire to contribute value to others. Such values, practiced over many centuries, impact biology and the genetics that increase intelligence. With the energy impulse idea and energy of desire for flight, humanity set in motion its intention to manifest it into the literal mass and matter of physical reality. Although the chemicals to make the steel for the fuselage and wings were already in the form of mass and matter, only the energy of directed thought could convert them into the mass and matter of an airplane. And with that intention, along with persistence and the additional energy-labor backing of money in the great catalyst of venture capital,

---

* Just as the speed of light is the ultimate speed attainable in the universe, when the perception of time stops, enlightenment is the ultimate attainment for humanity, at which point time also stops.

laws of nature were accessed and applied for the benefit of humanity in lift and propulsion. The result is the transmutation of the energy impulse idea of flight, manifested by humanity in the literal mass and matter of airbuses transporting people almost anywhere on Earth and even beyond. Such a tremendous contribution of value has enabled countless people to visit loved ones almost anywhere and to expand other relationships, business or otherwise.

Thus, application of the first law of energy should inspire optimism in the intelligent innovators of free societies to see that even the sky is not the limit, as manifested by the development of commercial space flight. Any free person with the energy impulse of an idea and the requisite energy in desire and persistence can transmute that thought into the mass and matter of reality, so long as it is consistent with the other laws of nature or physics. Look at all of the great technologies that have been manifested as a result of this law. Who could have imagined communicating across the world instantaneously with a few key strokes on a computer or even with face-to-face video via cell technology and the Internet? Actually, many have, as we have even seen expressed in the late 1960s series *Star Trek*.[3] From the impulse of thought energy and the energy in desire and persistence backed by energy-labor (money), the intelligent innovators made it happen in accordance with the first law of energy.

The second law of energy expresses the *thermodynamic arrow of time* and energy transfer, which in practical, real-world terms simply means this: As time progresses forward, energy disperses from a more concentrated state to a more diffuse state, or from relative order to disorder.[4] This is inevitable, as everything we generally perceive with our five senses in the physical world eventually decays or deteriorates, but it does so at varying rates, from instantaneous to billions of years, depending upon the composition of the entity (even the element gold decays). The statistical tendency to the dispersal of that energy or disorder and its quantitative measure is called *entropy*. We commonly see this in the long-term processes of aging. Look at most celebrities on television when they were in their prime, then look at them in middle to old age. That is the most visible and visceral method of understanding entropy. You may notice gray hair, wrinkles, a bloated face and body that makes them almost unrecognizable. Other examples include flowers wilting, wood rotting, and food spoiling. Obviously, things tend to decay—to become disordered—as time progresses. However, such decay or disorder may be resisted by applying energy of value. Those celebrities who consume energy of value in healthy food, and/or exercise consistently and properly by methods of value "age well." This is only resisting entropy, as systems need to be maintained since they tend to disorder as time progresses. This is the reason why economies develop to substantially include maintenance organs and corresponding goods and services. Just as the organs of the human body produce chemicals from consumed energy to assist the individual body and its cells when it deteriorates, the organs of nation-states or the economy do the same for the aggregate body and its cells of humans from consumption of goods and services. Countless examples of this include hospitals (and ambulances to repair damaged cells) and their corresponding medical products and services; health food stores and their corresponding health foods and food services; fitness centers and their corresponding goods and services; hair salons and their corresponding hair products and services; nail salons and their corresponding nail products and services; lawn nurseries and their corresponding products and services; and hardware stores and their corresponding products and services, etc. These are all in existence to resist the decay of entropy.

Entropy and the Arrow of Time

Entropy is known as the only quantity in the macroscopic world that picks a particular direction of time by increasing as time progresses.[5] The one directional nature of time occurring in the macro world we see is illustrated by the fact that you cannot un-break a glass, un-ring a bell, un-birth a baby, or un-kill a person. Time is nature's instructional device for humanity, so that we may deduce that our actions and behavior have consequences, without which we could not learn experientially in our evolution toward the enlightenment of virtue. For if we could go back in time, each person would simply correct their mistakes so that they would not have to live with the consequences, so the experiential impact would be limited. Instead we have both physical and emotional scars as a record to remind us of our behavior and the consequences. Time is *a record of our behavior.* Hence, we often judge people by their "track record." History is the aggregation of time, hence the term *learning from history*, for if time is a record of our behavior and history is the aggregation of time, *learning from our history* means learning from our aggregate behavior. Two salient facts provide further support that time is nature's instructional device for humanity: 1. Humanity is the only known animate system that measures and records time both internally and with external devices, and 2. The one-directional arrow of time does not exist at the atomic level—the world we can't see operating beyond the unaided human physical senses. At the atomic level, going back in time, an atom might move to the right, while going forward in time an atom might move to the left, with no qualitative difference in the actions of the atom.[6] Moreover, relatively recent studies have strongly suggested that the future influences the past, and vice versa.[7] Time is a construct of the human mind, designed by nature as a record or ethereal notebook of experiential behavior.* Studies of substantiated and credible near-death incidents consistently reveal that the subjects experienced their "whole life" flashing before them.[8] This is their track record or life history being reviewed for experiential impact learning. We have records of such anecdotal evidence because we have been divinely inspired to develop external devices which measure and record time. Such devices include wrist watches, calendars, yearbooks, still photo cameras, video cameras, and audio recorders. These devices mark and record our behaviors and experiences in time so that we may review and hopefully learn from our past behaviors by their emotive impact. Movies, television, and lyrical music are also created for the same purpose but teach us through the lessons of others. Time is endemic to humans, a "benevolent trick" from our source that makes us feel as if our existence is limited. This restricted view tests our behavior and its consequences. Why behave with virtue if we are going to die no matter what? The truth is that we are in school and we are eternal; otherwise, such complexity of life would be unnecessary and statistically impossible. The matter of our body is animated by the energy of our soul, and since energy can neither be created nor destroyed (first law of energy), it follows that the energy of our soul must be eternal. Physical death occurs when the matter of the body becomes compromised, at which point the energy of the soul vacates for transfer elsewhere.

Entropy and Virtue—Perception, Choice, Consequences

Nature has designed the universe so cleverly that the most efficient way for humans to resist entropy is through the attainment of virtue.

---

* Technically, time is a measure of motion, e.g., moving a hundred miles per hour. Everything is moving through space even when we are standing still, as the earth spins on its axis at a thousand miles per hour and revolves around the sun while the galaxies move through space.

This is not by chance, as enlightenment is our ultimate purpose, at which point time will cease for those who attain it, just as it does when the speed of light is attained. As previously noted, since energy always disperses over time, as open systems we are required to actively replace it through the perpetual cycle of energy consumption and expenditure. Otherwise we decay, disintegrate, and die. Entropy is nature's hedge against sloth. When we are lazy, we decay more rapidly. VIRTUE IS THE ANTIDOTE. Most of us have choices about the information and energy we consume, the amount we consume, and the methods by which we expend it. These choices determine the life, health, and prosperity of our system.

We must be discerning. Bad choices in consumption of both information and energy, along with bad choices in the methods of energy expenditure, do not bode well for life under the second law of energy. They result in toxicity, overindulgence, indolence, disease, atrophy, pain, misery, and death. Virtuous choices in consumption of information— aligned with truth as conducive to moderation, industriousness, and intelligent innovation—and healthy energy consumption, along with virtuous methods of expenditure, perpetuate and promote health, happiness, and prosperity. *The greater the value of the energy (and information) consumed and the greater the value in the method of expenditure, the greater the health and prosperity of the system.*

As advanced animate open systems, humans are designed to have perception, choice, and consequences in order to learn so as to ultimately achieve enlightenment to virtue. Again, our perceptions and choices in energy consumption and the method of expenditure, along with the consequences of those perceptions and choices, determine our health and prosperity, both as individual humans and human aggregates called nation-states. However, we are often blinded by the subjectivity of our perceptions and choices through indoctrination (as polarized cells) by our primary caretakers and/or culture, and this usually inhibits health and prosperity. Thus, the values of our cultures determine misery or prosperity, depending upon whether or not they align with the laws of nature and truth. If we could step out of ourselves and create parallel systems without the "free will" or "choice" aspect of advanced living systems but still functioning in accordance with the laws of physics, we could learn how open systems operate most efficiently and extrapolate that knowledge for the health and prosperity of humans and nation-states. Of course we have already created such systems, but we have done so without understanding or applying that knowledge to ourselves. The open systems we have created perceive value in energy, consume it, channel it through their organs, and expend that same energy just as we do. A simple battery-powered electronic device is an example of such an open system without choice, so we can use it for illustration of and comparison to living systems—humans and nation-states. Thus, the distinction is that inanimate open systems don't have choice and discernment in how they consume and expend energy, and although we may have created them, their processes are instructive to us, especially for understanding how to achieve nation-state prosperity. They are an expression of our concurrent knowledge of energy and science. The following illustrations should remove the naturally imposed filters that obscure the organs and rudimentary processes of nation-states (fig. 2).

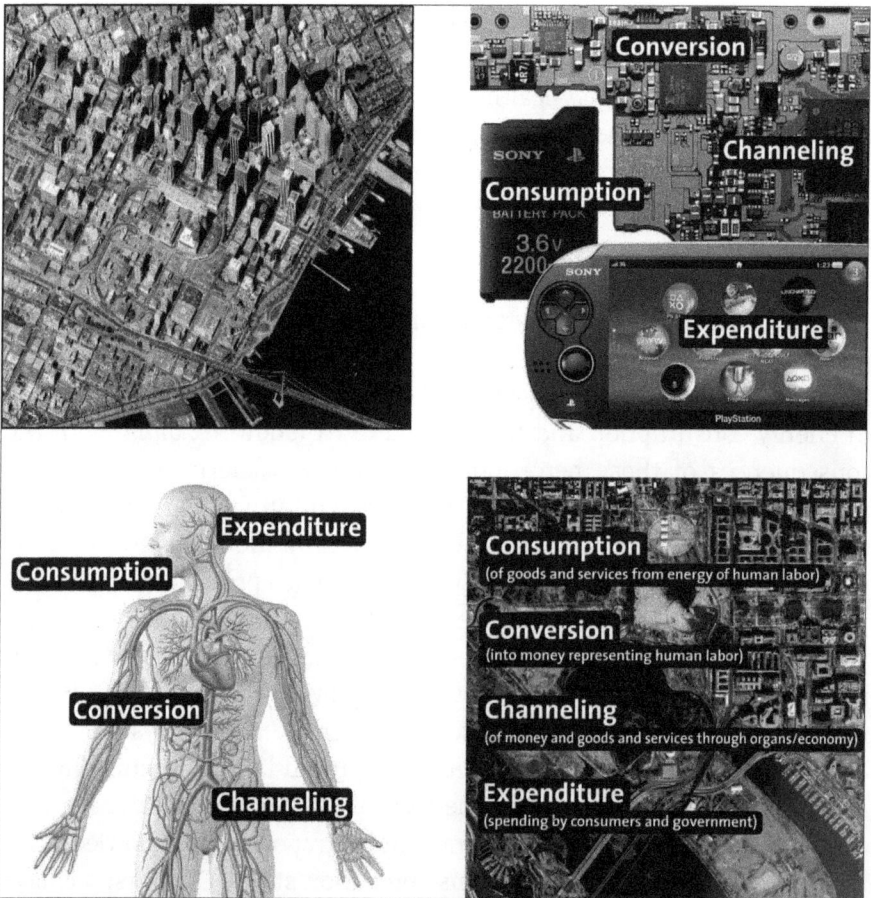

Fig. 2: Consumption of Energy, Conversion, Channeling, Expenditure.

Energy of Proper Form Perceived as Value for Consumption, Conversion, and Channeling through Organs: Mechanics of Open Systems

For energy to yield potential value to a system, it must be in the proper *form* to be perceived as value for consumption, conversion, and expenditure. *This is because each open system has an energy converter or coupling mechanism which channels the energy for expenditure/work.*[9]

Within battery-powered electronic devices, the form of energy for consumption is typically chemical-filled batteries, which is converted and channeled as electrical energy *through the circuits and transistors for expenditure/work, all regulated by the processor/brain* (fig. 3). If energy-rich orange juice is poured into the battery compartment, the system will not perceive it as value for conversion to electrical energy and expenditure to operate the device since the energy is not in the proper form.

Within humans, the form of energy for consumption is food/biomass, which is converted and channeled as chemical and electrical energy *through the body's organs for expenditure/work, all regulated by the brain/processor* (fig. 4). If a human consumes gasoline, the system may not perceive it as value for conversion to chemical and electrical energy and expenditure since the energy is not in the proper form.

WITHIN NATION-STATES, THE FORM OF ENERGY FOR CONSUMPTION IS HUMAN LABOR/GOODS AND SERVICES, WHICH ARE CONVERTED AND CHANNELED AS MONEY THROUGH THE ECONOMY FOR EXPENDITURE/WORK, ALL REGULATED BY GOVERNMENT (fig. 5, Also see Chapter 3, "Money": The energy of human labor is quantized in units called money). Goods and/or services for consumption that no one wants will not be perceived as value for conversion to money and expenditure/work since they are not in the proper form. Energy consumption and expenditure by nation-states is a bilateral simultaneous process of the individual citizens and the nation-states organs, which include the economy and government: (1) individual citizens consume food/biomass, expend that energy in labor to create or render goods and services domestically (GDP) and/or internationally, which when consumed by consumers is converted into money (quantized energy-labor), channeled through the organs/economy of the nation-state and expended or stored in accounts for expenditure (just as energy in fat is stored in the body). The perceived value of the goods and services consumed determines the amount of money (value of energy in labor/GDP), while the difference between the real value and perceived value of the goods and services is the degree of "toxicity" of the energy or labor; (2) governments whether national or local are also organs of the nation-state. They simultaneously receive a distributed portion or percentage of GDP through taxation of the productive labor of goods and services previously converted into money. Governments regulate or direct expenditures of that nation-state energy, as the brain regulates energy expenditure of the human body, via government spending on the legislative, judiciary, and executive branches in what *should solely* be for the purpose of protecting nation-state life, liberty, and property. But in order for the nation-state to consume and expend, the citizens must be productive in goods and/or services or GDP. THEIR LABOR IS THE SOURCE OF ENERGY WHICH DRIVES THE NATION-STATE, NOT THE GOVERNMENT. The government organ obviously derives its energy from the productivity of people, and not vice versa. Government can consume only what the people distribute to it, whereas the people can consume as much as they produce. Just as food is distributed to the different organs of the body as converted into the form of chemical and electrical energy, the energy of productive human labor is distributed to the organs of the nation-state body as converted into the form of money, including to the organ of government through taxation.

Toxicity

It is critical to understand that even if a form of energy is perceived as value and consumed by a system, it may still ultimately be toxic to its health and prosperity. Toxic battery energy may eventually corrode and damage an electronic device. Toxic foods may corrode the arteries or calcify the organs of humans, causing disease and death. Nation-states also consume energy from human labor in the form of goods and services that may be perceived as value but may in fact be toxic, as certain financial services or harmful products has proved, causing lasting damage to nation-states, as the U.S. economic meltdown of 2008 demonstrates (also, toxic ideologies or values consumed as information produce toxic cultures). Perceived value is the variant, because the *real* value of the energy consumed is critical to the health of any open system, e.g., *whether the types of goods and services are of benefit or detriment to a society or whether the values of the society are conducive to prosperity.*

Entropy of Systems—the Value of the Energy Consumed and the Value of the Method by which the Energy is Expended Determines the Health and Prosperity of the System

Battery-Powered Electronic Devices

Suppose you purchase a brand-new battery-powered portable video game loaded with a new, fully charged battery. If you leave town for a significant amount of time without having ever used the device, you may notice upon your return that the unused battery over such time became dead and inoperable, and calcification of sulfites may have manifested itself on the ends of the battery and into the electronic device to render it inoperable, as well. This is the result of entropy. Over time the concentrated chemical energy in the battery dispersed or decayed. When the fully charged battery was originally integrated into the electronic device, that device contained energy for consumption and expenditure (work). Had the electronic device been switched on so that it could perceive value in the energy of the battery, the device would have consumed that energy just as people consume food or nation-states consume energy from the productive labor of their people, and that energy would be expended as it channeled through the circuits and transistors as "work" of value to operate the device. But since the device was not powered on in our initial example, no work of value took place, while concentrated and somewhat toxic unused chemical energy remained in the fully charged battery within the device. When that energy was not expended as work of value, over time, entropy caused the energy to disperse, and the toxicity from the battery chemicals manifested itself on the battery and inside the device in sulfite form. So how do we get the device working again? Once the toxicity of the corroded parts is eliminated, the device needs energy to operate. It can't just be switched on and ordered to operate without a supply of energy. Therefore, energy of value in a battery, hopefully one that is cleaner, longer-lasting, and more efficient must be integrated into the device for its consumption. The best performing electronic devices or open systems will be those that expend the energy most efficiently—those that waste the least energy for longest duration of operation. As I will demonstrate, intelligent innovation increases the efficiency and value of energy expenditure. Thus, the method of expenditure is also critical to the operation of the device.

Humans

The human body operates the same way. When we consume food/biomass energy without expending it as "work" in proper exercise or some form of physical activity of value to the body other than just autonomous functions, over time, entropy causes the transferred energy (which created muscle mass) to disperse, causing atrophy or "flabbiness." This affects the health of the system in mobility, physical strength, and functioning. Moreover, if the food energy consumed consistently contains toxicity (as the battery's chemicals in our previous example), such as greasy meat, sufficient quantities may disperse in the body over time to manifest itself as plaque of the arteries, fatty mass, gout, or calcification of the organs, just like the plaque calcification manifesting itself on the ends of the batteries. This renders the system enervated and unhealthy. When the human body is in such a state, asking it to expend additional energy alone will not revitalize the body. When a runner is exhausted and near collapse after running a marathon, the runner cannot be revitalized by asking him to run an additional twenty-six miles. Instead, the runner must consume energy of value in healthy foods and liquids and must also expend it in a way that creates value to the bodily system. Punching a brick wall is a method of energy expenditure and an exhibition of effort, but it is not expending energy of value to the system. Proper physical resistance exercise for muscle tone and cardiovascular exercise to oxygenate the cells for endurance are methods of valuable energy expenditure. Thus, for the system to be healthy and prosperous, the value of the energy consumed and the value of the method by which the energy is expended determines the health and prosperity of the system.*

Nation-States

The same applies to nation-states. The energy of value consumed by nation-states is the productive energy labor of its people or GDP (de-

---

* Also, incessantly bad and stressful thoughts are sustained impulses of "bad energy," which if not successfully expended and transmuted as work of value causes stress to the system that disperses to manifest itself as disease. This is the operation of both the first and second laws of energy.

THE LAWS OF ENERGY — CHAPTER 4

rived from cultural values consumed and transmitted as information). Thus, only the cells (people) participating in commerce, not the government, can stimulate the economy. The government is an organ of the nation-state body needing sustenance, but it should not sap, overtax, or over-regulate the energy source which sustains it and the rest of the body nation-state—the creative labor of the people. The perceived value of their goods and services determines the amount of consumption and money it is converted into by consumers for further channeling through the economy. A portion of that productive labor (GDP) in money is also distributed to the organ of government, which consumes it through taxing the economy. If the economy is overtaxed, just like overtaxing the organs of the body, it may collapse. Thus, both the individual cells (people) and the organs of the nation-state (including government) both consume energy. When that energy is consumed, value must be created from it, or else it will dissipate over time in accordance with entropy. The consumer provides value by handing over money (representing the energy of human labor) for goods and services, but the government must also provide sufficient value for their consumption or taxation for a nation-state to be healthy and prosperous.

Money is the perfect example to demonstrate that value must be created when energy is received; otherwise, it will dissipate in accordance with entropy. As I have repeatedly stated, money represents the energy of human labor. When it is received but not used to create value, over time, it dissipates or loses its value. The example in the chapter "Money" is illustrative and worth repeating. If five $100 bills were hidden in a mattress seventy-five years ago, they will not have nearly the same purchasing power today.* However, if that same sum of currency was instead put to use as value to others in a bank account for lending instead of hidden in a mattress, it would have accrued interest to keep up with or even exceed inflation. This is how nature operates. *We must create value when we receive energy, or else that energy will dissipate.* In fact, that is the nature of capitalism. Humans consume food as energy, and they expend that energy in labor, attempting to create or provide value in goods and services for others. If those goods and services are perceived as value by others, they may be converted into money by consumers. The more value perceived by consumers, the more money the goods and services yield. The money received by the provider of the goods and services represents an amount

---

* *Paper* bills representing labor, not coins. Coins of scarce metals represent a different type of value.

of human labor that may be directed through the economy to create or provide additional value in employment and more goods and services, either through consumption or reinvestment. Thus, with each exchange of energy in goods and services for money, additional energy of value may be created to resist entropy of the organs—the economy—of the nation-state.

Unfortunately, nation-states that adopt substantial socialist or welfare state policies falsely perceive value to their system (consumption and transmission of toxic ideology) in government spending on something-for-nothing entitlements. In fact, government spending on such entitlements without the recipient's expending energy of value is not work of value from the government for its consumption in taxing others, but is simply the transference of energy from one part of the system to another, or in other words, the redistribution of energy without value creation. And energy dissipates without work of value. Socialists make the illogical and false argument that entitlements are of value since free healthcare or unemployment benefits "improve" the lives of people. However, as nature dictates, since the recipients of these entitlements did not perform work of value from what they received, the system did not resist entropy. Instead, without accountability, the entitlement recipients can continue with unhealthy habits, knowing that there is no financial/labor consequence to them in overindulgent eating, smoking, and drinking, nor is there much incentive to go to work when they get paid to sit at home. In fact, they usually become dependent and unfit to work as their abilities are also subject to the laws of energy with entropy. This entropy cycle continues with the values of a culture decaying to an entitlement dependency mentality. Like a baby seeking his bottle, without the milk from Momma he will scream and quake violently (see public employee labor unions and the Occupy Wall Street movement). This is the reality of a decadent society transmitting toxic values. Decadent of course means to "decay," which not coincidentally is the same essential meaning of entropy. We can see the decay of prosperity in direct correlation with the decay/entropy of American cultural values. Of course a nation-state has downtrodden people. Many of us have been there. However, individuals and charities are best suited to help them, for they are much closer to them than an impersonal government. Moreover, this is the test of virtue, our ultimate purpose. People with ability may ignore them, throw money at them to relieve their conscience (yet perpetuate their condition), or conscientiously and constructively assist them in direct confrontation of the issues that have brought them down and out (often their values). Only this last option is actual work of value to improve the diseased or damaged cell (the individual) through remediation of values and biological sustenance. This also tests the values of a culture. Enlightened people understand that entitlements do not work to improve the conditions of others in a sustained manner, as verified by ample empirical evidence.[10] This is because entitlement does not address the underlying cause—the *values* which cause impoverishment. Unfortunately, when government assumes the role of caretaker, it overrides the private charities that would normally fill that gap to address values, just as it did before politicians usurped that role in perpetual vote-buying cycles—"Give me your vote, and I will give you free stuff." This approach is largely responsible for the entropy or decay of American values and prosperity. Value must be given for energy consumption (money), or else the energy will decay (entropy), as we see with the over sixteen trillion-dollar U.S. national debt and the European debt crisis, caused by something-for-nothing entitlements.

Since government health and unemployment entitlements (*taking the productive labor energy of one and giving it to another*) is not work of value to the system nation-state, over time, entropy causes that consumed energy (from government taxation) to disperse as a net loss of unusable energy, and depending upon the amount of something-for-nothing entitlements, the system may become enervated and rendered unhealthy. But instead of weakened or diseased bodily organs, it is weakened economies in recession or depression, as America and Europe can attest with their resultant *quantity of entropy, which we call "debt."* REMEMBER, JUST AS CIRCUITS AND TRANSISTORS CONVERT AND CHANNEL CHEMICAL BATTERY ENERGY AS ELECTRICITY THROUGH ELECTRONIC DEVICES, AND HUMAN ORGANS CONVERT AND CHANNEL FOOD/BIOMASS AS CHEMICAL AND ELECTRICAL ENERGY THROUGH THE HUMAN BODY, THE ECONOMY CONVERTS AND CHANNELS THE ENERGY OF VALUES/LABOR/GOODS/SERVICES AND MONEY THROUGH NATION-STATES. Nation-states expend that energy-labor on both the cellular level (the people) and organ level (e.g., government). The nation-state organ of government for the United States of America, for example, currently expends (spends) much more energy than it consumes in taxable work of value (productivity or GDP). Obviously, a system cannot expend more energy than it consumes without affecting its health and prosperity. Just as a human must seek energy when it is enervated and out of food, so must a nation-state. Leftists/socialists argue to "raise taxes on the wealthy," or in other words to take more energy-labor from the most productive; however, this would enervate those who provide goods, services, and employment, as *the consuming entity always increases the entropy of the entity which it consumes (second law of energy)*. For self-preservation, the entity being consumed would either take their business (productive energy) abroad or park their money (store their energy) to prevent the coerced inequitable redistribution of their productive labor. This has in fact already occurred in America as a result of the highest corporate tax rate in the world. And when a nation-state does not have enough energy of value to consume in taxable productivity to keep the system running or prevent collapse of its organs (economy), it must borrow it from others, just like asking for food—only in this case the food must be repaid and may have "toxicity" in its terms on the way down through its system.

America as a nation-state used to have sufficient taxable productivity as energy for consumption to sustain itself, and its debt burden or entropy was also at sustainable levels which could be resisted. Unfortunately, over the past century, an unhealthy something-for-nothing entitlement society perniciously developed from within the system. This began with the values of the progressive movement of the early twentieth century, causing expenditures to far exceed consumable productivity (work of value), while simultaneously transforming American values as a culture from self-reliance to entitlement. The method of expenditure of the consumed or taxed productivity by the government became insufficient work of value to the system nation-state, as much of it was in effect only a transference of energy within the system (redistribution) and not work of value at all. And without work of value, that transferred energy dispersed or dissipated for a net loss of energy or debt (entropy) to the system nation-state, thereby weakening the system. This hit a crescendo in the 1990s and 2000s after the U.S. government declared that all people are entitled to home ownership regardless of insufficient successful contribution of energy of value to the system, or insufficient productive labor. The government consumed energy of perceived value (productive labor) by taxing money converted from goods and services and transferred it to those who could not successfully contribute sufficient value to the system so they could own homes. This was effectuated in the form of guaranteed loans through the government agencies Fannie Mae and Freddie Mac. Giving homes to people is the same as giving them the energy labor of those who built them. This would be fine so long as they could provide sufficient work of value to resist entropy, or debt, from the borrowed cost or labor of the homes. But even if they could not, their mortgage debt was still perceived to have value, represented by their future productive energy-labor to be repaid. The perceived value of that mortgage debt was further converted into securities called mortgage debt obligations, collateralized by the value of the homes, which was much less than the purported value of the securities. The difference between the two defines the toxicity level of the securities. These toxic securities were channeled by the organs or economy of the U.S. nation-state (and internationally) and insured by other private *organs* of the economy. The toxicity was so great that the government feared that the organs of the nation-state would collapse. As a result, it ordered the taxpayers to assume the debt in an additional entropy burden for the taxpayer to resist (the assumption of debt is a promise of a future quantity of productive labor at least equal to the quantity of entropy or debt). Unfortunately, at some point the increase in entropy became so enormous a quantity (sixteen trillion quantized units of labor) that the amount of energy of value or productive labor to resist was insufficient. Thus, the system could ultimately collapse unless intelligent, innovative industry develops to dramatically increase the value of productive labor or productivity (sufficient energy of value) in order to resist the great quantity of entropy/debt. The value of the method of expenditure (government spending) must also be more efficient so as to resist the enormous debt of entropy (reduce unnecessary spending substantially and pay down the debt). Government spending should be limited to the protection of the lives, liberty, and property of the nation-state.

If all this wasn't enough to weaken the system, the current neo-radical leftist U.S. administration would compound the something-for-nothing quagmire with the most expensive of all entitlements—health-care. Legislation would now require responsible citizens to pay for the irresponsible lifestyle choices of others. We all overindulge at times and make bad choices. But we should be solely responsible for the consequences of those choices so that we can learn from our mistakes in our individual path to enlightenment of virtue in order to become stronger individual cells for a strong collective body. And although Medicare and Medicaid have already corrupted those fundamental values, the new legislation would take it even further to fundamentally transform cultural values. Citizen Ascetic could work hard and abstain from smoking, drinking, and unhealthy foods only to have to pay for Citizen Hedonist's overindulgent, chain-smoking, bacon cheeseburger-eating, and alcohol-binging medical problems. Now that's social justice!

Instead of reducing or eliminating overspending on something-for-nothing entitlements, the U.S. chose to perpetuate the folly by borrowing additional energy-labor for consumption not only from its own people but from the people of other system nation-states. When a nation-state borrows money from another nation-state, it is borrowing energy to consume for survival, just as a broke hungry human would get food energy from others to survive. That energy is the productive labor of the citizenry of the system nation-state from which the money is borrowed. The U.S. currently borrows and consumes a significant amount of its energy/money from the labor of the citizenry of China. When energy/money is borrowed or consumed, work of value must be expended in an amount at least equal to the amount borrowed or consumed. Effort is not good enough, as the work/energy must be of value to the system, otherwise the energy disperses to debt (as with the 2009 U.S. "stimulus") in accordance with entropy. Unfortunately, much of the money borrowed by the U.S. is used just to pay the interest on the accumulated national debt. Then it dissipates after the interest payment without enough real additional value to the system nation-state other than entitlements and the perpetuation of additional entropy or debt. Therefore, no improvement of the condition of the system occurred with such borrowing. To save the nation-state and culture at the cellular level, the method of expenditure (government spending) must improve in order to be actual work of value rather than entitlements. Life, liberty, and property are all in jeopardy under current conditions, where the organs (the economy) of the system may collapse. The only energy source that can sufficiently resist or overcome the enormous entropy of debt is labor of increased value or productivity, and this stems from cultural values. Thus, only spending that resists entropy by paying down debt or otherwise supports or catalyzes intelligent innovative technologies can be work or spending of value at this point toward the protection of life, liberty, and property of the nation-state. Government spending or expenditure of energy (from consumption of human labor in taxation) must be substantially reduced so that current government consumption levels of that energy can be used as value to pay down the debt or resist the decay of entropy. This means government spending should solely be *for the equal protection* of the individual lives, liberty, and property of the nation-state citizenry.

Intelligent Innovation to Increase the Efficiency and Value of Energy (Evolution) and the Method of its Expenditure

Improvement upon open systems can be achieved by increasing the efficiency and value of both the energy consumed and the method of expenditure through intelligent innovation. This is basically what evolution is—increasing the efficiency and value of energy. Increasing the efficiency and value of the energy consumed and the value in the method which that energy is expended through intelligent innovation will improve the life of the system both qualitatively (more efficient energy) and quantitatively (less entropy). This applies to both animate and inanimate systems, as illustrated with battery-powered electronic devices, humans, and nation-states. But it is important to remember that the value of the energy consumed and expended derives from the value of each cell. The individual cells of energy must have value to expend for the health and prosperity of any system. Thus, it is imperative that the cells at the individual level are strong. The cells of a nation-state are the individual people. They must have strong values for sustained health and prosperity.

Battery-Powered Electronic Device

If through intelligent innovation we develop a battery consisting of cells that are more efficient, lighter, cleaner, stronger, and last longer than the cells of regular alkaline batteries, we improve the efficiency or value of the energy for consumption. Through intelligent innovation we may also improve the efficiency or value of the method of energy expenditure, as we may develop an improved processor in the "brain" of the battery-powered, portable electronic device (portable video game or cell phone) to efficiently regulate the amounts of energy expended so that less energy is required to operate the device (for nation-states, government has a similar role). These improvements in value of both the energy for consumption and the method of energy expenditure would substantially increase the duration and quality of use, as the energy would be consumed and expended more efficiently, without the toxicity of sulfite calcification in the battery powered electronic device.

Humans

The same applies to humans. However, unlike the inanimate electronic device, virtue would be critically tested with human consumption of biomass. As open organic systems, we must consume other life to survive. This is not a coincidence. Everything we eat that has value in energy was alive at some point, not just animals but fruits and vegetables, as well. *The test of virtue is our treatment of living things: humans, animals, and even flora.* Our treatment of other beings have consequences; mad cow disease, bird flu, swine flu . . . Coincidence? Our eating of animals per se is not immoral, it is our *treatment* of them, especially the intelligent life forms that feel pain and horror. Some believe that ephemeral, unnecessary, overindulgent pleasures of the palate justifies imposing horror on other living things. Virtue is poignantly tested here. As we intelligently innovated in scientific research, we not only discovered that free-range, antibiotic-free animals and organic fruits and vegetables are a cleaner more efficient source for energy consumption, but we also developed fruits and vegetables of improved biomass for consumption. Is it a coincidence that humane treatment of animals results in healthier food? We also developed techniques through intelligent innovation to improve the body's method of energy expenditure. Methods such as circuit weight training improve the human body system, because it not only builds muscles to resist entropy, it combines cardiovascular exercise to increase both duration and quality of life. BREAKING DOWN THE HUMAN MUSCLE THROUGH RESISTANCE OR WEIGHT TRAINING PLAYS EXACTLY THE SAME ROLE AS CREATIVE DESTRUCTION THROUGH INTELLIGENT INNOVATIONS FOR NATION-STATES. Just as older, inefficient goods and services are replaced with more efficient goods and services of greater value, older, weaker, decaying muscle is destroyed in favor of newer, stronger muscle to improve the strength and condition of the overall body, thereby increasing the value and efficiency of energy. The more we resist entropy in expending energy in proper resistance and aerobic training, the stronger the muscles and cardiovascular system for improvement over the original condition. Moderation in consumption and consistent physical expenditure in exercise to resist entropy is not easy. But such discipline is part of the test of virtue. We must remember that virtue is the antidote to entropy, and discipline is one of the most difficult of tests, but it is a true test of virtue nonetheless.

Nation-States

The same applies to nation states. In revolt against excessive taxation/consumption of their energy-labor by the organ of government known as the English monarchy, the Founding Fathers of the United States accessed the laws of nature to *intelligently innovate* a new nation-state chartered on the values of human liberty. Under the newly created U.S. Constitution, nation-state *consumption or taxation of citizen labor* was codified only to protect life, liberty, and property—not to coercively redistribute the labor of one person for the benefit of another without compensation.* This governing charter served the same role as the improved and more efficient processor of the portable, battery-powered electronic device previously mentioned in this section. However, for nation-states, instead of regulating the battery energy more efficiently, the improved form of government would provide liberty as the greatest conditions for intelligent innovation *to increase the efficiency and value of energy in human labor,* enabling the creation of goods and services for consumption and expenditure by others. Such optimized conditions designed for the individual cells of the open system fostered health and prosperity of the nation-state as never before in human history. The individual cells, the human beings comprising a nation-state, must be individually strong. Their *values* represent their value as individuals. The individual cells—the people—are the energy source of nation-states. Cells of weak values result in a weak energy source, while cells of strong values result in a strong energy source. Too often, excessive regulation imposed by national, state, and local government has constrained and enervated this energy source, discouraging intelligent innovation. The larger the government, the less freedom to channel innovative energy of the cells or citizens through the organs of the nation-state we call the economy. Conversely, the smaller the government, the more freedom to do so. Government should exist only to safeguard the natural rights to life, liberty, and property. Up until the early twentieth century, America provided the greatest freedom to intelligently innovate, as efficiency and value in expending energy-labor increased so significantly that it became known as the Industrial Revolution. Citizens were free to cultivate natural resources for the creation of goods and services of perceived value because of minimal restrictions,

---

* Although slaves were designated as property instead of life, the Founding Fathers provided the process for and remediated that form of involuntary servitude with the 13th Amendment. Also see Federalist Papers.

laying the foundation of intelligent innovation for the greatest prosperity in any nation-state in history.

To understand this mechanism at the most primitive level of humanity, let's look at prehistoric man. Instead of wasting energy and life chasing and wrestling animals to the ground for consumption, through intelligent innovation man learned to set traps and invent weapons such as spears. This conserved critical human energy needed for survival, as would the domestication of animals and agrarian farming. Similarly, in the process of evolution, to use a simple example, refrigeration saved a tremendous amount of time and energy in human labor. Unrefrigerated foods and beverages lasted only a certain amount of time before they became spoiled and rotten from the decay of entropy. Time and energy in human labor was required to acquire, prepare, and distribute additional foods and beverages for consumption. However, with the intelligent innovations of alternating current (AC) electricity and refrigeration, the efficiency and value of energy were substantially increased, as more foods could be stored and preserved for later consumption, conserving energy, life, time, and additional resources which otherwise would have been unnecessarily expended. The refrigerator and freezer slowed down the molecules of foods, delaying their dispersal or decay, and the time and energy conserved could then be used for other productive purposes and additional intelligent innovations. The refrigerator was intelligently innovated as a good for mass consumption by nation-state consumers, and therefore consumption of refrigerators collectively by many individuals of the nation-state increased GDP *because so much collective energy in human labor was saved to improve the quality of life for many individuals.* Thus, even consumption of refrigerators partially fuels a nation-state. This combined with all the other intelligent innovations purchased by consumers to increase the efficiency and value of energy in human labor increased GDP and tax revenues to the organ of government.

Increasing quantization of energy through decentralization for greater cellular (human) mobility and sufficiency has been characteristic of evolution (as opposed to collectivization), from analog to digital; from group barter to quantization of individual human labor by coins and paper money to individual computer blip transfers; from centralized switchboards to public phone booths to independent cellular mobile Internet devices; from mainframe computer to home PCs to individual mobile

Internet devices; from centralized printing stores to centralized office printers to individualized mobile laser printers; from movie theaters to VHS tapes to DVDs to individual streaming on mobile devices; from centralized libraries of hardcover books to mass distributed print paperback books to instantaneous electronic books digitally streamed to individual mobile devices; from centralized public radio music produced by records, cassettes, and CDs, to digital streaming of music on individual mobile devices; from centralized public network television to individual channels on the collective satellite dish and cable to the individual miniature satellite dish to Internet television digitally streamed on individual mobile devices, etc.

The greater *the value* of the energy consumed of human labor in goods and services (GDP) and the greater the value of the method of expenditure (government spending only to protect life, liberty, and property of the cells of the nation-state), the greater the nation-state system. Today, excessive regulations and the growth of inefficient crony-corrupted redistributive government has rendered the nation-state of America to life-support, as every dollar spent is borrowed to keep the system alive, and the trillions owed are all but impossible to pay back. The only hope for the U.S. is for the bloated welfare-state government to stop enervating the population and perpetuating a dependency culture, both of which have weakened *the values* of the cells. Instead, a small government which frees the population to develop habits consistent with both self-reliance and industriousness will strengthen the values of the cells to foster the intelligent innovations of the new technologies required for prosperity.

Intelligent innovation is the catalyst for the evolution of systems to improvement. If we want to improve systems and evolve, we must encourage, support, and revere intelligent innovation at the individual level, not vilify it. Those who have embraced intelligent innovation as a cultural value have improved the value, at the cellular level or individual level of the nation-state, for strong "energy cells"—the people. Look at nation-states that encourage intelligent innovation, then look at those that don't. The former achieve prosperity and optimism while the latter languish in poverty and despair. The nation-state region of the Middle East illustrates this disparity. A culture of only six million people that reveres intelligent innovation far exceeds a culture of over three hundred million in patents, technologies, scientific achievements, health, and prosperity. The internal stability and instability of their respective nation-states are also illustrative. Unfortunately, as a result of envy and indoctrination, intelligent innovators throughout the world are vilified as "exploiters" or "oppressors," even though the world greatly benefits from their contributions in raising the living standards of world populations. Ironically, the most vociferous lamentations against the intelligent innovators of the world come from those who most enjoy and exploit their contributions. They object to the intelligent innovators while they duplicitously drive luxury automobiles, fly jet planes, communicate on cell phones, enjoy tailored suits, luxury hotels, and fine cuisine—all created by the intelligent innovators and their aggregates called corporations.

Although we cannot stop the overall entropy or decay of the universe from increasing over time, as demonstrated, we can temporally decrease the entropy of local systems for maintenance, restoration, and improvement with the proper use of energy. But in order to do so, a system must first perceive value in an energy source. It then must *consume* that energy, convert it for use, and channel it through and *expend* it as work of value to its system. The higher the value of the energy consumed and the higher the value in the method of energy expenditure, the more resistance to entropy (disorder or decay) we have to improve the system. On a most visible level for open systems that exchange energy and matter, we see this highest value in top human athletes. They consume energy of the highest value (food/biomass), convert and channel it through their bodily organs as chemical and electrical energy, and expend that energy through daily physical training as the highest work of value to their physical system. You may notice that they have far more power, endurance, and overall better health than the obese, who generally consume low-value energy and expend energy in work of minimal value for subsistence functioning.

As a whole, the United States of America was founded on the greatest charter of values, and it is no coincidence that this has resulted in the greatest prosperity in human history. Those values have decayed or degraded over the past hundred years because of the indulgence-oriented leftist/progressive movement. As a result, America has become the obese nation-state (both figuratively and literally) once again demonstrating that the values of a culture determine its prosperity. The solution proposed by today's neo-radical leftist leadership in the executive and legislative branches clearly defies physics. They claim that increased government spending will stimulate and improve the nation-state economy. *This is the same as telling an obese person who has expended all of his energy chasing an ice cream truck, just before he collapses, that running additional miles will restore his energy and revitalize his body.* The runner cannot expend energy of value which he does not have. He must find additional energy of value for consumption.

The same is true of nation-states. The organ of government consumes energy as a portion of the productive labor of its citizens (taxation). That energy is then expended (government spending) ostensibly to support the health and prosperity of the nation-state. However, just like the obese person chasing the ice cream truck, when a nation-state over expends itself into a huge debt and deficit of energy, it may collapse. It can be revitalized only through the consumption of energy of value. But sufficient nutritious energy of value must be available for consumption. For nation-states this means sufficient productivity from human energy-labor, a portion of which the organ of government consumes to regulate the nation-state. However, consuming too much energy from those who produce will enervate the productive, reducing or eliminating their productivity. Therefore, tax rates must be low to moderate so that productivity and intelligent innovation can take place while government simultaneously consumes a portion as tax revenue for expenditure (spending) dedicated only to the protection of life, liberty, and property of its cells in resisting entropy or debt. This is also consistent with Arthur Laffer's infamous Laffer curve.[11] When taxation—the government's consumption of its citizens' productivity—is too high, government revenues decrease along with productivity. However, when government consumption of citizen productivity is low to moderate, government revenues increase. They increase because under such conditions, the productive still retain energy/money/labor to expend on intelligent innovation, and therefore do not need to conserve this energy in self-preservation from the consuming organ of government.

Moreover, it is immoral to tax different people at different rates. Each person should be treated equally and should pay the same flat percentage. A person with ten dollars should pay one dollar, and a person with a million dollars should pay one hundred thousand dollars. Otherwise, we promote the inequity that we are not to be treated equal. We should all be treated equally under law, regardless of our achievements.

We don't cut inches off the limbs of the tallest dominant basketball players, nor do we put weights on the legs of the fastest runners. If values determine the prosperity of a nation-state, what type of value system would
penalize or inhibit those responsible for prosperity? Envy, guilt, theft, and
preservation of depraved political power are not values which can sustain
prosperity. To punish success and reward mediocrity only weakens the
values of a culture. If the values of a culture determine its prosperity, the
values of the constituent cells or the individuals are paramount.

We see the highest value in energy expenditure by those whose
values are conducive to intelligent innovation. This is most evident in the
intelligent innovators' development of both communications and trans-
port of human cells, as months of arduous travel (energy expenditure)
are no longer required for either. The intelligent innovators who had the
values of freedom, self-determination, desire, persistence, self-reliance,
and responsibility sacrificed and expended their energy developing automobiles, airplanes, phones, the Internet and its many platform sites and
technologies for the greatest prosperity in human history. Such goods and
services have raised what we now take for granted as our standard of living, saving tremendous amounts of collective energy (and time) for both
human and nation-state systems. The intelligent innovators perpetually
increase the efficiency and value of human energy, thereby facilitating
evolution. Unfortunately, they have come under increased attack and vilification from power-seeking, indulgence-promoting leftist progressives
seeking captive dependents for votes. This has transformed the values
of the energy cells (individual Americans) from strong, self-reliant, intelligent innovators to weak dependents. Again virtue is being tested, as
the U.S.A. is at a crossroads—a nation-state of the free self-reliant versus enslaved dependents. Only a return to the strong values upon which
America was founded—the U.S. Constitution—can restore the prosperity of self-reliance and the liberty which it spawned.

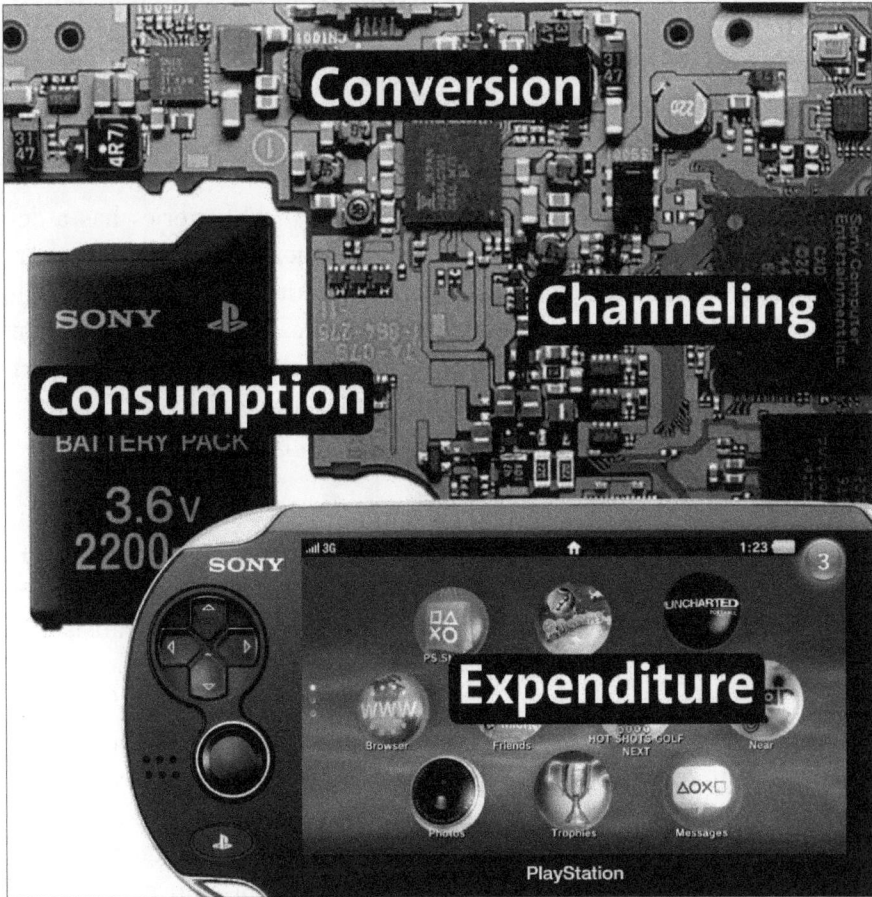

Fig. 3: (Images by Sony, PSP NGP)

Battery-Powered Electronic Device

- SYSTEM: Electronic device containing energy of fully charged alkaline chemical batteries within device.

- ENERGY: Transferred into the battery from chemical source upon production of battery, battery then integrated into electronic device—like food.

- ENERGY CONVERTER/ORGANS: Circuits and transistors

- ENTROPY: When little or no work of perceived value to resist entropy—electronic device system unused and left dormant for prolonged period of time. Energy remains latent in unused battery integrated within electronic device. Without use of the battery energy within the electronic device as work of perceived value to said device, *over time,* energy in chemical batteries disperses in accordance with entropy.

- TOXICITY: The source of energy in chemical batteries has a degree of toxicity. Therefore, when the energy disperses in accordance with entropy, calcification of a white substance called sulfite forms on the ends of battery. Calcification causes the system or device to become unhealthy. System may die, be restored, or even improved, all depending upon level of toxicity from battery chemical dispersion to circuits and/or transistors.

- WORK OF PERCEIVED VALUE: Electronic device system powered on, and energy is discharged as successfully contributed work of perceived value to system until the energy of the batteries has been fully dispersed or transferred through the circuits and transistors.

- INTELLIGENT INNOVATION TO INCREASE EFFICIENCY/EVOLUTION OF ORIGINAL SYSTEM TO IMPROVEMENT: New technique of efficient energy cell storage in batteries without toxicity and with less weight. More efficient and more valuable energy, results in healthier, longer life and improved performance. The processor or brain of the device may also be improved for more efficiency of energy regulation and longer use.

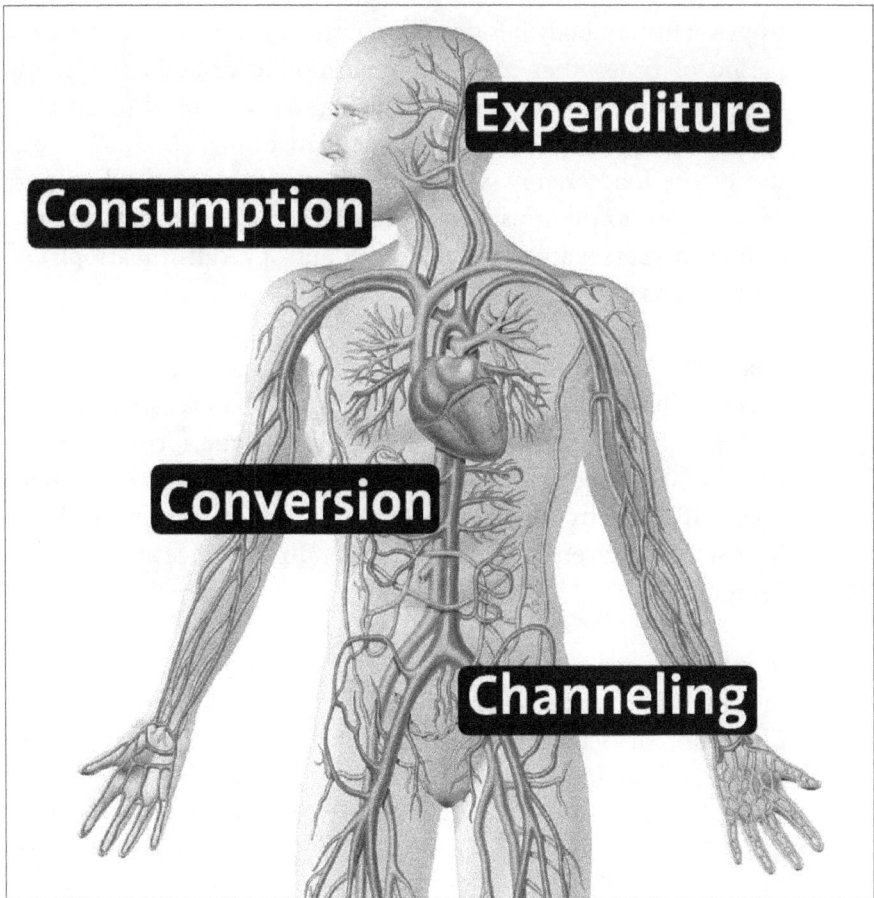

Fig. 4: (Image from anatomyonlinecourse.com)

Humans

- SYSTEM: Human body containing energy from consumption of beef.

- ENERGY: Animal containing energy from grass and grain consumption is slaughtered to make hamburger food, which is integrated into human body from human consumption.

- ENERGY CONVERTER/ORGANS: Bodily organs. They convert and channel energy through system.

- Entropy: When little or no work of perceived value to resist entropy—Human body lies dormant without exercise for prolonged period of time other than for consumption of additional hamburgers (beef), energy remains substantially unused (used only for autonomous functions) and latent in human body. Without use of the food energy within the human body as work of perceived value to the muscles in proper exercise, *over time*, energy in body disperses in accordance with entropy, causing atrophy of muscle mass.

- Toxicity: The source of energy in hamburger has a degree of toxicity. Therefore, when the energy disperses in accordance with entropy, calcification of substance called plaque forms in arteries and fat in other parts of the body. Calcification within organs causes the system or body to become unhealthy. System may die, be restored, or even improved, all depending upon level of toxicity from beef.

- Work of Perceived Value: Human body must properly exercise (not just effort) as work from energy received from hamburger. Effort not sufficient, cannot just punch a brick wall repeatedly, as this is destructive to body, and therefore not work of perceived value to body. Similarly, cannot just lift weights alone since it does not help cardiovascular system. Must successfully contribute sufficient work of perceived value to system for health. Examples include properly running/jogging until energy of hamburgers is expended through cardiovascular exercise. Running/jogging properly is successfully contributed work of perceived value to human body in maintaining muscles and providing increased oxygen to cardiovascular system.

- Intelligent Innovation to Increase Efficiency/Evolution of Original System to Improvement: Consuming food of less toxicity such as fruits and vegetables and employing exercise such as circuit weight training. Fruits and vegetables are not toxic to the system as hamburgers are, and the body functions more efficiently on this form of energy. Circuit training not only prevents atrophy of the muscles but actually increases muscle mass from its original state (analogous to *creative destruction* within nation-state economies) while utilizing the cardiovascular system, improving the overall condition of the body. In fact, the more contribution of directed energy as perceived value, such as proper weight training, the stronger the muscles, resulting in improved health, longer life, overall strength, and performance of muscle.

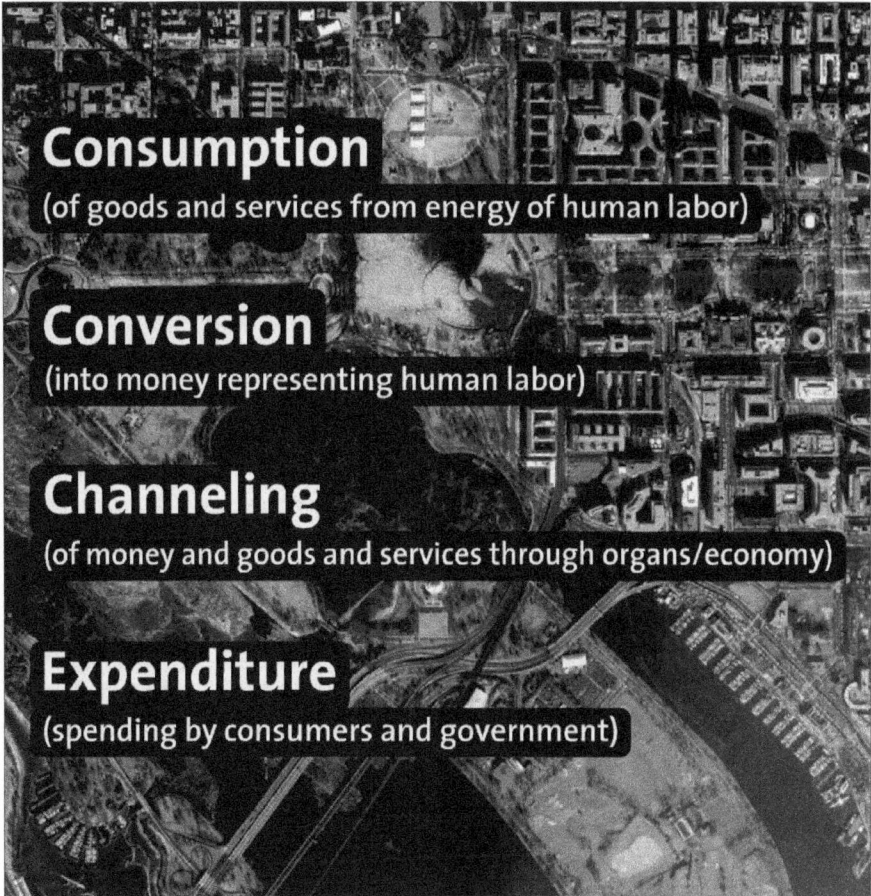

Consumption
(of goods and services from energy of human labor)

Conversion
(into money representing human labor)

Channeling
(of money and goods and services through organs/economy)

Expenditure
(spending by consumers and government)

Fig. 5: Inauguration in Washington (Satellite image by GeoEye)

Nation-States (United States of America)

- SYSTEM: Nation-State—the United States of America has a large deficit and debt of energy (human labor or productivity represented by money). It does not have enough energy of value (goods and services in proper form for conversion to money) or productive labor from its citizenry to function. Therefore, it borrows energy of value from the citizenry labor of the nation-state of China, represented by money called the Yuan.

- ENERGY: Labor of Chinese citizenry represented by money called Yuan transferred and converted to U.S. money at specified rate of conversion, and specified rate of interest owed, term of default, etc. U.S. government integrates it into U.S. economy by spending substantially on little to no value entitlements and interest on debt. Energy from human labor converted and represented by money channeled by U.S. economy.

- ENERGY CONVERTER/ORGANS: The economy. It converts and channels energy through system.

- ENTROPY: Little or no work of perceived value to resist entropy— the nation-state of the United States of America currently expends more energy represented by money than it consumes as work of perceived value (productivity). It expends so much energy/money (Over $16 trillion in debt) that it has an enormous "debt" of "work" owed from the transfer of borrowed energy (labor/money). The borrowed money/energy remains within the nation-state as it is just transferred through the economy substantially as entitlements to both citizens and non-citizens in free stuff from the government without any contribution of energy of value by most of the recipients. *The dispersion of this energy to debt is the process of entropy*, and there is not enough productivity or GDP to resist it sufficiently. Therefore, it is a very unhealthy system or nation-state. In addition, although unrecognized at the time, a toxic element of energy developed not from the expenditure of energy but in the transfer of energy from one part of the nation-state to another, which would put the nation-state on life support. This began when the government generally declared that all adults are entitled to home ownership regardless of insufficient contribution of energy of value to system (insufficient productive labor). The government consumes energy of perceived value (productive labor) by taxing money converted from goods and services of perceived value and transfers it to those who did not successfully contribute sufficient perceived value to the system so that they could purchase homes. This was effectuated in the form of guaranteed loans through government agencies Fannie Mae and Freddie Mac. However, the recipients of these homes and loans did not have the energy value or ability to pay for the loans or homes (not even down payments). To make matters worse, the mortgage debt was perceived to have value as energy/labor/productivity of these borrowers, and thus was further converted into a form of money/energy called mortgage debt obligations (securities), which was also channeled by the organs (economy) of the U.S. nation-state (and internationally). Without successfully contributed work of value in the form of enough productive labor to repay the energy/money in mortgage payments, *over time,* the energy disperses in accordance with entropy as the money is spent or disbursed into the economy by the seller of the home who received the money/energy from the enervated buyer's lender. However, little to no value in energy/labor/money was contributed from the enervated buyer (recipients of the homes and loans) to resist entropy or replace the dispersing loaned money/energy/labor.

- TOXICITY: The initial source of energy has a level of toxicity due to conversion rate, interest rate, and term for default. The level of toxicity spread further as some of energy converted into traded toxic securities called Mortgage Debt Obligations. Therefore, when the energy disperses in accordance with entropy, it burdens the taxpayers (since no payments of energy/money from "entitled" home recipients to resist entropy), causing debt and deficits to accrue to the nation-state as the energy (loans) cannot even cover the toxic housing debt and interest on the foreign loans (like sulfites on battery and plaque in arteries of human body). Borrowing becomes perpetual since taxes on productivity or GDP cannot cover the deficits and debts. The deficits and debt cause the system or nation-state to become unhealthy to where the debt and dollar bubbles may collapse. System may die, be restored, or even improved, all depending upon level of toxicity of loan debt (internally with Mortgage Debt Obligations and externally with loan of Yuan in initial conversion rate, interest rate, term of loan, amount of interest accrued as additional debt to the system).

- WORK OF PERCEIVED VALUE: Nation-State of United States of America must successfully contribute sufficient work of perceived value (productivity) in goods and services (GDP) for enough quantum units of energy/money for government to consume by taxation in order to discharge debt of system nation-state. Effort not good enough. Effort expended to develop goods or services that no one wants does not result in successfully contributed perceived value, and therefore will not yield sufficient energy/money to discharge debt of system or resist this form of entropy. Americans must successfully contribute sufficient work of perceived value in goods and services (productivity or GDP) to receive sufficient energy/money required to pay debt (taxes) in resisting entropy. The greater the perceived value in goods and services, the more quantum units of energy/money reciprocated back to the contributor of such goods and services. A percentage of this amount is taxed as government consumption of energy-labor to pay debt and maintain system or nation-state from debt and dollar collapse. But taxation must be limited, because it is the same as taking energy from an individual. If too much is taxed they become enervated and weakened, causing economic collapse. The most foolish statements are from Keynesians or those who say government spending will improve the condition of a weakened nation-state economy. This is the same as asking a runner who is out of energy to run even more to improve his organs and his overall health. What is needed is more nutrition or energy for the runner. For nation-states, more productivity or energy of value is needed, i.e., goods and services of greater value.

- INTELLIGENT INNOVATION TO INCREASE EFFICIENCY/EVOLUTION OF ORIGINAL SYSTEM TO IMPROVEMENT: Innovation in technology creating new industries of both efficient domestic energy extraction from seemingly inaccessible resources, e.g., hydraulic fracturing or "fracking," and renewable energy in solar and batteries. Just as steel and information technology increased productivity in labor and GDP as work of perceived value to system, so too with innovative energy technologies. Such additional perceived value would be converted to money domestically, and internationally as exports, both to pay debt, and if of sufficient perceived value to exceed debt obligations, then surplus to greater resist entropy.

Chapter 5

NATURAL CAPITALISM

Socialism: each according to *effort;* Communism: each according to *need;* Theocracy: each according to *the clerics;* Capitalism: each according to contribution of perceived *value.* Only one of the foregoing is consistent with the immutable laws of energy for healthy and prosperous open systems and does not require coercion by "elite" planner-rulers. The prosperity of nation-states begins with the value of the energy of the individual cells or the individual people, whether they are weak, dependent, captive recipients or strong, self-reliant, free producers. The latter requires some modicum of virtue in discipline and productivity, whereas the former does not. Nation-states are obviously aggregates of humanity, each culture reflecting values that are closer or further away from truth or harmony with nature's laws. Just as virtue is tested on the individual level and manifests itself in the health and prosperity of the person, virtue is tested on the parallel aggregate level of nation-states, for which health and prosperity are also dependent. While the individual is tested with gratification, restraint, and moderation, the nation-state faces the same challenges on an aggregate level. Liberalism/progressivism represents gratification, while conservatism attempts restraint, and of course the moderates represent moderation. This contention may be tested on every political issue from abortion to government spending, even though some complex political issues may superficially appear otherwise until thought through abstractly. Those advocating constant gratification or indulgence such as unrestrained spending reject truth as absolute, for without truth they may indulge without consequence, discarding the disparity in results from the values of discipline and moderation (see economic health of liberal/progressive State of California, moderate State of Florida, and conservative State of Texas).

The values of a nation-state's culture determine its prosperity, as such values manifest themselves in productivity levels and the aggregate value of nation-state labor for goods and services or GDP. Cultural values also determine nation-state entropy or debt levels, as virtue is an antidote to entropy. The virtuous are productive, moderate, and do not spend more than they have the ability to reasonably repay; otherwise, they find entropy or debt levels ever more difficult to resist. And since everything tends to disorder or decay in accordance with entropy, the value of energy or labor must constantly be increased. This is why economic metrics require constant growth of GDP for nation-states. Otherwise, a state of "recession" or "depression" is declared. Intelligent innovation increases *the efficiency* of energy in human labor and therefore its value as measured by productivity and GDP. Increasing the value of energy through intelligent innovation is also known as evolution. For nation-state prosperity, conditions must be evolutionary or conducive to intelligent innovation. Intelligent innovation is catalyzed by incentive. Incentive begins with the desire for happiness. Most believe happiness can be achieved through the gratification of physical/material needs and desires, which includes the creation and acquisition of property. Property is an expression of man's intelligence and ability to harness nature for survival, comfort, security, and prosperity. This distinguishes him from the rest of the animal kingdom. Only those who could benefit from the protective property of weapons, clothing, and shelter, or otherwise learn and discern through intelligent innovation would be rewarded with survival.*

In a sedentary society, gratification of physical/material needs and desires generally requires the cooperation or coercion of others to obtain their labor in goods and services. Even basic travel, food, and comfortable lodgings require the goods and services of others. The more labor one commands, either through cooperation or coercion, the more power and freedom one has to pursue the individual predilections that one believes will bring happiness. Thus, people generally seek the authority or influence to direct others as power, in small or large measure, depending upon the level of freedom they require to gratify the individual physical/material needs and desires which they believe will bring happiness. This is nature's bait and test, for our true purpose is enlightenment to virtue. Will we obtain the labor of others to fulfill our needs and desires through cooperation or coercion, and which will bring sustained happiness and/or enlightenment to virtue? The test is how we treat others in our pursuit of gratification. We must generally be oblivious to this test so that our actions are not predetermined. In the universal pursuit of happiness, there are generally three routes to obtain power to direct the labor of others to

---

* After surmounting the difficulties of survival, intelligent innovation of property became the elixir for prosperity, but only under conditions where such property was protected.

fulfill our needs and desires, and these routes are frequently intertwined: money, political leadership, and status-prestige. Each may be obtained through cooperation or coercion.

Deflection

Most nation-state systems are coercive and designed to preserve the power of the few elite at the expense of freedom for the majority of humanity. These elite keep the masses dependent by dispensing monthly pabulum, material and/or spiritual, under systems of limited opportunity and limited individuality. But such oppressive systems are inherently defective, as restive generations naturally emerge from the irrepressible human spirit. To prevent revolt and the toppling of elite seats of power, the true cause of oppression must be deflected. Therefore, an enemy is designated, internal or external, but such designation will always require promoting *envy* or vilification of the intelligent innovators who create, produce, and cause consumption of the evolutionary goods and services that gratify universally sought material needs and desires. Such vilification is the simplest and most effective method used to deflect revolt and anger against tyrannical government, because visual images of the material disparity between the haves and have-nots, *regardless of the cause*, easily evoke visceral reactions. The cause, values, and conditions which result in the prosperity of intelligent innovation are irrelevant to those without virtue, even though they result in improving their standards of living, in which they shamelessly indulge before lamenting the "evil" providers of such technologies. The massive axis of secular progressives, socialists, liberals, and their seemingly mismatched theocratic allies have a core unifying but largely unidentified commonality—the role of *truth* in their ideology. The leftist secular progressives, socialists, and liberals generally believe truth is relative, that it is not a constant, while the contemporary relevant theocracies treat truth with religious dissimulation (Koran 3:28), all to achieve an end—commonly expressed as *the end justifies any means*. For this axis there is no right or wrong in the treatment of others and no virtue, so long as they achieve their paramount goals of power (since no right or wrong exists to them in the pursuit of power, they will eventually turn on one another, even within their own insular organizations). This ideology attracts the overwhelming masses without virtue or values to the liberal indulgence that they are entitled to the fruits of another's labor, whether through redistribution or outright theft of resources. Since many would viscerally know this as wrong, the baseline of truth must be blurred through multi-generational campaigns of indoctrination, secularly with political correctness and theocratically with religious dogma. Such systems naturally and invariably result in impoverishment, enslavement, and inevitable populace discontent. Meanwhile, the coercive ruling elite are aware that the critical mass of intelligent innovators which produce prosperity naturally emerges from those cultures and nation-state systems which promote or provide to the masses the freedom, opportunity, and incentive to acquire and maintain large sums of money. Money is power and freedom because it commands the energy of quantized human labor, and therefore control of money is control of human labor and humanity. Thus, for the coercive ruling elite to deflect the populist anger of discontent in preserving their own power, freedom and the system of capitalism which produces the meritorious intelligent innovators and attendant wealth and power must be the enemy or oppressor. Otherwise, the true cause of oppression would be identified and discarded for systems of greater freedom, opportunity, and prosperity.

Capitalism and Democracy Cannot Secure Prosperity

The broadest and most equitable access to power for the most people is through capitalism. Generally, under capitalism, the more perceived value contributed to others, the more money and power to the contributor. Since value may be unlimited, the commensurate money and power may also be unlimited. Thus, capitalism provides for unlimited power to be accumulated through meritorious contribution, as perceived value is exchanged for human labor in the form of redeemable quantized units called money. *The elite planners cannot control those who accumulate power and freedom in such a manner unless they can limit their ability to accrue money and its attendant power.* Therefore, capitalism is vilified and attributed as the cause of economic failure, oppression, and the "obstacle" to world government. However, *the truth* is that capitalism is the obstacle to *control* by coercive elite planners seeking to maintain and expand their own power. Yet capitalism is the only system of trade which drives nation-state economies. *And this is a great natural irony; capitalism imperils their monopoly on power, yet without it poor economic conditions make them struggle to maintain such power.*

NATURAL CAPITALISM — CHAPTER 5   91

But *capitalism per se is not sufficient for prosperity.* Capitalism takes place in most economies. Just as capitalism took place in fascist Italy and National Socialist (Nazi) Germany, capitalism also takes place in the mixed economies of predominantly socialist Europe, America, China, and Venezuela. *Capitalism does not secure life, liberty, and property, and thus cannot secure prosperity.* A broad prosperity requires stability and incentive for intelligent innovation, which can be maintained only under those conditions where the fruits of labor are protected along with life and liberty. Those systems enabling freedom and incentive to develop one's individual talents for contribution of value to society have disparate results compared to systems which bring dependence to societal conformity of menial subsistence—prosperity versus misery. And true democracy can fare no better for prosperity. True democracy is a euphemism for mob rule or the emotional lynch mob. If the guillotine could speak, it would reveal that its blade was the only thing that true democracy kept fully employed during the French Revolution. True democracy provides a mechanism to institutionalize and execute upon emotion, enabling the tyranny of the majority to take what it covets and prohibit what it irrationally fears and prejudices. This is the proverbial lynch mob on a macro scale. Only a small percentage of humanity has ascended the ladder of enlightenment to virtue—respect for life, liberty, and property. The masses have not achieved such virtue, and therefore the tyrannical majority rule of democracy cannot protect life, liberty, and property—unless it is a *representative* democratic society *under charter or constitution which protects such natural rights through due process.*

Man's Birthright

Although it has rarely occurred in human history, paradoxically, life, liberty, and property are nature's birthright for humanity. As the intended recipients of such gifts, it is also humanity that has abridged and denied these natural rights, placing it at odds with nature's bequest. When conditions of open systems are inharmonious with the laws of nature, health and prosperity cannot attain. Picture a man sailing the seas alone who comes upon a deserted island of no nation-state territory but one that is fertile, with docile fauna and flora. He is free to do as he pleases. He may hunt, fish, or plant crops to live and to intelligently innovate property for both survival against the elements and material comforts. He is designed to *individually* reap the benefits of his industry and *individually* suffer the consequences of his indolence. This is his birthright—*individual freedom*. Only other men may take his life, liberty, and property should they come upon the island. He could spend months of arduous innovation and labor, cultivating and constructing intricate shelter of many comforts, but it could be taken away in an instant by the coercion of others. Without the protection of life, liberty, and property, he would think twice before expending such effort intelligently innovating, planning, and laboring for better living conditions. Should he be joined by others, of course the best resources or comforts become desired by many, so a system of governance must be instituted to minimize the natural tendency to disorder. Human energy of value must be expended to create a healthy and prosperous system from disorder. In crafting such a system, the nature of humanity must be cognitively synthesized; each person is of unique characteristics and predilections, each person is of different strengths and weaknesses. There is the industrious and the lazy, the ascetic and the indulgent, the creative and the conformist, the bright and the dim, the talented and the inept, the virtuous and the corrupt, and every permutation in between, each demanding liberation or mitigation through the tempest of social relations and virtue.

Each man has a meaning of purpose. Sustained happiness can be attained only when that meaning of purpose is identified and the pursuit of its fulfillment is endeavored. He must try and fail until he succeeds in order to develop the emotions and qualities of hope, faith, discipline, persistence, self-reliance, and cooperation, while overcoming fear, indolence, envy, and coercion.[1] This is the test of character, and each person is at a different level of enlightenment to the truths which constitute such character. Therefore, any system of governance cannot homogenize the masses if prosperity is to attain. Conditions must be such that the individual may develop and contribute, and for this freedom and self-reliance are required. The system must correlate with the truth of natural law in values and virtue for health, happiness, and prosperity.

Nature provides incentive for each person to distinguish himself from the rest of society by the identification, development, and contribution of one's unique gifts and talents. The greater one distinguishes himself by talents which contribute perceived value to society, the greater the status-prestige and labor of others in goods and services one may command. These are the trappings of power that people believe will bring happiness, while the means of self-development and contribution to others simultaneously produce the sine qua non for sustained happiness—self-worth. An individual cannot maintain happiness without self-worth. When living among others, self-worth is dependent upon whether one feels they are of value to society. Therefore, contribution of value to society is the best method for achieving self-worth, status-prestige, and happiness. The more value one contributes to society, the greater the chance of self-worth, status-prestige, and happiness. And when this is cooperatively achieved by a critical mass of people, prosperity is within reach. But prosperity can be attained and sustained only while the natural rights of each individual to life, liberty, and property are protected.

Natural Capitalism

Every five hundred years or so, an arrhythmia in the heart of nature pumps a convergence of genius, circumstance, and courage, and we are forever changed. Such convergence manifested itself most profoundly in the eighteenth century when a group of British expatriates seeking liberty from an oppressive monarch of the most powerful nation on Earth signed their own death warrant on a document called the Declaration of Independence. Their passion and courage for freedom and the individual pursuit of happiness overcame the strength of the world's strongest military, yielding a revolutionary, ingenious nation-state charter protecting life, liberty, and property with due process. Thus was born a constitutional republic called the United States of America, resulting in the greatest freedom and prosperity known to humanity—and the recipe was the first system of *Natural Capitalism* in human history.

Natural capitalism is a system of governance and trade under which the *natural rights* to life, liberty, and property are protected, unless otherwise forfeited by violating those same rights of others. Under such a system, the role of government exists for the sole purpose of protecting such natural rights. When the natural rights of life, liberty, and property are protected with due process, the natural result is that individuals freely gravitate to their interests, passions, and talents as the best suited to intelligently innovate related goods and services for others. And they are incentivized to do so in exchange for the equivalent perceived value of such goods and services in redeemable credits of human labor called

money. For those fortunate enough to live under such a system, nature
calls out to each:

"YOU SHALL RECEIVE POWER AND FREEDOM COMMENSURATE WITH
THE LEVEL OF VALUE WHICH OTHERS PERCEIVE YOU HAVE CONTRIBUTED."

The more people who perceive value from one's contributions or
the greater the perceived value of one's contributions to others, the more
money and power. More power means more freedom to do as one pleases,
as access to the goods and services of others increases. There could be no
more equitable a system, for it provides opportunity for all, regardless of
background or socioeconomic status, while simultaneously testing and
tempering virtue. This is nature's design, and orphans to inheritors have
answered this call in spectacular fashion. The world's most prolific intelligent innovators started with nothing under natural capitalism, some
under the limitations of its entropic dismantling. Yet through the first
law of energy, the thought energy in ideas of value were sculpted into
the mass and matter of goods and services for others. Thomas Edison,
Andrew Carnegie, Orville Wright, and Henry Ford had no formal education at all, while Steve Jobs, Bill Gates, and Mark Zuckerberg were college dropouts. Even the highly educated Sergey Brin started with nothing.
Yet they all contributed tremendous value to billions of people, as these
intelligent innovators delivered to the masses incandescent light bulbs,
steel, human flight vehicles, automobiles, personal computers, computer software, electronic social networks, and Internet information search
capabilities. *And nature lived up to its end of the bargain.* They were rewarded commensurately, for the world became their bounty. They earned
so much money or redeemable credits of other peoples' labor, as well as
status-prestige, that people gratified their needs and desires practically
wherever and whenever they so chose. As intelligent innovators they facilitated evolution by *increasing the efficiency and value of energy expenditure,*
changing the way we live while reducing the collective energy humanity
normally expended without such invention. They have made billions of
lives easier, and were commensurately rewarded. But they could not simply rest on their accomplishments, for the competition inherent of natural
capitalism kept them striving to maintain their status-prestige, yielding
further intelligent innovations for the benefit of humanity.

If a person has a good or service that may add value to the lives of others but lacks the resources of additional human energy or money to bring it to market, others are incentivized to cooperate and assist for a share of the possible returns. If the good or service is sufficiently developed or defined to convince others to put human energy or labor behind it (money), the laws protecting property under the system of natural capitalism, intellectual or otherwise, make it possible to have such goods and services vetted by experience. And experience is often rigid of convention, for it may be rejected hundreds of times. But with adjustments, desire, faith, hope, and persistence, it requires only one "yes" from the right person or the intelligent innovation otherwise required to bring it to market without capital.[2] Nature urges us under natural capitalism to cooperate with others to synergize *unique* and *individual* human energies for intelligent innovation, combining energy for more power. And natural human synergies in business enterprise have vastly improved conditions for humanity, as the greatest contemporary technologies have come from the collaboration of friends. Apple Computer (Jobs and Wozniak), Microsoft (Gates and Allen), and Google (Brin and Page) are the best known. But more importantly, the freedom and protections of natural capitalism provide the greatest trial of virtue, unlike coercive systems where decisions are limited and you do as you are told. Money is the bait or incentive, generally requiring the establishment of social relationships to acquire it. Under natural capitalism, whether those relationships are with business partners, employees, suppliers, clients, or customers, it is how we treat one another in these relationships to acquire the bait or money that we hopefully learn and grow to enlightenment.

But natural capitalism begins with the individual. It precisely parallels nature's call for each person to first improve himself and his condition, cultivating his gifts and talents in order fulfill his second duty to contribute those gifts and talents to humanity as equitable exchange for its perceived value in money or credits for the labor of others. *The scale of that contribution of perceived value generally determines the level of individual freedom.* Of course each person has different skills and talents, and each will contribute different levels of value to society. Because natural capitalism generally distributes rewards equitably upon contribution of perceived value, there will always be great but natural disparities in wealth. A small percentage of the most talented *or determined* will contribute greater value to society than others, and the commensurate rewards will be envied by those who contribute less value. Envy is a powerful and pervasive emotion to overcome, but people cannot be equalized. Nature's equitable hierarchy provides that even the less talented with greater virtues of industry and persistence may achieve what a more talented but less virtuous and less industrious person has not. And even though natural disparities in wealth are an immutable part of nature, natural capitalism results in the highest standards of living from which everyone benefits (today's "poor" have cell phones, flat-screen TVs, iPods. and automobiles). As nature's proven system, natural capitalism provides conditions of human freedom and opportunity for all to achieve unlimited success. But with freedom comes choice and responsibility—the latitude to experience different methods of acquiring the energy-labor of others in the form of money. Each choice has its consequences.

Trade, Inheritance, Theft

Nature has devised the system of natural capitalism so that the bait of money to achieve what most people believe will bring happiness may be acquired through three general modes: *trade, inheritance, and theft*. There are those who trade goods and services of value for money and others who scam goods and services of no value for money. There are those who trade in the stock and futures markets who provide value to companies and nation-state currencies with needed capital for growth, all in the hope of a return for such faith. Others game the markets without any contribution of value, "shorting" companies and nation-state currencies with willful bets on destruction for pure personal gain. Then there are those who inherit wealth. Many inherit lawfully and create value for others with such inherited energy. Others find that the laws of energy have divested them of their inheritance for not creating any value with it (entropy, the second law of energy). Finally, there are the seriously depraved, who would kill for inheritance or otherwise coerce money out of others through outright theft. Such choices and their corresponding consequences are the individual tests of virtue inherent of a free society. Variations of similar conduct and interpretive lessons are constantly displayed in television dramas, movies, plays, news stories, books, and lyrical music, all to stimulate introspective guidance.

Trade, inheritance, and theft all require relationships with others, whether personal or impersonal. The conduct of our relationships determines happiness, and if one were to achieve the goal of happiness and enlightenment to virtue through such relations, the *secret key* will always be the contribution of value and the aversion to coercion. And there's an inherent evolutionary mechanism for humans and nation-states to experientially evolve to such truths. That evolutionary mechanism is *perception and choice*.

The Mechanism of Evolution: Perception and Choice

Recall the way in which the laws of energy operate upon living open systems such as humans and nation-states: *the value of the energy consumed and the value of the method of energy expenditure determines the health and prosperity of the system.* This law of nature applies to both biological consumption and expenditure as an individual human being or as the economic consumption and expenditure as people of the human aggregate nation-state. As living systems, humans and the aggregate nation-state obviously *have perception and choice in consumption* in the various forms of biomass/food energy and the various forms of goods and services of human energy-labor. Humans consume not necessarily according to value but according to the *perceived* value. Each of the various forms of food/biomass as well as the various goods and services exists at a different level of impact to open systems, from harm to value, increasing or decreasing the entropy of the system, and this may be measured by the respective effects upon the individual human as measured by health and by the prosperity of the aggregate nation-state as measured by GDP.

Similarly, at least as adults, we generally have perception and choice about what information and ideologies we consume, internalize, and expend and from which our values and behavior are influenced. And while we may be indoctrinated as children, with the modern proliferation of information via the intelligent innovation of the Internet, adults of most cultures or subcultures are generally exposed to information and ideology of different polarities, albeit often distorted and to a *limited* degree. Information and ideology are ideas conveyed via energy. If we perceive them as value, we internalize them and become a polarized cell with an affinity for other such polarized cells. Polarized cells naturally aggregate as informal or formal organizations, e.g., political parties, criminal gangs, business clubs, terrorist organizations, subcultures, cultures, nation-states, international political groups, and NGOs (non-governmental organizations), etc. If the ideas or ideologies are aligned with truth, they are of *real* value. If they are not in alignment with truth but are internalized, they are only *perceived* value and become the opposite pole, which resists the struggle to truth. Thus, the ideologies we *perceive* as value and *choose* to consume, internalize, and expend determine health, prosperity, and position of advancement on the path of evolution to enlightenment. Some cultures *perceive* value in the ideology of mass murder through the suicide-homicide bombings of innocent babies and children, the suppression of women and minorities, and religious intolerance. Other cultures on the opposite pole cherish life above all else, education through the scientific method, intelligent innovation, freedom for women and minorities, and religious tolerance. Contrary to what substantivists/relativists teach in "higher education" institutions as cultural relativism, such cultures cannot be viewed as equal. Cultural relativism must be equated with moral relativism. Moral relativism cannot be justified in the realm of truth. There is right and wrong.

The two aforementioned cultures are obviously distinguishable by their patently different manifestations. One lives in general squalor and the other in general comfort. They *cannot* be the same unless they consume, internalize, and expend the same ideology and ideas. They are at different proximities to truth, and this distinguishes the relative advancement among cultures. When academia uses the term *advanced,* societies or peoples, *advanced* must be related to some objective end or goal. The "politically correct" cultural substantivists/relativists of such academia are usually unaware that when they use the term *advanced* societies or peoples, they are referencing their place in relation to other societies and peoples along the path of evolution to the goal of enlightenment to truth. Truth necessitates right and wrong conduct. Those who believe that there is no truth or right and wrong cannot logically condemn those who would terrorize and kill their most cherished loved ones. Cultures and nation-states are not equal. Those that are in alignment with truth are more advanced or evolved than those that are not in alignment with truth. Regardless of what relativists say about truth, *the truth* is that consumption of poison or toxicity by open systems infects its cells, causing its organs to weaken for potential collapse. Whether the open systems are individual humans or aggregate nation-states, and whether the organs are of the human body or the economies of nation-states, the perceptions and choices of "value" for consumption, internalization, and expenditure, including ideologies and ideas, determine each system's proximity to enlightenment and the corresponding levels of health and prosperity. Such perceptions and choices are commonly known as "values."

The Human Constant

The core values of natural capitalism from which the United States of America was formed (and optimized between 1865 and 1913) is the formula or recipe for prosperity. The people who made the United States the greatest country in human history came from different cultures and ethnicities, but they embraced the transcendent values of freedom, self-reliance, industry, intelligent innovation, and contribution, all inherent of natural capitalism. Such values are in alignment with truth for the health and prosperity of open systems. However, *no matter what nation-state system*, humanity will always be the constant, and that constant consists of individuals of varied levels of virtue, from the honest and good to the corrupt and depraved, each at different levels of enlightenment.

Most participants of the U.S.'s free-market economy do contribute some measure of value. But this situation has become precarious, as American values have changed to an entitlement culture exacerbated by corruption. This is reflected by the depressed economy. Nevertheless, at least fifty percent of the population currently contribute value. But they do so not because they are so enlightened to know that the goal of happiness requires the self-worth of feeling of value to society through such contribution. Nor are they aware that the laws of energy for the health and prosperity of nation-state systems require energy of value from the human labor of goods and services. *The reality of humanity is that most people are not so enlightened, and but for the threat of punishment, they would try to acquire money, power, and happiness by any means.* Therefore, some regulation is required to inspire confidence in the system in order for them to participate. There must be a degree of protection from those with the least virtue.

Even so, people must still be free to create without emasculation by government planners and regulators. Regulation must not inhibit freedom, participation, growth, and prosperity. Thus, for a just prosperity to attain, a delicate balance between regulatory protection and freedom of enterprise must be achieved. Such a balance is difficult to maintain, because power corrupts. Regulation cannot change that different people will always be of different grades of character and virtue. In fact, planners and regulators of legislative, executive, and judicial authority themselves are obviously human and subject to those same grades of character and virtue. This is why the U.S. Constitution prescribed a nation of *laws* and not men. But since government must consist of men, it would be *limited* to certain enumerated powers with three branches checking one another from the incentive of preserving the power of their own branch and their individual seats of authority within it. Recall that power commands the authority to direct or influence the labor of others for the gratification of needs and desires, an authority that may be acquired not just through money but through political leadership and status-prestige. Many without virtue seeking the equivalent of money in political power and its consequent status-prestige make, carry out, and interpret the laws and/or regulations. To obtain and preserve such power, they have perverted and exploited the greatest governing charter in human history at the expense of the citizenry. Power would intersect with the ugly emotion of envy, and property would no longer be protected. And as goes property, so goes liberty, and vice versa. Votes would be bought to institutionalize envy, decay values, destroy culture, and subvert merit and truth. Natural capitalism would be compromised, and American values perniciously transformed from self-reliance to dependence, weakening the economic organs and the nation-state body. Even the greatest society would not be immune to the timeless, universal root of human conflict—the haves and have-nots.

Chapter 6

THE HAVES AND HAVE-NOTS

It's one of the most important and contentious issues confronting humanity since time began, and the basis of most human conflict, including politics, economics, and war. Most information and indoctrination including education, the news media, entertainment, and values, all derive from it. Yet most people don't have a clue what it's *really* about as layer upon layer of herrings in red obfuscate the simple truth buried underneath. Despite the nomenclature and demagoguery, the true ideological battle of the haves and have-nots is not about who *has what*, as it is predominantly portrayed. *It's about the morality and virtue of how we obtain the labor of other human beings—by cooperative exchange of value or by coercive taking.* Instead, a complex confluence en masse led by those seeking power over the envious, the guilt-ridden, the useful idiots, and those who want to be taken care of, have effectively perverted truth by shifting the substantive argument from how the labor of other human beings is obtained to the straw man of who has the most labor of other human beings in goods and services. As the late paragon of the neo-radical left, Saul Alinsky, summed up the methodology from his luxury penthouse in Chicago:

> *"One acts decisively only in the conviction that all the angels are on one side and all the devils on the other."*[1]

All the haves become devils and all the have-nots become angels in the demagoguery of *oppressor and oppressed.* By this method, the neo-radical *international* left, led by George Soros, Hillary Clinton, and Barack Obama, have entrenched a narrative which eliminates the distinction within freedom and capitalism between the intelligent innovators who meritoriously contribute tremendous value in goods and services to humanity in exchange for money and power and those who achieve money and power without meritorious contribution of value. Once merit is extracted from the argument, everyone is on equal footing, and no one should have more than another. There would no longer be any difference between those who earned their wealth and those who coercively took it.

All those who have power to acquire the most goods and services of others, regardless of cause, are the oppressors; those who don't have such power, regardless of cause, are the oppressed. Such sophistry defines the ideological line between left and right and the organizations aligned with each. It also provides cover and justification for those seeking to attain and maintain power to implement their platform of taking from the haves and giving to the have-nots. And only those to be divested would resist, for the materialistic patina as illuminated by the contrast between the haves and have-nots elicits emotions of envy which compromise the ability of the masses to grasp truth, morality, and virtue.

The truth is that all goods and services come from human labor. They don't just magically appear for grabs as most are impaired to think. People actually sacrifice and work hard to develop and produce the goods and services which improve our life. Nature taunts us with the want of gratification in the display of material goods and services such as houses, automobiles, electronic gadgets, and fine cuisine so that most would believe materialism to be the path to happiness. Even the most physically appealing of the opposite sex naturally gravitate to those who have the most freedoms of gratification and the most material security for potential offspring. Therefore, the fruits of other people's labor are universally sought, most often without regard for *how* they are obtained. This is nature's method of testing character and virtue, for the bait laid and the path taken to it are paramount. Each individual faces life's great challenge: to discern truth experientially through perception and choice. Those manipulating truth in an already difficult hunt will be held to account.

Natural Hierarchy

The natural hierarchical structure of human society provides that *no matter what the system of governance*—capitalism, socialism, communism, or theocracy—only a small minority will have the most concentrated wealth and power over the labor of the majority. This immutable principle is critical to our understanding. Whatever your belief system may be, equality of outcomes is impossible to attain. All systemic attempts to homogenize the socioeconomic status of unique individuals *always* benefits a small class at the expense of the masses. This is a law of nature. Although each historic attempt to equalize outcomes may initially seem to be a just and romantic cause of exchanging the traditional underdog have-nots to haves, and vice versa, it is instead exchanging THE METHOD of obtaining the labor of others, from commerce to outright theft. And as history reveals, criminal mass murder is often part of the process. When envy of the masses combines with the political power of the State to cheat nature's equitable hierarchy, a ferocious correction informs us of the vulgarity. Romanticizing such movements with the perverse language of "social justice" is how it is legitimated, even though no one can convincingly explain how stealing from those who contribute the most value to others and giving it to those who don't is any type of justice. Only the pain of the inevitable, barbaric reality and the eventual financial collapse associated with such collective robberies alert us to the inequity before fools of subsequent generations repeat the same misguided blunders. Whether it's the guillotine of Robespierre's French Revolution or the millions murdered under Mao, Stalin, Hitler, Castro, and Che, history is usually ignored. But once the phony justifications and clouds of sophist obfuscation to justify such indulgent theft are removed, the real substantive issue becomes a simple choice: whether the labor of others is obtained under conditions of freedom, opportunity, high standards of societal living, and general prosperity or whether it is obtained through tyranny, dependence, and general misery.

Ideological systems for the governance of nation-states are the systemic manifestations of *values* for how human labor in goods and services is to be obtained. Under *any system*, as long as human beings are present there will always be the corrupt and the virtuous. But even the most idealistic class warriors would find that the choice in ruling hierarchies is a simple one: a class of generally meritorious intelligent innovators who preside over freedom and opportunity, or one of bureaucratic corruption that manages dependence and misery. Unfortunately, the latter has prevailed for most of humanity, notwithstanding nature's display of lessons throughout history.

Control of Labor/Money

Recall that people seek access to the labor in goods and services of others through power in the forms of any or all of the following intertwined methods: political leadership, status-prestige, and money. Although money provides the broadest access to goods and services for the masses, most people don't acquire enough of it for the freedom to do what they want when they want. Only a minuscule minority—those who have contributed tremendous perceived value to humanity, inheritors, and those who otherwise gambled or gamed the system—have achieved such freedom primarily through money. While money is power or influence over human labor, it is the SYSTEMS of nation-state human governance that generally *control the masses and their labor* (unless it is a *fictional* system of freedom where life, liberty, and property are protected from the politicians). Those who would control systems of nation-state governance would control the masses and their labor. Of course, political leaders and their benefactors control nation-state systems of human governance. But as the contemporary Marxist political leader of the most powerful nation in the world, U.S. President Barack Obama, along with his benefactor and frequent White House visitor—international radical left financier George Soros—both understand, there is one group they cannot control and whom they envy—*the intelligent innovators.* The intelligent innovators have earned the most power and money by contributing tremendous value to humanity with great technological and evolutionary innovations. The number-one and number-two nation-states in the world for top innovations are the United States and Israel.[2] In Obama's words:

> *"I do think at a certain point you've made enough money. . . ."*[3]

And in Soros' words:

> *"The main obstacle to a stable and just world order is the United States,"*[4] and *"The main stumbling block is Israel."*[5]

Obama, Soros, and their acolytes envy the intelligent innovators because they gave commensurate value for the power they earned. Neither Obama nor Soros earned a dime through value to others in the balance, and they feel empty as a result. They made their money by destruction and coercive taking. Obama's game is to take money from those who earn it and *"spread the wealth around"* to those who don't.[6] Soros' game is arbitrage—destroying nation-states by shorting their currencies and taking the spread in profits. He foments revolutions with that money and strategically advances his power via the chaos and suffering. Soros has orchestrated financial crisis and pain upon millions in England, Russia, Thailand, and Malaysia, and is doing so now to acquire his greatest prize—the United States of America. He was also convicted as a felon in

France for insider trading. But the greatest year of his life, according to Soros himself in an interview on the American national television show *60 Minutes*, was as a child, confiscating the property of fellow Jews in 1944 Hungary. *"I rather enjoyed it,"* he said.[7] He advocates taking from the haves and giving to the have-nots to discharge his burden of guilt for his unearned wealth. As a destructive and depraved miscreant, he knows, deep down, that he is of no value to society. His public proclamation, for which he titled his authored article in the *Financial Times* in 2010—*"America Needs Stimulus Not Virtue"*—succinctly sums up his character and international mission, as well as the world's ideological line of division.[8] *Stimulus* is a political euphemism for taxing those who have and giving to those who have not. Government is the depraved have-nots' coercive power agent of theft. Such coercion is antithetical to virtue. Only the virtue of self-reliance, responsibility, and *voluntary* charity can restore the health and prosperity of nation-states. Entitlements, dependency, and forced redistribution cannot. This is generally the same historic philosophical divide and administration of good and evil only with different players for the experience.

Exploiting the divide of haves and have-nots is the universal bread and butter of the amoral seeking to attain and maintain power and control. This always happens at the expense of humanity and its greatest expressions of freedom—intelligence and property. The intelligent innovators present "the main obstacle" and "the main stumbling block" to the unfettered power of megalomaniacs who cannot earn meritoriously through contribution. With the indispensable assistance from the corrupt international Marxist media, the masses are indoctrinated to "learn" that not only are they not responsible for any impoverishment they may have ever suffered, but that they will no longer suffer from want. It was the oppressor "haves" (except for those particular haves seeking coercive political power over them) who forced all the have-nots into oppressed conditions, and once the masses cede their liberty to government leaders and their acolytes, along with the authority to seize the haves and their property, utopia can commence. For ceding such liberty to government, the have-nots are promised cradle-to-grave security as their take in the institutionalized robbery of the haves. However, in the words of Margaret Thatcher, *"they always run out of other people's money."*[9]

The perennial lesson most famously expressed by Ben Franklin essentially states that those who would trade liberty for security *deserve* neither.[10] However, this can be better expressed as nature actually codified it: those who trade liberty for security *get* neither. Once liberty is given up, it is impossible to have security. *Nature will not allow both.* *Someone* has to provide the labor for the material security they seek in goods and services. It does not just appear out of thin air. Unless people are willing to volunteer those services, *labor must be compelled* to render them, and that never ends well for anyone. There is nothing to prevent those who have been given absolute power from using it against those who traded it for security. This is the true oppressor-and-oppressed relationship, as leadership oppresses the have-nots into dependence and the productive would-be haves to compelled labor (even if such labor is compelled through taxation). Ceding the gift of self-determination to another for material security is one of the weakest and most depraved acts of humanity. It is an affront to nature's bequest. Liberty requires responsibility. Responsibility yields character. Ceding liberty is ceding character—and revealing it, too.

Unique Individuals

It is worth repeating by encapsulation critical truths regarding happiness, prosperity, and wealth disparity which perpetually go unheeded. As unique individuals born with different innate abilities and temperaments, we subsequently develop different values and skills. As nature constantly hints, individual abilities and skills are designed for the benefit of humanity, for when passion, talent, and vocation intersect with contribution, happiness attains. In a free system where government is limited to protecting the life, liberty, and property of its citizens, an unlimited pie of wealth may grow from the unlimited creative energy of productive human labor—the more value each person contributes to others, the more money and freedom. Although the environment we are born into often determines the steepness of our climb, nature compensates for such factors. The greater the difficulties surmounted, the stronger the yield of character and the more gratifying the success toward the goal of sustained happiness.

Exceptional Minority/Intelligent Innovators

Just as the natural hierarchy of the human animal allows only a tiny minority of *any* society to have the most power to obtain the labor of the majority in the form of goods and services, the laws of nature also dictate that only a tiny minority of humanity can be exceptionally talented or *determinedly* accomplished in any field, whether it's basketball or rocket science. *But this does not insure success for the naturally gifted, nor does it preclude success for those born not so gifted.* Both values and the intangibles determine success—desire, hope, faith, discipline, persistence, diligence, experience, judgment, and readiness for opportunity. Development of these qualities requires human energy of value.

The potential of the exceptional minority comes from every race and creed, and it may also emerge from any socioeconomic class or background. However, conditions of values, ideology, culture, and nation-state levels of freedom determine the volume that surfaces. Since each person is naturally different, each will naturally contribute different levels of value to society, and in a society of true social justice, compensation commensurate with the level of perceived contributed value naturally results in disparities of wealth—from poor to rich. This is the unavoidable truth of immutable logic. Only the exceptional minority will contribute the most value to others. That exceptional minority is largely comprised of the *intelligent innovators.* They create from nothing the property which improves conditions for humanity, whether it is the polio vaccine or the cell phone. Since they contribute the most value to society, they should be compensated commensurately, as free market forces naturally determine the demand for such goods and services.

Intelligence and Property

Intelligence and property distinguish humanity from the rest of the animal kingdom. Those who use intelligence to innovate goods and services foster evolution. Under natural conditions of freedom and the market economy, nature provides incentive and reward for the use of intelligence to contribute value to others—commensurate compensation in money and status-prestige. The more value perceived by others in a good or service, the more labor others are willing to sacrifice in the form of money to obtain it. Those systems that attempt to equalize income through wealth redistribution artificially devalue intelligent innovation by equating it with service labor, thereby marginalizing humanity's advanced distinguishing features of intelligence and property. This is the same as taking away the speed of cheetahs or the strength of gorillas— the qualities that allow them to prosper. Freedom exposes each unique individual as exceptional, inept, and each degree in between, because under true freedom, people are not *required* to labor for others, as the paternalistic state mandates. In a truly free society, people must be self-reliant, which generally requires each family provider to either give value or steal to obtain goods and services for survival. Under such a meritocracy, individual incomes are general barometers of society's perceptions of each person's contribution of value *at that particular time of the contributor's life.* Freedom provides opportunity and incentive to demonstrate distinctive intelligence in value creation for others and to be compensated commensurately as others perceive such value. Under such freedom, the unfortunate would be assisted through voluntary charity and advice, as a moral, but not legal, obligation. Those who cannot earn a satisfactory wage either continue to try until they do, evolving during the process of trial and error, or else they shift to the dark side.

The Dark Side

Moving to the dark side begins with envy, anger, and resentment, and then proceeds to incitement against the intelligent innovators. It then evolves to include expedient coercion of others through collective criminal enterprises, including mob-controlled labor unions. Such collective labor unions are universal, and they coercively take with violence and corruption what they were otherwise mentally unfit to achieve under the rules of a civil society. Their universal symbol of the fist represents such violence, and it is no coincidence that communist and socialist organizations (including Occupy Wall Street) use the same exact symbol (often in conjunction with the color red and the collectivist star), as they are just a larger aggregate of the same human pathology (fig. 6-9). Violence is the lowest animalistic element, used when the intelligence of reason ceases to function. "Workers of the World Unite" is a euphemism for "we believe we are mentally unfit to contribute the same value and to receive the corresponding income as the 'enemy' who puts food on our table, the intelligent innovators, but by banding together in an animalistic, physical display of force, intimidation, and the purchase of politicians to limit freedom and the market in which intelligent innovation thrives, we can achieve similar results."

Fig. 6-9: Fist representing collective physical force instead of individual intelligence. Top: Communist fist on red collectivist star, union fist with collectivist star. Bottom: Union fist for workers of the world unite, Occupy [Wall Street] collectivist (99%) fist.

Just as only a small tyrannical class benefits under collectivist nation-state systems, the small tyrannical class of union leadership becomes very wealthy at the expense of its members and does not participate in service labor as their members do. Again, the intelligent innovators of business enterprise who create the greatest value to society in goods and services as well as employment, and who receive commensurate compensation, are the designated enemy. Most people don't realize that the extreme manifestation of this ideology is expressed in a book called *Mein Kampf* by Adolph Hitler, with union membership limited to Aryan Germans.[11] Of course the designated enemy in that book is the intelligent innovator Jews. The brutal National Socialist (Nazi) government obviates the necessity to purchase politicians to pass legislation that limits individual freedom. "The heart of Hitler's case against the Jews is that through their superiority over Aryans in capitalist finance and trade [the Jews' general mastery of capitalism], they were cheating the law of survival of the fittest. They had found an individualist route to power without making the sacrifices necessary to achieve collective strength as warriors. They were circumventing the mandate of nature that requires all creatures to gang together and fight for their own survival."[12] Marxism and its variants are just the institutionalization of this ideology, but it says the enemy is *not just* the Jews but the intelligent innovators of goods and services from all races. Marxism generally requires the intelligent innovators to labor for others. However, as history has proven over and over, such systems never work, because the intelligent innovators required for prosperous productive societies are suppressed and marginalized under such conditions which limit freedom and incentive. *If intelligence and property distinguish humanity at the top of the animal kingdom, Marxism and its variants are anti-evolutionary.*

Service Labor and Intelligent Innovation

Contrary to Marxian deceit, service labor and intelligent innovation are usually two different things, and a free-market economy painfully exposes this truth to the masses whose vocation has thus far been limited to the former. Productive service labor of a good or service in the free market is generally less valuable than the productive creative labor of intelligent innovation of such goods and services. This is because service labor is reliant only upon an able body and a functional mind, whereas intelligent innovation is reliant upon exceptional thinking. There is no shortage of able bodies and functional (arguably) minds on the planet. However, the same cannot be said for exceptional thinking. Naturally, by definition, exceptional thinkers comprise a miniscule percentage of the world population. Since that which is scarce *and* in demand has greater general value than that which is plentiful and readily available, the value of service labor is limited (unless artificially increased through *coercion* with collusive sick-outs, strikes, and violent intimidation against the freedom of those who would provide labor—the workers who are demonized as "scabs"). As such, we cannot honestly equate the value of the creative labor of the intelligent innovator of the polio vaccine with the service labor of the person who cleaned up after each experiment. Both are labor of value, but the service labor of the cleanup person could be quickly replaced without preventing the development of the vaccine. Could the intelligent innovator of the polio vaccine be so easily replaced? The same is true of the cell phone. We cannot equate the value of the creative labor of the intelligent innovator of the cell phone with the service labor of the person who assembles its parts on the production line. Again, the latter may be easily replaced whereas the intelligent innovator may not. Notwithstanding this fact, even the Marxist view of labor logically requires that the intelligent innovator who may have spent thousands of hours in labor and dollars for medical/scientific education and training be compensated more than the service labor of those who did not expend years of labor in training.

The intelligent innovators clearly contribute the most value to humanity, which is not to say that those who create less value are not necessary. Most intelligent innovators were once service laborers of the unexceptional majority but believed they could innovate or improve upon the products and/or services for which they performed such service labor, e.g., Henry Ford once worked for Thomas Edison. We should all earn and learn through service labor unless or until we figure out a way to contribute greater value to others. Unfortunately, universal minimum wage laws have restricted such freedom, discriminated against minorities, and increased the misery of unemployment, especially for the least skilled. The truth of such a misguided doctrine unjustly provides that if someone can't deliver the hourly productivity of the current arbitrarily government-set minimum wage, they don't deserve any job. If conditions of freedom and competition were permitted to flourish, starting with apprenticeships for the least skilled, the *opportunity* to become an intelligent innovator would be available to all, including the people who clean up after each experiment and assembly line workers. Sadly, most have been indoctrinated with values that are contrary to such truth. Instead of celebrating and examining the qualities, characteristics, causes and effects for emulation of intelligent innovation and contribution, those comprising the pot without virtue exploit the unexceptional majority for power by calling the kettle of intelligent innovators black.

Responsibility vs. Compelled Labor

The fundamental root of conflict within most political systems, and the differences between most political systems, is the degree to which people take responsibility for themselves versus the degree to which others are *compelled* to labor for them with entitlements. This also defines the degree that each society permits individuals the *freedom to choose* what one does with the fruits of his labor—individual freedom versus collectivism. This has traditionally been expressed as class warfare between the have-not majority and the have minority. Even though each person is different and contributes different levels of value to others, the have-nots naturally want the same amount of stuff as the haves. Unless the have-nots can increase the perceived value of their contribution to others or the haves voluntarily divest themselves, the freedom of the haves must be taken along with their property for the have-nots to have the same stuff. This is artfully accomplished with government redistribution programs—entitlements—disguised by perversion of the term *human rights*. Under such circumstances, the haves are compelled to labor for the have-nots, without redefining *human rights* to include the term *compelled labor of others*. The have-nots are *not* compelled to work for the haves in business or industry because they may quit to start their own business or leave at any time. However, the haves are always compelled to work for the have-nots through statist redistribution. So who is really being exploited?

When one is compelled to labor for another, liberty and responsibility are curtailed. Healthcare is illustrative of this fact. When people advocate a government service such as free healthcare as a human right, they are stating that they have the right to compel others to do labor for them for life, regardless of whether a lifetime of overindulgence in chain-smoking or overeating caused the ailments. Someone else must pay the consequences for such bad decisions. Some people consume and expend in ways that are detrimental (of little or no value), while others consume and expend in ways that are disciplined and beneficial (of value). Unless doctors are willing to volunteer their services, their labor must be compelled, or else the doctor must be paid by money from the taxed labor of others. It would not matter that many of those others developed the responsibility and virtue of discipline to exercise regularly and refrain from overindulgent consumption; they must labor for the overindulgent bad decisions of the entitled, claiming their "human rights" to other people's labor. If they were responsible for their own ailments, some number—however small—would refrain from overindulgence to avoid paying nature's consequences for lack of virtue. However, the reality is that their overindulgence doesn't stop at the cause of their ailments but continues with the taking of medical services paid for by the labor of others. People obviously also have congenital health issues for no fault of their own. However, in a free society of natural capitalism, health insurance would be available for under $100 per month. But the cost of music and cable TV are more important priorities to the uninsured, especially when government can compel others to labor/pay for the uninsured's health care. Under such circumstances, *government is actually compelling others to labor for the uninsured's cost of music and cable TV*. Such values become cultural, so they inhibit prosperity and decay virtue to an entitlement/dependence mentality. Similarly, an unmarried couple taking state benefits may decide to have five or more children. Under nanny-state societies, which comprise most of the world's notions of "advanced" governing systems, including those of the United States and Europe, others must pay to raise these children. The responsibility of the parents is ceded to the state. This cannot be fair to the families who have fewer children. Moreover, the kids are likely to grow up without the strong and weak force balance of a nuclear family since only single parents may be eligible for robust state payments. The children are forced to exchange the paternity of a father for the paternity of the state. Enculturation of statist dependence and the decaying weak force of a one-parent family become their values, as they know no others. When the children grow up, they are statistically likely to become impecunious and to perpetuate the vicious cycle; they will vote for the variant of the Marxist party who will insure their monthly pabulum, their dependence, and re-election of the vote-buying politicians who enslave them. As for the nation-state, once a critical mass of dependents manifest, prosperity cannot attain in a demoralized society of serfs who are increasing an already great entropy of debt. This is abject immorality, as no one is served but the small class of political leadership without virtue.

Who Will Take Care of the Sick, the Poor, and the Unfortunate?

Of course the natural question then comes up: "But who will take care of the sick, the poor, and the unfortunate?" The intelligent innovators of the *relatively* freest nation-state in the world, the United States of America, are the richest people on Earth. This is not a coincidence, as they lived under relative conditions which enabled them to contribute the greatest relative value to humanity. The intelligent innovators who have contributed the greatest value to humanity, e.g., Andrew Carnegie of the Industrial Revolution or Bill Gates of the computer and information age, have somehow been enlightened to the secret that *"all energy is only borrowed, someday you must give it back."*[13] Remember, money represents the quantized energy of human labor. The amount of money they have earned, donated, and pledged to return upon their death is so tremendous that it would take care of the needy, and even if it didn't, churches and other charities would make up the difference. Why? If the values of freedom and responsibility characteristic of natural capitalism were permitted to flourish, the character of the nation-state would produce a responsible and prosperous society instead of corrupt pigs feeding at the government trough. Not only would many more wealthy people donate to charities and compete for the status-prestige of donating the most, but naturally, greater productivity would develop and less needy people would exist, under such values of virtue. If charities and organizations claiming to do public service are legitimate and worthy, they would not need government funding. They would get funded organically, while illegitimate political causes where politicians and their cronies rob the populace (see ACORN) might not be, because individuals generally monitor the hard-earned dollars they control. Unfortunately, government has largely usurped the roles of charity and corruption, increasing taxes to pay for both. Therefore, people aren't as charitable as they would be if they were not compelled by government. The character of successful people is such that if they are compelled to do something, they will expend great effort, time, and funds to avoid such coercion, especially if the funds were generated by their labor and they know that much ends up in the hands of the corrupt. Unlike government, charities don't just hand out checks to people who spend it on indulgent and addictive things which perpetuate their condition. Charities are the closest to the people and have an interest

in assessing and ameliorating the conditions of the downtrodden by identifying and addressing the root causes. Government, on the other hand,
perpetuates the problems by keeping people dependent. Politicians get
their power by keeping people enslaved and promising they will deliver
their fix each month in return for their votes. If by chance or strength of
will the dependent become productive, they will lose eligibility for their
fix, and often revert to the indulgent monthly check rather than the dignity of hard work and productivity. It's a sad cycle of dependence that
weakens the cells of the nation-state and inhibits health and prosperity.
Welfare state/socialist government instills the values and perpetuates the
conditions of poverty. As Milton Friedman so lucidly stated:

> *The capitalist system, the private enterprise system in the 19th century
> did a far better job of expressing that sense of compassion than the gov-
> ernmental welfare programs are today. The 19th century, which people
> denigrate as the high tide of capitalism, was the period of the greatest
> outpouring of eleemosynary and charitable activity that the world has
> ever known. [The welfare system] has destroyed private charitable ar-
> rangements which are far more effective, far more compassionate, far
> more person to person in helping people who are, really, for no fault of
> their own in a disadvantaged situation.*[14]

The poor, the sick, and the unfortunate will always be with us.
Most people may become any or all of the three at any time. This tests
the morality and virtue of *individuals* who are in a position to help. The
virtues of freedom breed a far more compassionate society than those of
statist tyranny.

SECTION II

VALUES AND VIRTUE

Chapter 7

THE BIOLOGY AND GENETICS OF VALUES

The Transmission of Information: Indoctrination and Enculturation

As complex as the world appears to be, the key to health and prosperity for both humans and nation-states is as simple and evident as the truth of cause and effect. To recap the preceding section, individuals and nation-states are open systems governed by the laws of physics, as they both exchange energy and matter. Both require consumption and expenditure of energy for survival. This is because everything tends to decay or disorder over time in accordance with the second law of energy. To resist such decay, nature requires us to consume energy of value and to expend that same energy by a method of value. Such energy is the raw material from which open systems are sculpted, and its levels of value determine health and prosperity. Therefore, we must learn and discern *what* is of *value for consumption and expenditure*, not only in food energy but, most importantly, TRANSMITTED INFORMATION FROM OTHERS. Such information may be harmful rather than of value, depending upon whether or not it is in alignment with truth for health and prosperity. Cigarette smoking is not in alignment with truth for lung health, no matter who transmits such information, as carbon monoxide is inconsistent with oxygenation. Similarly, most present methods of human governance are not in alignment with truth for prosperity because they are inconsistent with the virtues of intelligent innovation. Instead, they indoctrinate *envy, entitlement* to the labor of others, institutionalized *theft* from the most productive, and *demonization* of the very source of prosperity—the intelligent innovators. Such transmitted, consumed, and expended information is harmful rather than of value, resulting in unhealthy debt, dependence, and misery rather than health and prosperity. Our perceptions and choices in what we consume, both in biomass energy as well as transmitted information from others, and how we expend them in lifestyle, define our values. Such VALUES determine the health and prosperity of the open systems we know as humans and nation-states, depending upon whether they are of VIRTUE.

The Energy of Value for Nation-State Consumption and Expenditure—Productive Human Labor

Just as the bodily organs facilitate the health of the individual, so too do the organs known as the economy for the nation-state. The human body requires the energy of food/biomass, which is converted into liquid form and channeled through the organs for functioning. Similarly, nation-states require the energy of goods and services, which are converted into "liquid" form (money) and channeled through the economy for functioning. Just as the health value of food and its conversion to energy through the organs substantially determines the health of the person, the value of goods and services converted to money through the economy—GDP—substantially determines the health of nation-states. As everything tends to disorder or decay, economies must have constant growth of GDP; otherwise, the entropy of recession or depression manifests. To resist the decay of entropy, nation-states must consume and expend the *energy of value* known as PRODUCTIVE HUMAN LABOR. These are the *goods and services* which improve the quality of life with medicines, nutrition, technology, the arts, etc. Meanwhile, the nation-state organ of government simultaneously consumes a portion of that productive human labor through taxation and expends it on what *should only be* services to protect the integrity of its individual cells—the life, liberty, and property of its citizens. However, through indoctrination and enculturation, we have been socially conditioned into an immoral value system which mandates "public servants" to take from one group and give to others, while they reap the commissions of power and material extravagance by such theft, e.g., the Imperial U.S. House Speaker Pelosi's "Congressional Air Force" special Gulfstream jet plane travel home,[1] and her participation in an IPO while presiding over pending legislation that would have hurt the company. That legislation never made it to the House floor.[2]

The Kings and Lords Return: Servants to Royalty, Masters to Serfs

Funds from the selective taxation of human labor is collected and deposited in a feeding trough where government pigs and their sycophantic co-conspirators overindulgently feed in self-interest—all at the expense of a broad prosperity. This occurs throughout the political spectrum, from left to right. Whether it's subsidies for a favored constituency or outright crony capitalism, legalized bribery or lobbying are standard values for nation-state governance. In fact, as the world painfully experiences nature's inevitable correction for humanity's corrupt and interdependent entitlement cultures, even the seat of government for the nation-state which historically represented the cause of world freedom—America—used its own financial crisis as a pretext to indulge in an unparalleled five trillion-dollar feeding frenzy upon the labor and fruits of others. Washington, D.C., is supposed to be the servant's quarters for its fifty states. *Instead, it has become the wealthiest region in the entire nation.*[3] The American Revolution was supposed to have ended the rule of kings and lords by charter. In fact, upon the formation of America, Ben Franklin was asked whether that charter resulted in a monarchy or a republic, whereupon he presciently quipped, *"A republic, if you can keep it."*[4] Sadly, Americans couldn't. The servants became royalty, and the masters became serfs. In setting the standard for a culture of corruption, self-serving political leaders of both the American left and right have personally profited in the financial markets upon pending legislation for which they had privileged information and influence unavailable to their public masters.[5] Until they were recently exposed, elite legislative officials made no laws against enriching themselves on such insider information as they did for the public they ruled. Thus, many public servants enter government impecuniously but exit as wealthy multi-millionaires even on a government salary.[6] And their excessive indulgences extend to those salaries, as well, increasing their own while the private sector's decreases. Even non-elected public employee salaries far exceed private sector pay for similar positions, and this is in addition to lavish benefits, all funded by taxpayers who have no such conferred benefits.[7] When the servants are compensated more than the estate holders, cultural values are seriously compromised. Although people throw the term *government* around as if it were an inanimate object, governments are comprised of people who have their own values and self-interests. In regulating the conduct of the citizenry, public servants effectively legislate their own values and self-interests into cultural values for everyone else. They are a small class with great power. "Power tends to corrupt, and absolute power corrupts absolutely."[8] Thus, those who advocate government which does any more than protect the life, liberty, and property of its citizens advocate the unmerited benefit of a *corrupt* small class at the expense of cultural values and prosperity.

The Elixir in the Fuel of Prosperity: Intelligent Innovation is Dependent upon Cultural Values

The value of energy in human labor for each particular nation-state is dependent upon its level of intelligent innovation. While productive human labor is the fuel of prosperity, intelligent innovation is the elixir which determines the grade of octane. It not only generates technologies to improve the health and well-being of humanity, but it also provides employment with factories, advertisers, distributors, wholesalers, retailers, resellers, repairs, etc. *Intelligent innovation drives evolution, and it is dependent upon CULTURAL VALUES.* This logically implies that since each culture has different values, some are more evolved than others. Although this should be patently obvious, most "advanced" Western nation-states, from their educational institutions and media to the highest levels of government, refuse to acknowledge this truth, and they affirmatively indoctrinate students and the populace to the contrary. A cursory examination of the prosperity levels for each nation-state empirically belies such false propaganda. These prosperity levels reveal the relative proximity of cultural values to the enlightenment of universal truth, i.e., whether their cultural behavior is conducive to prosperity. They also demonstrate that political correctness, relativism, and substantivism are dangerous for their patent conflict with truth. But the politically correct relativist/substantivist would reflexively counter that all cultures are equal but of different substances and that some prosper and others don't because of the natural resources of the land they happen to inhabit. Really? So how could it be that approximately three hundred million people of a particular culture concentrated in the Middle East sit on the greatest wealth of proven oil reserves, yet their general populace lives in squalor, is generally illiterate, and are of the lowest level of achievement based on the number of patents per capita in the world, hold an insignificant number of scientific awards, and innovate relatively few contributions to humanity (unless the skill of terrorism counts). At the same time, a miniscule culture of less than seven million people sits on barren land surrounded and frequently attacked by the aforementioned three hundred million people yet live in relative luxury, have the highest literacy rates in the world, have the fifth highest number of patents per capita in the world, and receive at least twenty-five percent of the prestigious international scientific prizes. With more engineers and scientists and more scientific papers per capita than any country in the world, this tiny culture as a nation-state, even without its diaspora, is second in the world in intelligent innovation.[9] Moreover, they list the third most companies on the NASDAQ technology index after the U.S. and China.[10] The U.S. and China have over 1.5 billion people combined. *How could such a tiny nation-state contribute such a great concentration of value to humanity in technology, science, and medicine, even while laboring under diplomatic boycott, perpetual terrorism and a siege of envy by its neighbors and much of the world?* The answer would be much more evident if not for the obfuscations of the cultural Marxism that we call political correctness. Nevertheless, the answer may be found in what relativists/substantivists inadvertently refer to as the substance of a culture. That substance is just a politically correct term for the *values* of a culture. The *politically* incorrect truth, again, is that *cultural values determine prosperity,* depending upon whether or not they are conducive to intelligent innovation. *Cultural values conducive to intelligent innovation and its resultant prosperity are values of virtue.* Such virtuous values include education of truth, freedom, self-reliance, cooperation, contribution, and respect for and protection of truth, life, liberty, and property. Cultures which promote contrary values are not virtuous and thus cannot maintain prosperity. Ignorance, tyranny, dependence, coercion, entitlement, and general disrespect for truth, life, liberty, and property inhibit intelligent innovation and prosperity, resulting in general misery. These are all values of the *immoral* family of coercion: the sisters of socialism/progressivism/liberalism and their ugly cousins—dictatorship and theocracy.

So Where Do Cultural Values Come From?

Inherent Cosmological Void

Each individual is born with an inherent cosmological void. Nature requires us to fill that void in order to satiate the discomforting insecurity of our mysterious presence on the earthly plane. This is by design to insure that we seek knowledge in our ascent to enlightenment. Nature abhors a vacuum, especially one of such critical significance as to determine our orientation in the world, and thus the cosmological void will be filled one way or another. Of course our initial caretakers, who are tasked with the process of nurture and orientation, generally fill that void by the indoctrination of their values. For most of human history, this transmitted information usually included religious mores or spirituality of a purported divinity. This constitutes our world view until we gain perspective with experiences of our own, which either corroborate or conflict with those initial values and create natural adjustments. As time progresses, we inevitably modify our views until, hopefully, we ripen with enlightenment to virtue. However, some people proceed in the opposite direction and rot with depravity, infected by and/or infecting others. Just as a table stands on the integrity and strength of its legs, our cosmological security is determined by the integrity and strength of our world views, whether they are rooted in a solid foundation of truth and logic or the quicksand of self-indulgent rationalizations. Truth, cause and effect, and logic are anathema to the latter, posing a great threat to a precarious cosmological security. Threatened by truth, cosmologies not based on an immutable foundation will naturally collapse, and thus may be readily identified by their base characteristics of survival—coercion, subterfuge, and violence. Calling something a religion does not immunize it from mortal scrutiny. Religions must be examined for their values to determine whether they are in alignment with liberty or tyranny, virtue or depravity. The cultures they produce are the litmus.

Biology and Genetics

Yet if filling the cosmological void with ideological content was the only basis of one's world views or politics, most nation-states would be politically homogeneous, without left and right views or political upheavals. However, we know that every nation-state inevitably oscillates politically. To understand this we must begin at the cellular level of nation-states— the individual. Obviously, each person is unique, with DNA and personality distinct from all others. This is biology and genetics, both of which, to a degree, influence us sociologically, including where one ends up on the ideological political spectrum—from liberal indulgence to conservative restraint. As scientific studies have indicated, the brain functionality of those on the left of the political spectrum generally require the stimulation of novelty and chaos and have a high tolerance for uncertainty and incongruent information.[11] This is the side of disorder or increased entropy of indulgence. Those on the right side of the political spectrum generally require structure and certainty and have a low tolerance for incongruent information.[12] This is the side of order or decreased entropy of restraint.

Many variations and permutations obviously fill out the variable political spectrum. Of course, we are all human and share common traits, but the *dominance* of certain traits and values which compose unique individuals designates our proximity on the political spectrum. This is not static. We are here to learn and evolve. Thus, age and experience are transformative factors of healthy political evolution. Myopia and idealism may evolve to perspective and reality as the results of cause and effect come to light with age. Liberal indulgence is a natural and an important experience when we are children, adolescents, and young adults, because we soon learn that such indulgence without restraint has consequences. If you drink too much, you get a headache. If you spend too much you go into debt. This is why young adults are generally on the indulgent political left. They haven't yet acquired sufficient impactful experience of perspective to drive them below the patina of issues. They generally have no property yet to protect and they want the free stuff stolen and offered most often by the left. They look to the expedient or indulgent solutions to societal issues. However, those who remain left at true middle age (around forty) and later either retain a congenital myopia and never cognitively process at sufficient depth to ascertain cause and effect, or they disregard it for indulgence and/or power. Thus, the famous truism: "If you're not a liberal at twenty, you have no heart; if you're not a conservative at forty you have no brain."

To illustrate this polarization of indulgent emotion on one end and experienced restraint of reason on the other, the political issue of gun violence in America is apt. The indulgent and expedient solution of the left would be to ban or limit arms at the expense of the 2nd Amendment freedom to keep and bear arms for defense. However, with emotional restraint and the discipline to dig deeper, they may come to the conclusion that if someone wants to kill another person, a gun ban won't prevent criminals from obtaining guns or using a myriad of other means to kill. If they have the discipline to dig even deeper they would further find that other countries have more guns per capita, yet don't have such gun violence. If they dug farther to the direct source of the gun violence and could restrain the indoctrinated emotions of idealism and political correctness, they would find the unpleasant truth—most American gun violence is an ethnic issue. And if they dug even deeper within that ethnic issue for cause and effect, they would find that it's about *values*, or a lack of them, because of the absence of sufficient parental guidance.*

Left and Right are merely positions of instinct in the human animal—*tendencies for indulgence and restraint*. All humans exercise both, but values trend toward one or the other, left and right respectively. And just as there is physical overindulgence, there is also cognitive overindulgence. With the former, overconsumption of feel-good "comfort food" in total disregard of truth in cause and effect may pain and disease the body with toxicity. With the latter, *overconsumption of "feel-good" idealism in total disregard of truth in cause and effect may pain and disease society with toxicity*. For example, "feel-good" idealism says that everyone should own a home, but the truth is that not everyone is productive enough to merit fulfillment of ownership responsibilities. Government policy directing private industry to authorize home ownership for everyone under taxpayer guarantees, regardless of creditworthiness or ability to pay, is toxic and proves itself to be a painful disease for society. Most recently, that disease manifested as the Great Recession. Virtuous values of restraint were ignored in favor of overindulgence.

Values Influence Biology and Genetics

Values are literally facilitated and expressed through cognition and volitional brain function, which directly influence biology and genetics. Practicing values consistent with truth and logic, generation after generation, cumulatively and incrementally yields increasing access to latent brain potential and/or mutational evolution of intelligence. The closer the cultural values are to truth and logic, the greater the intelligence of the culture. Just as dominant physical mannerisms become genetically encoded to manifest in progeny, thought patterns of dominantly practiced cultural values may manifest over great time spans that we can't perceive but in accordance with the first law of energy, whereby the energy of thought and mass/matter are transmutable. On a nano time scale,

---

* Although individuals who had sufficient parental guidance have committed gun related massacres, they are extremely rare and a result of defective aberrational minds. However, such massacres would be prevented or mitigated if vigilant lawful citizens were permitted to bear arms to defend themselves, their families, friends, and others. Moreover, gun murders are highest where guns are banned, e.g., Chicago, Illinois. This is because the law abiding people cannot defend themselves under such a disadvantage, and criminals know it. Only criminals violate the gun ban for use against the lawful— whose political representatives stripped them of their ability to defend themselves.

this is akin to practicing a sport consistently and becoming skilled at it over time as a result of repetition and adjustments, assessing feedback of current performance, and *intending* gradual changes until proficiency is achieved. Contrary to the fallacy of *random* mutations naturally selected for adaptation proposed by the theory of natural selection,[13] mutations of increased intelligence over great time periods are *intended* in our dominant thoughts, which we express through cultural practices.

Fig. 10, Leaf-shaped Katydid mimicking a dying leaf, morphing parts of its leaf shape "dying" brown on one end, and healthy vivid green on the other. (Animal Highlights, Belize, 2007, Jun 25, 2007 by Tim)

Cultural practices adopted by a culture which are in sync with truth advance that culture toward enlightenment by the degree of truth embraced and practiced. To clarify by an example of *intended* rather than *random* mutations, we can look to nature to identify this process; the mutations cannot be *random* which enabled many marine and terrestrial species' inherent morphing capacities, wherein they produce colors and patterns at will which strikingly replicate an illusion of their surrounding environments. The odds are impossible for such complexity to *randomly* appear in genetic programming. A species born with the general appearance of its surrounding environment is one thing, but to have the ability *to morph colors at will* is quite another. The former could support the *random* mutation theory of natural selection whereby the organisms born matching the color of the environment survived while those that were conspicuous predators and prey died off. However, complex morphing capabilities and complex shapes indicate the design of *intent,* as the leaf-shaped Katydid strikingly illustrates (fig. 10). Blending into the environment *at will* to avoid detection for both predators and prey increased the efficiency or value of energy for self-preservation, i.e., excessive energy would not have to be expended to hunt or to evade hunters. The coherent likelihood is that over great periods of time, in its limited capacity within the limiting laws of physics, desire was incrementally willed into manifestation and locked into genetic code; then some species could visually blend into their environment at will in order to consume energy (prey) or to avoid being consumed as energy (prey). As for human beings, the mechanism of survival and prosperity is *intelligence and innovation. Enculturation and indoctrination of human values should therefore be those which foster intelligent innovation—values of virtue.* Intended dominant thought patterns of virtue perpetuate a cycle of cultural values, which manifest intelligent, innovative minds.

Indoctrination and Enculturation

Enculturation of values takes place via peoples' consumption of information inculcated by primary caretakers, ethnic and societal tradition, religious authorities, government authorities, education, and the media. Those values derive and are adopted from influential individual conduct. Each individual is motivated by pain and pleasure, fear and desire. Fear of want and its resultant pain motivates, as does desire for pleasure. In addition to how we treat ourselves, such motivations generally necessitate the establishment of relationships with others, and it is our individual conduct toward both ourselves and others in avoiding pain and seeking pleasure that defines our values. *Fundamental individual conduct derives from, and must be viewed by, its position between the humanistic poles of indulgent gratification and disciplined restraint.* It's indulgent and much easier to take someone else's money than to have the virtuous restraint to labor for it. It's indulgent and much easier to go to the race track all day and watch TV at night than to have the virtuous restraint to go to school during the day and do homework at night. It's indulgent and much easier to eat cake and candy than to have the virtuous restraint to eat spinach and grains. The levels of virtuous restraint from indulgence generally yield corresponding levels of health and prosperity, while eliciting the virtues which reveal our values, e.g., self-reliance, education, etc. Too much indulgence causes decay and disease, and too much restraint causes an unhealthy rigid conformity which inhibits the creativity of intelligent innovation and growth. This is the natural struggle of left and right inherent in each human being. We all naturally seek indulgence, pleasure, and avoidance of pain to gratify physical/material needs and desires in pursuit of happiness. But to maintain health and prosperity a tilted balance whereupon restraint, even if painful, must exceed indulgence, as we must always be one step ahead of the decay of entropy. This requires the discipline of restraint from instinctual overindulgence, or productive energy of value, which decreases the decay of entropy. Indulgence is as natural as the decay of entropy. Anyone can indulge in pleasurable junk food and let the body go, as the muscles atrophy on their own. It takes disciplined restraint in diet and exercise to manifest a healthy and prosperous body. This is why we glorify professional athletes, because they had the discipline to develop and maintain their talents at an extraordinary level. *Our values generally determine our levels of indulgence and restraint.*

On the scale of one to ten, with one being liberally indulgent and ten being conservatively restrained, humans and nation-states must be at a minimum of a six to maintain health and prosperity. Thus, the most prosperous nation-state in human history consists of a center-right populace, six or above on the aforementioned scale, and in its greatest prosperity was much more conservative. The decline is the waning legacy of humanity's greatest governing *charter of values*—the U.S. Constitution. Although it has been indulgently ignored, circumvented, and subverted by corrupt, elitist politicos, its values of virtue, which protect individual life, liberty, and property, when adhered to, require self-reliance and co-operation, resulting in the prosperous American spirit. Those values are no more, as America has decayed to an entitlement society of indulgence. Those without merit or substantive accomplishment have become the lionized ideal, and this is reflected in the decay of virtue and the corresponding decline of prosperity. Nature designates the arts and entertainment as a cultural mirror, displaying contemporary values for all to see. The culturally selected and celebrated talentless personas of contemporary entertainment known as "Real[van]ity" television are intended to remind us of where we are as a culture. Everyone generally desires attention and love, and this naturally motivates us. But the virtuous method to attain it is through exceptional achievement which provides value to others. This usually requires hard work and sacrifice to develop talents or skills. Attention would be warranted as delayed gratification when the fruits of one's accomplishments are performed or displayed as value for others, entertainment or otherwise. However, this has now devolved to the immediate gratification of "Just look at me. I demand that you just look at me. I'm eating, now I'm walking, I'm going to the bathroom..." Similarly, but more saliently reflective of the decline in contemporary American values is the chosen leader of the people. Out of a nation-state of hundreds of millions of people, America's current selection is an individual who has previously never held a real job, run a business, or accomplished anything of substance. He has only indulged the vanity and narcissism of writing about himself in not just one but two "autobiographies"* *before* becoming the U.S. president.[14] The nation-state effectively elevates *and perpetuates* the values of its selected leader, as they are proliferated from the platform and influence of the highest office in the land. America continues to stagnate because *the values selected* in its highest executive, who administrates such values, are antithetical to virtue and prosperity. President Obama was indoctrinated through enculturation with the false premise that the unaccomplished must be oppressed and that the accomplished must be the oppressor.[16] His spiritual advisor reinforced this message in the sermons sans virtue of the church which Obama frequented for decades.[17] This message is indulgently gratifying for many, because it absolves the unaccomplished of any responsibility for their life. They just perpetually blame the accomplished "oppressors" and racism, while simultaneously and duplicitously advocating racism (Affirmative Action) in order to leverage influence. These indulgent values are not grounded on the solid foundation of truth. Ironically, they were patently belied when an "oppressed" minority was democratically elected to the most powerful office in the world by a diverse, albeit uninformed, guilt-ridden multicultural majority of varied and disparate socioeconomic strata. As a prodigy and professor of Alinsky doctrine and values, Obama generally does not believe in virtue, only power and any means to achieve it. His psychological development can be traced through the stimuli of his real world experience—going from school to school of Marxist-Alinsky influence (the American universities), creating a local power base through Alinsky "community organizing," and rising straight to power.[18] But this is the

---

* Investigated and found to be substantially false[15]

power of government, not the power of merit. In achieving power without having contributed meritorious value to others, Obama maintains a deep-seated, contemptuous envy of those who have achieved power through merit—the accomplished intelligent innovators of business:

> *"If you got a business, you didn't build that. Somebody else made that happen."*[19]

That "somebody else" to which he is referring is government, which built much of the nation-state infrastructure. Of course, the business owners "made that happen" through their labor in taxes, and such infrastructure could have been built much more efficiently through private enterprise.

However, the final dispositive factor which formed Obama's values derive from his genetic/biological predisposition between the poles of left and right—indulgent gratification to disciplined restraint. Instead of promoting virtuous values of merited accomplishment—the disciplined restraint of giving value to others in goods and services as cooperative exchange for money—Obama promoted the opposite pole of indulgent gratification: ENVY AND DEMONIZE THE ACCOMPLISHED INTELLIGENT IN-NOVATORS OF MERIT AND COERCIVELY DIVEST THEM TO PARITY WITH THE UNACCOMPLISHED AND UNMERITED "ENTITLED." For him, this is the role of government, to "spread the wealth around."[20] This indicates a serious deficiency of virtue and values. If he does not understand that wealth is generally the result of innovation of value and productive labor, then such abject ignorance is not a virtue for leadership of the free world. If he does understand wealth creation, then his call for theft and redistribution are also not virtues for leadership of the free world. Yet these are the values which he literally proclaimed and executed with great influence in the most liberally indulgent manner in American history. This is significant because it sets the bar for the rest of the world:

> *"Only a virtuous people are capable of freedom. As nations become more corrupt and vicious, they have more need of masters."* —Benjamin Franklin[21]

Indulgence/Restraint

Indulgence and restraint are the balancing polarities of humanity and its aggregate nation-states. However, the balance must tilt right to prevent decay and collapse as explicated by the laws of energy. The values of virtue which determine health and prosperity derive from the side of restraint. For nation-states, this means that life, liberty, and property should not be indulgently plundered but protected. The nature of the human animal majority acts on instinct. This would insure the indulgent values which have kept humanity enslaved throughout history. In the one prominent movement where indulgence (to plunder) was restrained and life, liberty, and property were protected by charter, the *values of virtue* as transmitted through the U.S. Constitution resulted in the greatest freedom and prosperity the world has ever known. But as everything tends to disorder, those values of virtue would be obfuscated, blurred, and supplanted through indoctrination and the enculturation of indulgent values, creating the presumption of *entitlement to the labor of others as a "human right."* This mindset necessitates the adoption of the other interdependent values of indulgence and the repudiation of the antithetical values of virtue:

- *Dependence is indulgent, because no discipline or virtue is required to receive a monthly entitlement check derived from another's labor, whereas self-reliance requires the discipline of productive labor or contribution of perceived value in exchange for food, shelter, and clothing.*

- *Ignorance is indulgent, because it does not require the virtuous hard work, discipline, and tedious study of education.*

- *Tyranny and coercion are indulgent values, because it's easier to dictate and force others than it is to gain cooperation and consensus through the virtuous hard work, discipline, and responsibility required of freedom.*

- *Disrespect for life, liberty, property, and truth are indulgent, because it is easier to mislead and coerce property, liberty, and life, rather than to earn and sacrifice honestly through enterprise which contributes value to the life, liberty, and property of others.*

And if truth conflicts with personal goals and desires, it's indulgent to say there is no truth. Without truth, there can be no right and wrong, only subjectivity—the ideal condition for leftist elites to indulge in coercive power. Of course the Right also indulges but does so generally from the corruption of power, not substantive policy. This is an important distinction. As a matter of policy, nature designates the Right to represent general *restraint* on most issues and the Left to represent general *indulgence* on most issues. America's broad multicultural populace and its representative government provide a prime political sampling of unequivocal proof that INDULGENCE is the denominating *policy* of the Left:

- ABORTION: The sex was great, but the care of another life is too much of a responsibility and requires too much sacrifice, so it's indulgent to abort a fetus.

- AFFIRMATIVE ACTION: When individuals don't qualify on merit or content of character for something coveted, indulgently reward them based upon the meritless happenstance of their race.

- ANTI-RELIGION: Judeo-Christian religion usually promotes values of restraint, which inhibit indulgence. Moreover, religion jeopardizes allegiance to indulgent elite liberal directives and statist groupthink and encourages a higher moral authority of natural rights and the restraint to maintain them.

- BIG GOVERNMENT: It is indulgent to use the jackboot of government force to take from others what one cannot legally or morally take on his own without threat of jail or harm from defense of property. Those who support big government vote for politicians who will legislate and authorize State force to indulgently appropriate the labor of others and its fruits and place them into the hands of those who did not earn it.

- A "LIVING" U.S. CONSTITUTION: Leftists and progressives abhor the limitations which the Constitution imposes on the indulgent taking of other people's liberty and property. Therefore, they indoctrinate others to believe the falsehood that changing and evolving times require a "living" Constitution which changes with the times, and without any requirement to comply with the Amendment process for such changes. A "living" document would provide the subjectivity and discretion required to indulgently feast on the property of others, while choosing which liberties to grant or revoke. However, the "living" Constitution indulgence is another weak cosmology which cannot withstand truth and logic. Although times change and evolve, the immutable principle of protecting life, liberty, and property do not. Changing and evolving times really means that there will always be new and different *forms* of property and liberties, but they must nevertheless be maximally protected to insure stability and prosperity. *Changing and evolving times require new applications, not new principles.* To protect life, liberty, and property from plunder is to protect prosperity. To discard such principles is to discard prosperity.

• Gun Control: It is indulgent to assign the cause of killing to an inanimate object rather than the person responsible. Truth and logic dictate that guns don't kill without people, but people kill without guns. The subtext for gun control is that indulgent government coercion of the masses is jeopardized when the populace has the ability to bear arms in defense of liberty.

• Universal Healthcare Entitlement: It is indulgent to believe that people have a "human right" to compel the labor of doctors, nurses, and health care professionals. Involuntary servitude is not only immoral but is prohibited by the 13ᵗʰ Amendment.

• Illegal Immigration: Even though many law-abiding applicants spend years and a lot of money and waiting in the hopes of gaining citizenship, it is indulgent to allow illegal aliens to just skip the application process and violate the existing laws by which others abide. Illegal aliens are rewarded by the party of indulgence with entitlements and the right to vote for a government which takes the fruits of labor from lawful citizens and gives them to lawbreakers.

• Progressive/Graduated Taxation: The Leftist media and educational institutions have been so effective with indoctrination as to compel the Left, the Center, and the Right into a groupthink on progressive taxation. Therefore, a real scenario may bring refreshing perspective from the reference frame of fairness:

Three American brothers decided to give a wedding anniversary present to their parents. They wanted to pay off the mortgage on the family home in which they all grew up and shared until each left the nest, because their parents still lived there and would retire there. One brother had received federal student loans for college, but he partied too much, failed most of his classes, and dropped out of school. He got a service job, from which he saved $1,000. The second brother also received federal student loans for college, but he had skipped the indulgent college parties, and since he was not that gifted, he had studied hard to graduate. He was able to get a good job, from which he saved $100,000. The third brother had decided to take a risk and skip college altogether, which was his prerogative in a relatively free country. He struggled as he bounced from one service job to another. While laboring at one of those jobs, he came up with an idea to improve upon the services the company provided. His boss didn't believe that the idea was feasible. So he took a risk again and quit his job to start his own company. He borrowed money from previous customers who believed in his idea. After many attempts to get his idea to work, years of sacrifice with no leisure time, he was able to perfect his idea and create a multi-million-dollar company. As a result, he saved $1,000,000. Because each of the brothers valued the virtue and sentiment of sacrifice in gratitude for the nurture of their parents, they respectively chipped in the following amounts to pay off the balance of their parents' home mortgage: $100, $10,000, and $100,000. Even though one brother chipped in almost $100,000 more than another one, they agreed that this was fair since each made an equal sacrifice—ten percent of what they had.

This is how the flat tax, otherwise known as the "fair tax," works. When told about the three brothers, most people naturally understand its inherent fairness, even to the extent that many actually believe this to be the prevailing U.S. tax code. It's not. In 1913, just after the U.S. Constitution was amended to allow a personal income tax in addition to consumption taxes (16th Amendment), the father of leftist progressivism, Woodrow Wilson, signed into law the progressive/graduated tax.[22] This paradigm shift institutionalized corruption and indulgence on an unprecedented scale, providing those in power with subjective discretion to legislate different tax rates and different exemptions for different groups, all depending upon who pays the right politicians and lobbyists the right amount. The constitutional protection of liberty and property, which had produced the greatest prosperity ever known, was circumvented. The indulgent majority without values now had access to the property and labor of the minority. The Constitution was supposed to protect everyone, especially the minority from the animal indulgences of the "mob" majority. But Ben Franklin's warning was prescient. We didn't really keep the republic. Instead, the majority could now take the property and labor of the minority by vote. They need only vote for the politician who promised to steal from the minority and redistribute it to them. That's what happened to America. This provided politicians with another route to power for which they could create a party platform based on theft. But with such indulgent values, a minority of the minority—the wealthiest—could also buy politicians so that they could indulge in tax exemptions. Thus, the wealthiest corporation in America with close personal ties to the Commander in Chief paid *no* U.S. taxes in 2010 and in fact claimed a credit on total worldwide profits of $14.2 billion, while small businesses struggled to survive under a corrupt labyrinth of a tax code.[23] The progressive/graduated tax code is an expression of leftist values: The more value you give to others in goods and services, the greater the *percentage* you will be penalized (unless you pay off the right politicians for an exemption). If we are all to be treated equally as human beings, increasing the *percentage* owed for some and not others is immoral, discriminatory, and violates equal protection, regardless of what any politically appointed hack jurist may rule. So who could be against a flat/fair tax which treats everyone equally and where the richest naturally pay billions more than the poorest? The overindulgent and corrupt.

- UNIONS OF THE PUBLIC SECTOR: Although volumes could be written about the corrupt indulgences of public employee unions, including their long history of coercion, violence, organized crime, discrimination, hypocrisy, meritless tenure, and indoctrination of false propaganda upon the people, the following is sufficient to illustrate why the left, as policy, supports public employee unions. Public employee unions require federal, state, or local government agencies to coercively take union dues from *all* public employee paychecks, whether they want to be in a union or not (except in right-to-work states), and the forcibly coerced money is used to pay off leftist politicians in campaign donations. In exchange, the leftist politicians in power authorize unearned pensions for public employees, labored for by ordinary taxpayers—pensions of such extravagance that they have bankrupted many municipalities. While almost everyone else (non-public employees) scrimps, saves, and invests for retirement, public employee unions simply buy politicians who kick back public employee pensions from taxpayer labor of up to ninety percent of their annual salary for the rest of their life.[24] And if that wasn't enough indulgence, when the public employee dies, their spouse, who also didn't earn it, gets the pension for life.[25] Such pensions kick in relatively early, at a time when those working in the private sector have many more years on the job before retirement.[26] In addition, they also receive special "Cadillac" health insurance plans and are specially exempted from the costs and limitations of Obamacare, for which they aggressively lobbied enactment for a majority that didn't want it.[27] Such overindulgence at the expense of others was another coercive overreach, because not nearly enough productive taxpayer labor currently exists to pay for it. As imminent layoffs of public employees approached for lack of funds, almost a trillion dollars in "stimulus" money "intended" to save the economy instead went to public employees and their unions as payback for the ground game they provided in getting Obama elected and his socialist agenda enacted (government control of automobile, banking, housing industries, etc.)[28] This delayed their layoffs for years so that dues from their paychecks could continue to bankroll leftist politicians to further grow and entrench government. As a result, the "stimulus" of nearly a trillion dollars of taxpayer money was used to coerce the public into unwitting support of corrupt leftist politicians. Interestingly, unions were originally intended to obtain a greater percentage of *company* profits for the workers. However, since government does not generate profit the way a business does, public-sector unions were used instead as the admission ticket to the feeding trough in Washington, D.C., where they joined the other pigs indulging themselves on stolen taxpayer money.

Nature and Overindulgence

The aforementioned leftist values are not values of virtue but of *overindulgence*. Nature does not allow overindulgence with impunity. Overindulge in food and increased toxicity and nature responds with the decay of diabetes, cancer, and other diseases. Too much energy expenditure without nourishing energy of value and the body collapses. The same applies to nation-states. Overindulgence in consumption by government taxation (in order to indulgently spend by redistribution) is harmful because it enervates the very source of productive energy, increasing the entropy of the productive to the extent that they flee for self-preservation. Overindulgence in nation-state expenditures, and nature responds with the decay of debt and currency devaluation to weaken the productive. You can't cheat nature on the important things. There can be no cure for non-congenital diabetes or cancer, only prevention and mitigation, as such painful diseases are nature's indicators of overindulgence or toxicity. This is why early detection is the most effective deterrent—the underlying *cause* is addressed. When nation-states overindulge themselves into too much debt, indulgently printing more money, as they typically do, cannot be the solution. Nature won't allow it. Printing more money without corresponding productivity in human labor devalues the currency in proportion to the additional amount printed. *This is nature's way of telling us to address the cause— overindulgent borrowing and spending, and not the effect of entropy's decay in debt.* Thus, the values of virtue—the discipline of restraint—are required for health and prosperity. But the overindulgent without virtue could not bear such restraint, and through enculturation and indoctrination, falsely equate ending entitlements to oppression and abuse of "human rights." Hence, with an entitlement culture beginning at childhood, everyone gets a trophy. Ironically, the very people crying oppression *are* the oppressors. The overindulgent professional left and associated professional victims groups are motivated by commissions and power on the amount of loot they bring in from the theft of others. In order to maintain this crime syndicate and preserve such power, leaders of the professional left and professional victims groups must have oppressed victims. So they keep their followers enslaved by a dependence mentality through indoctrination and the enculturation of blame, hate, envy, and entitlement. These become their values, which are inconsistent with virtue, and thus the enslaved remain impoverished. But what about the enslaved who want to be emancipated by truth, dare to express that wish, or seek escape from the Democratic Party Plantation for a life of dignified self-reliance and contribution? They would be treated the way the Democratic Party treated slaves before Lincoln's Emancipation Proclamation and the Union abolished slavery: any slave who talked about freedom or escaping would be skinned in front of other slaves so they would conform to the rules.[29] This is exactly what today's Democratic Party does to blacks and other minorities they want to enslave for votes, especially those who dare to seek escape and become self-reliant libertarians or conservatives. They vilify them, call them names, won't debate the issues, and otherwise disparage and intimidate them so no one escapes the leftist plantation of dependence and servitude to the masters who dole out the bread stolen from the labor of others.

Values of virtue necessitate the development of skills, responsibility, and contribution to others. However, this might render the minorities productive, independent, and healthy. This is unacceptable to the professional left and professional victims groups, as they would be rendered irrelevant and powerless. Consequently, they must perpetuate dependence and misery and designate an "evil" enemy to deflect blame and anger. This was the platform of the Occupy Wall Street (OWS) group, which the left organized and funded to vilify the "one percent" that provides for most of the "ninety-nine percent." The unabashed values of the aspiring OWS theft cartel and their deep-pocketed, leftist sponsors delivered a clear message: *take from those who earn.* And when they inevitably run out of other people's money as a result of the exorbitant debt and bankruptcies they created, the professional left and professional victims groups become indignant and enraged at the prospect of any debate about whether to continue their immoral cycle of conduct. This is because their power is *dependent* on the promises of *coercive* taking from one group and redistributing it among another. Merited power derived from the *cooperative* exchange of value renders them irrelevant and unemployed, unless they would adopt such merit. The overindulgent left argues with deceptive euphemisms, saying that it's a "revenue" problem (not enough loot stolen from the productive) instead of a spending problem (redistribution). They have become so immoral that their solution to the problem of overtaxing and overspending is not to decrease overindulgence but to increase the amount of money they steal from the productive, who already pay most of the nation's taxes. They model and aspire for the failed values of Europe; amoral, entitled, dependent, bankrupt, and riotous. And they actually achieved it: It's called California, New York, Michigan (Detroit), and Illinois. These states serve as exhibits of leftist ideology, unequivocally demonstrating the failing results of indulgent theft of the productive. If subtitles of truth appeared as closed captioning during a televised tirade of a prominent self-proclaimed socialist U.S. Congresswoman, they would stream "How dare you stop me from stealing from others?! If we're broke, we just need to steal more from the productive. It doesn't matter that those I steal from already pay most of the nation's taxes. My constituents have a right to compel others to labor for them, and I won't stay in power if I can't keep them dependent on what I can steal. And without power I won't be able to continue steering millions of dollars in taxpayer money to support my husband's banking business" (Corrupt U.S. Congresswoman Maxine Waters). No subtitles were necessary when she loudly proclaimed that those advocating reduced entitlements, small government, freedom, and adherence to the U.S. Constitution "can go straight to hell."[30] She also publicly called U.S. House leaders on the right "demons."[31] The tone and tactics of this senior leftist congressional leader epitomize leftist American values. As of this writing she was scheduled to be tried on charges of corruption.[32]

PEGIT—The Fascinatingly Complex Psychology of Leftists

At first blush it may appear that leftists are solely motivated by indulgence, but it's much more complicated than that, as they are comprised of different elements of different psyches. Long-sought answers to perplexing and seemingly irreconcilable leftist positions reveal a fascinatingly complex confluence of conditioned values. We must always remember that human beings are members of the animal kingdom. And just as other animals are domesticated through conditioning or training, so too are human babies, adolescents, and adults. Recall that each person comes into this earthly plane with a vacuum which must be filled so that the person feels cosmologically secure. Our individual political orientation is naturally polarized by genetics and biology to a limited degree, but when we arrive as babies our mind is generally malleable so that indoctrination and enculturation have the greatest influence. As inherently inquisitive beings, we want to know our source and *purpose*. We want to believe our existence has meaning and that we continue on after our earthly episode(s). Religion or spirituality generally satiates this yearning, filling that void for security. Most people are generally raised to believe that our actions have consequences, that our mortal conduct determines our afterlife, and that we derive from and are answerable to a greater power. However, the *elite* leftist leadership that sets the agenda generally rejects this as irrational fantasy and an impediment to anything-goes indulgence. They adhere to secularism. Nevertheless, as humans they cannot escape the fact that they still have an inherent cosmological void which must be filled with purpose. *Yet without divinity or a higher power, they can know nothing greater than themselves*, and thus, it is the ego which is vacuumed into the void. In the ultimate indulgence, they assume the role which the higher power normally fills and become omniscient or elite. In the words of the godfather of elite leftists:

> *"I carried some rather potent messianic fantasies with me. . . . I fancied myself as some kind of a god. . . ."* —George Soros[33]

But it gets even more complex. Guilt is generally nature's mechanism for flashing alert signals to warn humans about improper behavior requiring corrective action. Guilt does not tell what type of corrective action to take, for that would dictate behavior rather than experiential and consequential choice. Receiving money from the labor of others that is not earned or that is otherwise obtained without commensurate contribution often causes guilt. Guilt is caused by our improper treatment of both ourselves and others. Guilt has always been a part of Judeo-Christian values. The holiest day of the year for Jews is their day of atonement for sins—Yom-Kippur. But for most of Western civilization during most of the last two thousand years, Jesus served to absolve humanity of its sins through his death on the cross, as people could discharge their guilt vicariously for their human transgressions. However, with the secularization of Western society and its great diminution of piety, a deep pathology manifested itself, especially in those most culpable for behavior worthy of guilt. After two thousand years of moral reflexivity in Judeo-Christian guilt, those who no longer believe in the metaphysical realm for such absolution have no place to discharge their moral burden. As Wilfred Mclay so brilliantly articulated:

> *Guilt itself turns out to be exceptionally crafty, a born trickster and chameleon, capable of disguising itself, hiding out, altering its size and appearance, moving its location. And yet it remains difficult to dislodge, managing to tighten its hold even as it is undergoing protean and unpredictable transformation . . . the conventional means of finding that absolution—or even of keeping the range of one's responsibility for one's sins within some kind of reasonable boundaries—are no longer generally available. Making a claim to the status of certified victim, or to identification with victims, however, offers itself as a substitute means by which the moral burden of sin can be shifted and one's innocence affirmed. . . . And almost none of it has occurred consciously.[34]*

Secular elite leftist progressives therefore find or create the oppressed and oppressor in "a game of projection and displacement, of offloading our toxic wastes onto one another, a game in which everyone is pinning his own guilty tail on someone else's vulnerable donkey."[35] And because they don't believe in a metaphysical realm or anything greater than themselves, there can be no consequence to their actions. As their ruthlessness to other human beings who disagree with them demonstrates, they don't really care about "victims" or the "oppressed," but just use them as a moral release for their failure of virtue. Without a higher moral authority, there is no right and wrong or rules for them, *only power.* And with the belief in a limited existence and no existential purpose, they must find one, especially those assuming the role of their discarded deity. Just as Superman needs crime for purpose, elite leftists need victims. With each shrill cry of racism, sexism, or oppression they become more relevant and meaningful. They see everything through the lenses of racism, sexism, and oppression, not with altruism but with a vanity which discharges their guilt and elevates their relevance, self-worth, paternal purpose, and power. No matter how many times paternalistic big government ideology has tried and failed, their ego informs them that they will be the first elites in human history to deliver utopia:

> *"This was the moment when the rise of the oceans began to slow and our planet began to heal."* —Presidential candidate Barack Obama[36]

Fig. 11: Fabian Socialist glass mural at London School of Economics. Molding their World to their Heart's Desire.

In the words of their ideological forebears—the Fabian Social-ists—they will "mold the world to their heart's desire" (fig. 11).[37] Secular elites project their omniscience and egoistic power through the state and as the state, hoisted on the backs of the masses. Instead of the natural *individual* freedoms to choose, learn, and grow from decision-making, the elites know what is best for you. They want to determine your values and control your actions. However, secular leftist values cannot withstand the scrutiny of logic and its consistent history of murderous failure. *It can only appeal to emotion.* Therefore, power-seeking elite leftists appeal to and enlist the most emotionally vulnerable as a power base: 1. those who *envy* the successful; 2. those who feel *guilty* from an empty success; 3. use-ful *idiots*; and 4. those who just want to be *taken care* of. This provides the support necessary for power to rule nation-states and the world. But are these the *values of virtue* which would produce freedom and prosperity? Are these the character-building values we should aspire to as individuals and cultures? These values of the left are most easily remembered in the acronym *PEGIT*—Power-Envy-Guilt-Idiots-Taken Care of. The *P*'s and *G*'s of the acronym are distinct from the *E I T*'s. They represent the "omni-scient" elites who would influence and direct everyone else. The *P*'s and the *G*'s are often the same people. Those who feel *G*uilty or unfulfilled because of the way they obtained great wealth are also in a position of, or are seeking to attain and/or maintain, *P*ower. An alliance with the "op-pressed" provides both with something they each covet: The "oppressed" get power without having to earn it, and the *P*'s and *G*'s get to identify with them as their champions while projecting and unloading their guilt onto a designated enemy "oppressor." Together, they ceaselessly work to divest and redistribute the wealth of the "oppressor" (those who earned it) while futilely coercing a society into the equal outcomes of which they were "deprived." Often, such *P*'s and *G*'s accumulated their wealth from sinecure occupations. Sinecure literally means "without cure" of soul and refers to occupations that require little labor or responsibility. Successful professional actors and musicians fit this category, as they make millions playing dress-up and make-believe or jamming out with enjoyable music. Many if not most are "royalty" who inherited their crown from their royal parents, who were also actors and musicians in the entertainment busi-ness of indulgence—"See me, hear me, please!" But when they notice oth-ers who toil in tedious manual labor for a weekly paycheck totaling less than what they tip their chauffeur, they feel guilty. However, such guilt is not justified insofar as what they earn financially. In a free-market econ-omy, money is voluntarily exchanged for goods and services perceived as value. Professional actors, musicians, and other artists provide goods and services which significantly impact the emotions of those who will gladly pay for such talent. They developed their talents and took chances against great odds to make it. Even those who made it because of their paren-tal connections are probably the most qualified anyway, genetically so in looks and talent or from growing up in the business. And because the en-ergy of the artist's humanistic expressions may be captured or transmut-ed into the mass and matter of digitized and quantized mediums—CDs, DVDs, books, etc.—they are able to distribute value to billions of people in perpetuity, and thus they should be compensated commensurately.

The Pathology of Destruction

In stark contrast, a virulent strain of *pathological P*'s and *G*'s or guilt-ridden leftist grew up with privilege and security *without* contrib-uting commensurate value. They are the most dangerous and destructive people on the planet, e.g., Castro, Che, Mao, Marx, Engels, terrorists Osama Bin Laden, Bill Ayers and Bernadine Dohrn, along with the heirs of *The New York Times* and *The Washington Post*. They have caused the greatest torment to humanity through the indoctrination of falsehoods, enculturation, misery, and murder. Lecherous heirs of the Rockefeller, Kennedy, and Heinz (John Kerry) families in the U.S. Congress would have done similar damage while depleting the wealth of their forebears, but they were limited by what little regard the U.S. Constitution still holds. *Nature informs us through the lessons of history that great power without merit is one of the most dangerous mixtures on the planet.* As David Rockefeller wrote in *The New York Times* on August 10, 1973, upon returning from China, "The social experiment under Chairman Mao's leadership is one of the most important and successful in human history."[38] *Sixty million murdered and impoverished.* That's success? It is to a guy in an insulated bubble who inherited his security and comforts. To indulge their own vanity, the pathologically guilt-ridden and their depraved values have been forced upon generations, as they could not understand the toil of those who started with nothing to achieve wealth, including their disconnected patriarchs. Their life of unearned privilege in contrast to the toil of the masses catalyzed their stated intent of lifting the poor to prosperity through the coerced divestment of others. However, such means are not the values of virtue which could yield the society of merit required to sustain a broad prosperity. They could produce only a society of entitled, meritless, and destructive miscreants like themselves. However, viewed as a practical means of self-preservation, their tactics are certainly effective in diverting the populace pitchforks. But this would not be necessary if they weren't so publicly resentful and intolerant of the prosperity of merit and individual achievement which enabled their family wealth. They passionately lament and demonize the successful intelligent innovators of merit as if they were railing against the very relatives who provided their privileged life. And maybe they are. Instead of embracing values of virtue to achieve meritoriously, the pathologically guilt-ridden would divest those of earned privilege in a vain effort to eliminate that which causes the shame, envy, low esteem, and guilt of their unearned privilege. They empathize with those of unmerited power, and would create an alliance with coercive dictators and destructive financiers of their ilk to accomplish common objectives—everyone should be the same except for the coercive elite, who find esteem in knowing what's best for everyone else.

The False Choice

Contrary to leftist propaganda, most people, regardless of political orientation and socioeconomic status, want prosperity, because living standards increase along with commerce to promote a positive atmosphere for all. The real issue is *how to get there*; through *freedom, responsibility*, and *enterprise*? Or *coercion, entitlements*, and *government control*? Big government leftists cannot win that argument, neither by precedent nor principle. Therefore, *the leftist tactic is to appeal to emotion with false choices*. If you don't want government health care, you want people to die; if you don't want government-run education, you want ignorance, etc.

> *"It is as if the socialists were to accuse us of not wanting persons to eat because we do not want the state to raise grain."* —Bastiat[39]

As if there are no free-market solutions. The facts cannot be rationally denied, only ignored and suppressed. Any enterprise government tries to run is usually a disaster, especially in comparison to free-market-based solutions. Remember the government-controlled economies of the Soviet Union, Maoist China, Cuba, and North Korea? These are not stupid people; They just have stupid values. Leftist ideology consists of values which are inconsistent with prosperity. Even government-run enterprise in the nation-state best known for its innovative business culture—the U.S.A.— has a one hundred percent failure rate, as all are broke and deep in debt. Whether it is Amtrak, the U.S. Postal Service, Fannie Mae, Freddie Mac, Medicare, or the Social Security Administration, big government is too inefficient, unaccountable, and corrupt—all the wrong values for prosperous enterprise. Although the facts cannot support leftist doctrine for an enduring prosperity, the nature of *PEGIT* insures that such "trivialities" would be no obstacle to the left:

> *"Give me just one generation of youth, and I'll transform the whole world."* —Vladimir Lenin[40]

Chapter 8

EDUCATION AND THE MEDIA

Our mind is largely a product of the transmitted information we consume, channel, and expend. After education by our primary caretakers, we get most of our information and values from government, school, and the media. In fact, most of the elite government planners that dominate the world are products of Western liberal education and media. They don't usually toil in labor as most of the rest of the world does, causing a degree of guilt and separation from the masses. They go from school to school and then straight to government to mold the world in their aloof leftist images. But not every elite leftist can rule as a government planner. Such executive power is reserved for a select few. The rest of the elite leftists find their places in the world's Ministries of Information—Education and the Media—where they can exercise the most power or influence in brainwashing the masses while maintaining their omniscient and paternalistic purpose. Consistent surveys demonstrate that most of the West's college professors and media journalists providing the world's information are leftists or have voted for leftist politicians.[1] Because they control the majority of information which the world consumes, they have tremendous influence over the values which individuals and cultures embrace. Although truth is absolute and immutable, "prophets," teachers, journalists, and entertainers serve as filters through which such truth pours to the masses. If the filter is biased, corrupt, defective, or dirty, some truths may be blocked from coming through while others become tainted and distorted enough to poison those who consume it. Tainted information creates tainted and destructive people and cultures, both of which may be infectious to others. Since these filters may allow some truths to come through, they accord credibility to the source for continued consumption. However, withholding other truths denies context for accuracy, resulting in a distorted and untrue picture of reality. This is like lacing healthy food with slow poison, and serving it to the masses. The transmitted information we consume is stored in, carried by, and modulates, our energy. Toxic information manifests toxic minds, cultures, and energy. As stated previously, our perceptions and choices in what we consume, both in energy as well as transmitted information from others and how we expend that energy and information in lifestyle defines our values. Such *values determine the health and prosperity of the open systems we know as humans and nation-states, depending upon whether they are true to virtue.*

EDUCATION—K-12 and Indoctrination U.

K-12

Leftist values transcend and influence culture. The multi-cultural bastion of America is the prime example. Although America was founded on individualism and freedom, organized indoctrination on a national level begins with public employee union-controlled K-12 education of the Marxist creed. These powerful unions have been wildly successful in advancing *only* their own interests:

> *"When school children start paying union dues, that's when I'll start representing the interests of school children."*—Albert Shanker, president of the American Federation of Teachers.[2]

Shanker's values represent those charged with inculcating America's children and influencing their future, and thus his words should be recalled when pondering the devolution of the great American culture. Sadly, these self-indulgent leftists have controlled the makeup of the corrupt and controlling school boards with whom they bargain at the expense of schoolchildren, taxpayers, and cultural values. Their tremendous financial and logistic contributions to leftist politicians on local, state, and national levels echo the teachers union president's statement that the interests of the teachers take precedence over the schoolchildren. And politicians have definitely reciprocated for their own interests as well, insuring that teacher employment and financial security are based on how long they have been contributing union dues (a percentage of which is "tithed" back to the politicians) rather than on the value or efficacy of teaching ability. Indoctrination of Marxist principles begins with the teachers themselves. The largest teachers union in America—the NEA—recommends on their website that their teachers learn Alinsky doctrine, including the Lucifer-dedicated, *Rules for Radicals:*

"NEA recommends the following Saul Alinsky books to those members of our Association who are involved in grassroots organizing, especially Association Representatives (ARs) — also known as building reps or shop stewards — and leaders at local affiliates."[3]

Teachers are heavily influenced by the public employee unions and their Marxist ideology; *band together and coerce rather than earn on merit.* They advance the long game of their agenda by indoctrinating young, impressionable minds with revisionist history in order to promote a society where individual merit is subverted for coercive redistribution. And as socialism is based on effort rather than value, Marxist unions have influenced their teachers to grade schoolchildren on effort rather than value/results. In addition to everyone's entitlement to a trophy, *there is even an honor roll for effort.*[4] Marxist values are indoctrinated at an early age so that when they become adults, *entitlement to the labor of others* becomes as natural as Occupy Wall Street. Thus, American children no longer have a clue about the Founding Fathers and the guiding principles of freedom and prosperity. Traditional American values of individual achievement seem unrecognizable in the classroom. That sublime but lost culture was so envied worldwide that cultural remnants in the form of movies and memorabilia are routinely found in the ruins and possessions of toppled dictators. The land of opportunity has become the land of the lost. Schoolchildren are even coerced to sing collective praises and write poems styled on the socialist likeness of "Dear Leader" Obama.[5] The traditional leftist playbook has gained great traction. As a noted National Socialist and previous *Time* magazine Man of the Year honoree once said, "Give me the youth . . . let me control the textbooks, and I will control the state" —Adolf Hitler[6]

Indoctrination U.

"Those that can't do, teach. Those that can't teach, teach gym."
—Woody Allen, *Annie Hall.*[7]

Of course this is a humorous oversimplification. The brightest leftists naturally gravitate to intellectual pursuits such as academics, while the brightest conservatives go into practical applications such as business, engineering, and the free professions.[8] While participants of the private sector sink or swim on their ability to create perceived value to others, college teachers are insulated in an ivory tower, secure for per-petual pontification:

> "Personally I like the university, they gave us money and facilities, *we didn't have to produce anything.* You've never been out of college, you don't know what it's like out there. *I've worked in the private sector—they expect results"* —Dan Aykroyd, *Ghostbusters.*[9]

This largely explains why college campuses have become leftist/Marxist indoctrination camps. Under the private sector of self-reliance, individu-alism, and meritocracy, those who "do" get all the glory and pay, while those who teach are relatively marginalized. Socialism not only elimi-nates this marginalization but actually elevates teachers for their ability to regulate uniformity in thought. The evidence of this is on full display at most college campuses, where an intolerant leftist/Marxist groupthink fervently squelches all dissent. And because teachers are entitled to per-manent employment with tenure, those seeking such tenured security are pressured to conform their research and professorships to the ideol-ogy of the influential leftists who would approve them. Ironically, tenure was developed to encourage the free exchange of ideas, so that teachers would not have to fear losing their job for unpopular speech. However, this has been perverted by the indulgent dictates of the left, who would discard principle for submission to Marxist groupthink, which discour-ages free speech. Pressure to conform by stifling free speech isn't lim-ited to university staff, as a speech code miasma pervades the classroom, student body, and the whole school's milieu. While genocidal dictators are warmly courted and doted upon to visit and lecture on campus, those advocating freedom and human rights are violently attacked or intimi-dated into staying away.[10] Similarly, in what the capitalist philosopher Ayn Rand called "a means of forestalling debate and extorting an opponent's agreement with one's undiscussed notions," leftists employ *"The Argu-ment from Intimidation,"*[11] which:

> *is not an argument, but it is a method of bypassing logic by means of psychological pressure . . . The essential characteristic of the Argument from Intimidation is its appeal to moral self-doubt and its reliance on the fear, guilt or ignorance of the victim. It is used in the form of an ultimatum demanding that the victim renounce a given idea with-out discussion, under threat of being considered morally unworthy.*

The pattern is always: "Only those who are evil (dishonest, heartless, insensitive, ignorant, etc.) can hold such an idea"...."Only those who lack finer instincts can fail to accept the morality of altruism."—"Only the ignorant can fail to know that reason has been invalidated."—"Only black-hearted reactionaries can advocate capitalism."—"Only war-mongers can oppose the United Nations."—"Only the lunatic fringe can still believe in freedom."—"Only cowards can fail to see that life is a sewer."—"Only the superficial can seek beauty, happiness, achievement, values or heroes."[12]

Yet again, leftist values of indulgence: just skip the merits of the argument and go straight to coercion. This particular pattern of "argument" is necessary to maintain the logically indefensible, and it has been so consistent a leftist tactic that it has been informally codified with a descriptive acronym: "SIN"— *Shift* the subject—*Ignore* the facts—*Name* call.[13] However, most undergraduates new to the college indoctrination process are not yet sophisticated enough to have learned the SIN tactic. Thus, when leftist-indoctrinated cosmology is challenged with truth and logic, they don't yet know how to respond. It is in this raw form that the folly of contemporary leftist values is most evident and exposed. Students attending prestigious universities must generally have demonstrated exceptional capacities to reason and articulate. Many such students, if not the overwhelming majority, are relatively young advocates of immoral leftist political practices promoting racism and theft, such as Affirmative Action and redistribution of wealth. Thus, it is reasonable to believe that leftist young students who can reason at such scholastic levels would readily subject their prestigious institutions of academia and athletics to the same type of practices—*or at least informally articulate why such practices shouldn't similarly apply*. Yet stunning videotaped experiments at such institutions reveal the contrary, eerily exposing the fingerprints of the indoctrination process endured by students of the K-12 and college experience.

Petition to Redistribute GPA Scores

To expose the coercive immorality of income redistribution inherent in the Western world's progressive/graduated tax code, intellectually sober students at the University of California-Merced and De Paul University pretended to conduct petition drives to institute the same system on campus, but they did so for grades instead of income. They proposed to redistribute the top ten percent of grade point averages "to those having trouble fulfilling graduation requirements." This was recorded on camera and is available on YouTube.com.[14] All the students on camera agreed that the top ten percent of U.S. income earners should have their money/labor taken and redistributed to those earning less. But they did not agree to sign an analogous petition to take and redistribute the grades of the top ten percent of GPA earners to those earning lower grades who faced the threat of not graduating. They were oblivious that their spontaneous objections were identical to the classic responses of those opposed to income redistribution:

> *"You're gonna take away the incentive for people to work hard";*

> *"It isn't fair, I work for what I have";*

> *"Then maybe they should study more";*

> *"So why don't they ask the people that do get the 4.0's advice to help them out?";*

> *"It's an indication of performance";*

> *"GPA affects job prospects and grad school and all those things in the future";*

> *"That's not my fault, I work my ass off."*

All their life they were indoctrinated into labeling those with such responses as "irresponsible, greedy, racists." However, when their own labor was to be subject to leftist redistribution under a fictional scenario not contemplated by leftist indoctrinators, they too would become "irresponsible, greedy, racists." Not a single student could articulate *how* redistribution of GPA was any different from redistribution of income. *This is because both GPA and INCOME are quantized measures of the perceived value of individual labor.*

Petition to Apply Affirmative Action to Basketball Team

To expose the invidious racism of leftist Affirmative Action programs, students at University of California-Riverside pretended to conduct a petition drive to implement race rather than just performance as criteria for selection to the men's basketball team. This was also posted on YouTube.com.[15] Although the student population at the school was only nine percent black, the men's basketball team was over ninety percent black. The students sponsoring the petition drive argued that Asians and other races should be included for diversity on the basketball team. Each student requested to sign the petition was asked whether they supported Affirmative Action. All those on camera *reflexively* responded support for Affirmative Action in hiring and school admissions but adamantly refused to apply it to athletics. Not a single student at the prestigious institution of "higher learning" could articulate *why* performance shouldn't be the sole criteria for school admissions and employment as it is for athletics. Their spontaneous responses are identical to the classic responses of those they were taught to label as "racist" for *the same opposition* to Affirmative Action in school admissions and employment:

"It should be about talent, not about race";

"You're kinda enforcing the whole race thing . . . choose him because he's good, because he has that skill";

"In this instance . . . I think skill should be the dominating factor. I support [Affirmative Action] academically and professionally but not in athletics";

"I think that sports are different."

But the most chilling revelation was the sense of blind indoctrination—intelligent adults unable to provide any basis for a belief, almost like programmed machines. Reason from the "petitioners" short-circuited their programming to the extent that, in their own words, they *"don't really feel comfortable."* That uncomfortable feeling was both the intended fear from their indoctrinators and a wavering cosmological security of false programming traumatized by the kryptonite of truth and logic.

After students leave campus and enter the real world, indoctrination and enculturation will continue, but it will be done by the elite leftist mainstream media.

THE MEDIA—News and Entertainment

News

The natural and primary role of a healthy free press is to seek and report the truth as an independent entity, with vigilance for undue influence and corruption. They are supposed to be a check on the abuse of power. Theoretically, there is great incentive to adhere to this valiant role. Those who expose truth at the expense of the powerful are rewarded with attention and status-prestige, which translates into advertising dollars and consumer response. However, if this was ever the case with the mainstream media, it is no longer. For the uninitiated, the role of journalism as taught to students and "professionals" of the most prestigious and influential Western schools of journalism is to:

"afflict the comfortable and comfort the afflicted."[6]

This logically requires that truth be secondary or incidental. Obviously, many if not most of the "comfortable" earned it, while many if not most of the "afflicted" reaped what they sowed, as well. After a lifetime of leftist indoctrination, aspiring journalists also get their pedigree from ultra-leftist professors. Thereafter, they immediately occupy an insulated bubble similar to the secure ivory tower from which their mentors pontificate their alternate reality. Most journalists have no real world experience in the market economy other than the parentage of their adoptive media family. They remain disconnected from those who "do" to *make* news through real-world toil. Journalists are supposed to be the witnesses, not the players, unless and until they expose subverted truth, corruption, or abuse of power. However, to advance in their career they seek attention to the same degree as an insecure entertainer does. They also know that the information they provide shapes the attitudes, prejudices, and ultimately the values of people. Most journalists have much different values from the rest of the world. Those values come from the rigidly maintained leftist/Marxist groupthink of an elitist subculture. Any ideological deviants are quickly banished and vilified without discussion or debate of the merits. The groupthink agenda, at least in America, is set by the descendants and wealthy family heirs of the founders of *The New York Times* and *The Washington Post*. Living off inherited wealth, they generally never had to struggle, sacrifice, or take risks to survive. To make matters worse, they were spawned by parents of weak character who were already ashamed of who they were—Jewish. Thousands of years of anti-Semitism had an effect on many such Jews seeking to appease the establishment to gain acceptance. Suppressing relevant news for a personal agenda was nothing new to *The New York Times* and *The Washington Post* families. They even made it policy to suppress Hitler's mass murder of their own people in Europe so they wouldn't sound too Jewish or parochial. Children of those with such an identity pathology have a striking tendency to become self-hating radicals,[17] and in the instance of several generations of such media magnates, these rich and powerful socialites of great privilege and influence feel emptiness because of their unearned wealth and status. In the role of world witnesses, they must report on both the "afflicted" downtrodden and the "comforted" intelligent innovators of industry who actually earn their living providing value to the masses in real goods and services. This is quite a contrast for the elites of inherited privilege and a constant reminder that exacerbates their own guilt. We all need to feel that we are of value for self-esteem and happiness. Trapped in sociological quicksand, they use their platform and control of the mainstream media to influence values and culture in a way that assuages their guilt. Their unearned wealth, status, and power, combined with the nature of being witnesses instead of players, manifested a serious pathology; divest the "comforted" intelligent innovators of industry ("the evil capitalist corporations" and the masters of capitalism, including "the Jews" and "Israel") of their wealth and redistribute it to the "afflicted." This would make them feel a perverted sense of value and self-worth. They further overcompensate for their guilt by contriving a moral superiority, one they think is more sophisticated and advanced ideologically than everyone else's. And those seeking such status-prestige of "sophistication" quickly adopt and promote the same manufactured cosmology to join the groupthink leftist social club. By looking down upon others they elevate their own esteem, but they must eschew any viewpoints to the contrary for self-preservation. It is through this distorted lens that information is filtered to become the news. Most significantly, almost all of the Western mainstream news organizations get their news from and are ideologically influenced by their "sophistication." In fact, the elite mainstream media people are so provincial that if it isn't in *The New York Times* or *The Washington Post*, they generally don't know about it.[18] This is astoundingly verifiable:

1. ABC *World News* anchor Charles Gibson admitted that he had no clue about the "pimp/prostitute" video sting of the taxpayer-funded community organizer group ACORN. This was one of the most relevant and dramatic stories of 2009, containing all the elements of a ratings bonanza. In a radio interview with WLS-AM Chicago, Gibson was asked about that story. Here is the brief self-explanatory transcript:

> Don: *Okay, here's my news question. A Senate bill yesterday passes, cutting off funds to this group called ACORN. Now, we got that bill passed and we have the embarrassing video of ACORN staffers giving tax advice on how to set up a brothel with thirteen-year-old hookers. It has everything you could want—corruption and sleazy action at tax-funded organizations, and it's got government ties. But nobody's covering that story. Why?*
>
> Gibson: *HAHAHAHAHA. HEHEHE. I didn't even know about it. Um. So, you've got me at a loss. I don't know. Uh. Uh. But my goodness, if it's got everything including sleaziness in it, we should talk about it this morning.*
>
> Roma: *This is the American way!*
>
> Gibson: *Or maybe this is just one you leave to the cables.*
>
> Roma: *Well, I think this is a huge issue because there's so much funding that goes into this organization.*
>
> Gibson: *I KNOW WE'VE DONE SOME STORIES ABOUT ACORN BEFORE, BUT THIS ONE I DON'T KNOW ABOUT.*
>
> Roma: *Jake Tapper did some blogging on it. I know he's blogged at least once on this scandal.*
>
> Gibson: *You guys are, uh, really up on the website.*[19]

The mainstream media also didn't think it was relevant to disclose that Obama worked for the community organizer group before becoming president, filing a federal lawsuit on ACORN's behalf.

2. CBS veteran news anchor Bob Schieffer admitted that he was unaware of the 2009 New Black Panther Party voter intimidation case stemming from an incident on election day in 2008. The story had everything for the all-coveted ratings. Videotaped outside a Philadelphia polling station on election day 2008 were two billy club-wielding members of the New Black Panther Party, all decked out in full jackboot paramilitary garb. Witnesses alleged that they yelled racial epithets while pointing their billy clubs at white voters to intimidate them. After receiving several complaints from these voters, the current Justice Department of the Bush administration brought a voter intimidation case against the Black Panther defendants. In refusing to answer the charges, the defendants lost by default. However, when President Obama took office the case was mysteriously dropped. As a result, the bipartisan U.S. Commission on Civil Rights issued subpoenas to Justice Department prosecutors Christopher Coates (Voting Section chief) and J. Christian Adams to testify about why the case was dismissed after they "basically won the case." Adding more drama to the story, the Obama administration ordered them to *defy the subpoenas* and refuse to testify. Instead, they defied their own superiors by complying with their subpoenas. *Their testimony revealed that they were pressured into dropping the case and told to ignore cases where the perpetrator was black and the victim was white.* Adams was fired by the Obama administration for testifying, while Coates invoked the Whistleblower Protection Act, stating that "there have to be certain common standards that we are bound by and that protect us all . . . For the Department of Justice to enforce the Voting Rights Act only to protect members of certain minority groups breaches the fundamental guarantee of equal protection..."[20] Coates was no right-winger. He previously worked for the ultra-leftist ACLU. Yet the Obama administration still shipped him out to the South Carolina U.S. Attorney's office as retribution for his testimony. Fresh from these events, Shieffer hosted Obama Justice Department chief Attorney General Eric Holder on his Sunday morning program *Face the Nation* for the full half-hour. *Shieffer did not ask a single question about the case.*[21] A week later, Schieffer was interviewed by CNN's Howard Kurtz, and the first question he was asked was why he didn't ask Justice Department chief Eric Holder a single question about the New Black Panther

Party voter intimidation case.[22] Shieffer's response: *"I didn't know about it."*[23] Apparently, his entire CBS staff didn't either. And even if they did, they could assert partisan privilege, as did the leftist publication *Newsweek* magazine, which stated that the New Black Panther Party voter intimidation case wasn't newsworthy and that it "hurts the Obama administration."[24] If it's factual and hurts the Obama administration, how could it not be newsworthy? And how could it not be newsworthy when Justice Department lawyers testified that they were pressured to drop the case and to ignore cases where the perpetrator was black and the victim was white? So many more egregious examples of leftist mainstream media bias exist that it would require volumes to list. Yet these are the media sources where Americans and many other Westerners have traditionally received their news. The mainstream media is militantly left, as is the Obama administration, and they are mostly reluctant to cover stories which impede both their ideology and those in power seeking to advance it. They have constructed an alternate reality which is inconsistent with truth, but their cosmological security is dependent upon it. To preserve that security, those who represent or advocate truth are ignored or taken down, but no discussion on the merits can take place for fear of truth and logic. If they are cornered or pinned down for discussion, they avoid truth by employing the previously discussed "SIN" tactic—*Shift* the argument, *Ignore* the facts, and *Name* call.

The End of the Mainstream News Media—Corruption, Collusion, and Conspiracy to Advocate

Before Barack Obama announced his 2008 U.S. presidential candidacy, much of the lack of reporting, as well as the reporting on things that advanced the leftist agenda was "merely" bias, possibly unintentional. Maybe the mainstream media were just not mindful of stories relevant to views different from their own insular groupthink. They routinely refer to non-leftist television guests as conservatives and lobbyists (implying an agenda), while rarely if ever similarly identifying leftists as liberals or lobbyists (implying impartiality), thus indicating a blind spot or inadvertent bias. However, once leftist salvation from guilt and suffering arrived in the announced presidential candidacy of the ideal oppressed minority, leftist indulgence was unrestrained, and bias turned into outright advocacy, corruption, and conspiracy.

"After hearing him [Obama] speak I felt this thrill going up my leg.... that is an objective assessment."

"If you're actually in the room when Obama gives one of his speeches and you don't cry, you're not an American."

—Chris Matthews, NBC[25]

Dean Singleton, the chairman of both the Associated Press and MediaNews Group, respectively the most widely distributed news service in the U.S. and the owner of scores of newspapers throughout the U.S., made the following speech at the AP's annual meeting and luncheon on April 3, 2012, when he introduced President Obama:

Two years later, in 2008, as a presidential candidate, he spoke again to the AP luncheon. In a Q and A after his speech, I asked him a question from the audience related to how he might deal with Obama bin Laden, if elected. *In his always genteel way*, he asked, might you be referring to Osama bin Laden? It was a slip of the tongue heard around the world. Thanks to the delights of our digital age, and YouTube in particular, I won't soon escape that embarrassing moment, even four years later. But we do have the answer to the question. Today [pauses for laughter], there is no mistaking his name and even I can't mess it up. It's Mr. President. President Obama made history as the first minority to be elected president. Even many who opposed his election felt proud of our country as he took the oath of office. *As president, he inherited the headwinds of the worst economic recession since the Great Depression. He pushed through Congress the biggest economic recovery plan in history and led a government reorganization of two of the big three auto manufacturers to save them from oblivion. He pursued domestic and foreign policy agendas that were controversial to many, highlighted by his signature into law of the most comprehensive health care legislation in history. And the budget plans proposed by the president, on the one hand, and Republicans on the other hand, aren't even on the same planet.* Many Democrats believe that his agenda doesn't go far enough and most Republicans believe it goes way too far. While we thought the 2008 White House race was rough and tumble, the 2012 race makes it look like bumper cars by comparison. Our country has become more polarized. The one percent and the ninety percent are at each others' throats. Campaigns are now funded by secretive, multi-million dollar super PACs. What's next? Giga-PACs? The only thing anyone seems willing to compromise on is—well, I can't think of anything. *Really, who would want this job in the first place? We're very honored today to have the man currently holding the office and aspiring for it for another term.* And, with apologies to Al Green, my new favorite singer. Ladies and gentlemen, the president of the United States of America.[26]

Media corruption has been endemic through most of world history because they have traditionally served as an arm of the State. However, America was to be distinctly different. Free speech and a free press are the *very first* amendment to the United States Constitution.* It has been part of the American DNA and values. These values made Americans unique in world history. Such freedom brought worldwide envy and admiration, as well as unparalleled prosperity. Humanity had finally reached a turning point of freedom with the arrival of the American experiment. As a country to the right of center, America has obviously had its ups and downs over its two-plus centuries. No one can truthfully deny the wrongs of the past, and guilt is a natural mechanism for correction. But it can also overcorrect. The guilt-fueled leftist mainstream media has inflicted decades of collective punishment on generations of those captive to television and newspapers—an endless stream of politically correct groupthink-filled programming and print. Those who are aware of this traditionally fled to talk radio for alternative viewpoints grounded in reality. But the leftist mainstream media was mostly in control of influencing American values, and although extremely biased, they seemed to be acting in good, albeit pathological, faith. Suddenly, the advent of the Internet presented a great challenge to their control and the ethics to maintain it. Although the mainstream media establishment had the advantage on the new medium, as well, people now had alternative information sources which were immediately accessible in real time. Print newspapers struggled to survive and adapt as the masses fled to the Internet. Losing control brought out the worst in the mainstream media, and once the messiah of the neo radical left arrived in 2008, America would

---

* Amendment I of the United States Constitution: Congress shall make no law respecting an establishment of religion, or prohibiting the free exercise thereof; OR ABRIDGING THE FREEDOM OF SPEECH, OR OF THE PRESS, or the right of the people peaceably to assemble, and to petition the Government for redress of grievances. [emphasis added]

ring a dramatically different tone. As worshippers at Obama's altar, the mainstream media became his minions, and no sense of decency would constrain a corrupt advocacy of leftist depravity. The mainstream media were all in for America's takeover. They knew what was best for everyone, and would set out to shape history. Values and virtue would not even be feigned. Truth, honor, and integrity were ideals of another left. In concert with the Marxist university indoctrination camps and the Alinsky tacticians, the mainstream media corps would assist the same radicals from the American counterculture of the 1960's straight into governing power. Although they traded their beads and tie-dyed T-shirts for executive suits and judicial robes, their radicalism remained virulent.

The neo-radical left gained full control of the White House for the first time in American history. With no other authority to restrain them—*they* became the authority. They would answer to no one, neither the Congress nor the U.S. Constitution. Who else could refuse a subpoena to testify before a bi-partisan U.S. Commission on Civil Rights? They have no red lines or morality, just power. They are self-avowed Maoists and Marxists. As Obama administration White House Communications Director Anita Dunn stated in a televised speech to high school students, the mass murderer Mao is one of her two favorite political philosophers "that I turn to most."[27] And Obama administration czar for manufacturing policy, Ron Bloom, proclaimed "We kinda agree with Mao that political power comes from a barrel of a gun."[28] President Obama's green jobs czar, Van Jones, a self-avowed communist, was videotaped at the Power Shift '09 conference yelling "We want a new system. We want a new system . . . give them [American Indians] the wealth, give them the wealth."[29] President Obama's Federal Communications Commission chief diversity czar, Mark Lloyd, has advocated media reform, praising Marxist Hugo Chavez's nationalization of Venezuelan media as "an incredible revolution."[30] Nevertheless, with all their power, they still largely operate with stealth and subterfuge. This is because of the one thing that could stop them—exposure to the people. If the mainstream media *reported* their radical Marxist views, comments, and associations, they would be voted out by a great margin. This is why the mainstream media's abdication is so grave. Their role and responsibility to humanity is to disseminate the unvarnished facts and truth so that the people can make informed decisions. Instead, the mainstream media decides what information the people should know, not only filtering out facts and truths inconsistent with their desired outcomes but intentionally influencing outcomes that affect the whole world. Exposing the facts and truth to the people has tremendous impact on power. Only forty years ago, two courageous mainstream media reporters exposed the corrupt Nixon administration in the Watergate scandal.[31] Today the mainstream media is at least as corrupt as the Nixon administration they brought down then.

Ministry of Information

After over two centuries of a free and independent American press, the mainstream media would be willingly co-opted by the White House as its new "Ministry of Information." Together they meet weekly to coordinate their agenda, talking points, and the political hit squads they use against those they cannot control. In this, too, George Soros, the frequent White House visitor and advisor, would be instrumental. To put him in context, his modus operandi for fomenting revolutions is important to understand. He manipulates the core mechanisms which determine power. In a democracy, the vote determines who gets power. The secretary of state for each of the fifty states in America certifies the person whom each state voted for, including the president and members of Congress. To take advantage of that procedure, in 2009 Soros started the Secretary of State Project in order to place radicals in the position of secretary of state so they would "certify" his candidates as "the winner."[32] However, the timing of this particular project was bad, as a successful populist uprising called the Tea Party movement took hold to resist a coercive and out of control leftist government, "shellacking"[33] the Left in the 2010 mid-term Congressional elections. But Soros fundamentally understood power, and would not be deterred because of the bad timing of this particular project. He was in it for the long game and knew that the media not only affected the vote, but also directly affected public policy. Stories, reports, and editorials, whether based on truth or not are consumed by political leaders as well as the public. The media obviously influence values and the corresponding political proponents of those values. Because money represents energy in the form of human labor, Soros injects an unlimited amount of energy in human labor into the mainstream media in order to push America's center-right culture to the left. Soros has at least succeeded in solidifying his ultra-leftist ideology in the platform of over thirty mainstream media news organizations, including *The New York Times*, *The Washington Post*, the Associated Press, ABC, NBC, and

CNN.[34] All of them have personnel on the board of Soros-funded media operations, despite the Society of Professional Journalists' ethical code— "avoid all conflicts, real or perceived."[35] He has also funded the taxpayer-subsidized National Public Radio to keep them on the left.[36] Soros has fully infiltrated the news media from the roots to the fruits, funding journalism schools, journalists, investigative journalism, industry organizations, news outlets, blogs, books, TV and radio stations, online operations, and start-ups.[37] Although America has been a center-right country, for many of the last several decades the mainstream media news organizations have overtly and effectively promoted only leftist values on the television airwaves. Whether through ABC, NBC, CBS, CNN, or PBS, they have maintained a constant bombardment. Those feeding stations are equipped only with leftist kitchens and leftist chefs. Only recipes flavored with leftist guilt can be cooked and served from those kitchens. However, in 1996 a new kitchen opened and used an original recipe—balance. And people couldn't get enough of it. Broadcasting information and opinions from both sides of the political debate on one television station appealed to American sensibilities and caused an exodus from the mainstream television media. Fox News achieved better ratings than ABC, NBC, CBS, and CNN, while beating all the cable news channels combined.[38] Even though it was only one television station, and a cable one at that, the left needed *full control* over the masses. Accordingly, Soros would coordinate strategy with the radicals of the Obama White House. In an unprecedented White House assault on a news organization, the Obama administration attempted to delegitimize Fox News, publicly proclaiming on many occasions that "it is not a news organization" and banning them from the five-member White House press pool, which they had been part of along with ABC, NBC, CBS, and CNN since 1997.[39] The Obama administration also urged the other news organizations through intimidation—press access to the President—to disregard Fox News.[40] Fearing the appearance of collusion with the White House that could further affect their ratings—already below Fox's—the other four networks would not consent to the ban.[41] The White House had to relent or lose their four mouthpieces. However, the White House would send officials to make the rounds for interviews on all the Sunday morning network and cable news shows, *except Fox*, repeating their scripted mantra, "It is not a news organization."[42] Meanwhile, Soros ramped up his efforts with Media Matters America, which he funds both directly and indirectly through his front groups, such as the Open Society Institutes and Moveon.org.[43] Unlike his Secretary of State Project, which generally failed, Media Matters America was tremendously successful and damaging to American discourse. Spirited political debate and advocacy has always been the American way. However, the tactics of the neo-radical left were not about debating the issues but about deliberate subterfuge and assassinating voices of dissent. In the words of the founder and CEO of Media Matters America, David Brock, their mission was "guerilla warfare and sabotage."[44] Masquerading as a media watchdog with a non-profit tax-exempt status, this organization duped most of the public into believing they were non-political. But as with most conspiracies of more than two people, they were exposed. But the mainstream media would ignore this, not only because it served their political interests, but because they were in collusion to corruptly influence elections and public policy. However, in February of 2012, the *Daily Caller* published an exposé that included leaked internal memo(s) from Media Matters America employee Karl Frisch to his bosses, CEO David Brock and president Eric Burns, revealing the sinister specifics of the plot:

> The progressive movement is in need of an enemy. George W. Bush is gone. We really don't have John McCain to kick around any more. Filling the lack of leadership on the right, Fox News has emerged as the central enemy and antagonist of the Obama administration, our Congressional majorities and the progressive movement as a whole . . . We must take Fox News head-on in a well funded, presidential-style campaign to discredit and embarrass the network, making it illegitimate in the eyes of news consumers . . . We should hire private investigators to look into the personal lives of Fox News anchors, hosts, reporters, prominent contributors, senior network and corporate staff . . . We should look into contracting with a major law firm to study any available legal actions that can be taken against Fox News, from a class action law suit to defamation claims for those wronged by the network. I imagine this would be difficult but the right law firm is bound to find some legal ground for us to take action against the network.[45]

They also undertook "an elaborate shareholder campaign" against News Corporation, the parent corporation of Fox News:

This can take many forms, from a front group of shareholders, to passing resolutions at shareholder meetings or massive demonstrations are [sic] shareholder meetings . . . We should also hire a team of trackers to stake out private and public events with Fox News anchors, hosts, reporters, prominent contributors and senior network/corporate staff . . . If we need to buy tickets for events that these people will be speaking at, so be it. "Detailed opposition research" on the network's staff and executives, attacks against Fox News employees on Facebook and other social media, mailing anti-Fox News literature to their homes and placing "yard signs and outdoor advertising in their neighborhoods."[46]

Media Matters America staged highly effective publicity campaigns to remove non-leftist media personalities, including libertarians, providing grants of hundreds of thousands of dollars solely to silence all opinions critical of leftist dogma. Harvesting the killing fields of political correctness, which they helped create, Media Matters America disseminated daily press releases of misleading, false, and out-of-context quotes of those whose voices were targeted for assassination. The mainstream media wrote articles based upon those false press releases, as if they were true. The populace accepted them as fact and shunned those who were targeted. Media Matters America and their followers also targeted the advertisers of the voices to be silenced with mass emails and intimidating boycotts, urging them to drop their sponsorships. Many advertisers fled, and the assassinated lost their job. Media Matters America does not discriminate upon political orientation, only speech which they disagree with; liberal (NPR's Juan Williams), conservative (CNN's Lou Dobbs), or libertarian (Fox's Glenn Beck) were all attacked. Media Matters America and their multimillion-dollar budget exist only to vilify, destroy, and *ultimately silence* any person or entity which publicly presents a viewpoint inconsistent with their radical agenda. They scour every statement and written document of those targeted for assassination, searching for politically incorrect sound bites which they can take out of context for press release. Yet even more disturbing was that Media Matters America conducted weekly meetings with the White House and NBC to write the narrative for the White House press secretary and for NBC's nightly cable newscasts.[47]

But this was not the first time the non-mainstream *Daily Caller* exposed corruption in the mainstream news media. The *Journolist*, a listserv of over four hundred leftist journalists, professors, and activists, illustrated the leftist media conspiracy.[48] In the midst of the 2008 campaign for the Democratic Party's presidential nomination, the mainstream media-fueled Obama juggernaut perceived a potential derailment. Obama had previously gushed about the close relationship he had with his spiritual advisor and pastor, Reverend Jeremiah Wright. Suddenly, videos of some of Wright's sermons became public, wherein he dramatically denounced white people and "goddamn America." Obama had attended the hate-filled, incendiary sermons for decades. Almost a year after the videos surfaced, ABC News hosted a debate between Obama and Hillary Clinton, both candidates for the Democratic presidential nomination, moderated by Charles Gibson and George Stephanopoulos. Anchor Charles Gibson asked Obama why it took him so long to disassociate himself from Wright, and anchor George Stephanopoulos (who previously worked for Clinton) asked Obama, "Do you think Reverend Wright loves America as much as you do?" As *The Daily Caller* reported:

> Watching this all at home were members of *Journolist*, a listserv comprised of several hundred liberal journalists, as well as like-minded professors and activists. The tough questioning from the ABC anchors left many of them outraged. 'George [Stephanopoulos],' fumed Richard Kim of *The Nation*, is 'being a disgusting little rat snake.' Others went further. According to records obtained by *The Daily Caller*, at several points during the 2008 presidential campaign a group of liberal journalists took radical steps to protect their favored candidate. Employees of news organizations including *Time*, *Politico*, *The Huffington Post*, *The Baltimore Sun*, *The Guardian*, *Salon* and *The New Republic* participated in outpourings of anger over how Obama had been treated in the media, and in some cases plotted to fix the damage. In one instance, Spencer Ackerman of *The Washington Independent* urged his colleagues to deflect attention from Obama's relationship with Wright by changing the subject. Pick one of Obama's conservative critics, Ackerman wrote, 'Fred Barnes, Karl Rove, who cares — and *call them racists*.' Michael Tomasky, a writer for *The Guardian*, also tried to rally his fellow members of *Journolist*: 'Listen folks–in my opinion, we all have to do what we can to kill ABC and this idiocy

in whatever venues we have. This isn't about defending Obama. This is about how the [mainstream media] kills any chance of discourse that actually serves the people.' Richard Kim got this right above: 'a horrible glimpse of general election press strategy.' He's dead on, Tomasky continued. 'We need to throw chairs now, try as hard as we can to get the call next time. Otherwise the questions in October will be exactly like this. This is just a disease.' (In an interview Monday, Tomasky defended his position, calling the ABC debate an example of shoddy journalism.) Thomas Schaller, a columnist for *The Baltimore Sun* as well as a political science professor, upped the ante from there. In a post with the subject header, 'Why don't we use the power of this list to do something about the debate?' Schaller proposed coordinating a 'smart statement expressing disgust' at the questions Gibson and Stephanopoulos had posed to Obama. 'It would create quite a stir, I bet, and be a warning against future behavior of the sort,' Schaller wrote. Tomasky approved. 'YES. A thousand times yes,' he exclaimed. The members began collaborating on their open letter. Jonathan Stein of *Mother Jones* rejected an early draft, saying, 'I'd say too short. In my opinion, it doesn't go far enough in highlighting the inanity of some of [Gibson's] and [Stephanopoulos's] questions. And it doesn't point out their factual inaccuracies . . . *Our friends at Media Matters probably have tons of experience with this sort of thing, if we want their input.*' [emphasis added]

—*The Daily Caller*[49]

Most Americans are astoundingly unaware of this systemic corruption, just as they have been unaware of the systemically corrupt international media from which they also get their news. However, it appears that those abroad, those on the outside looking in, understand how the American psyche and values are manipulated by the leftist mainstream media. After Syrian dictator Bashar al Assad came under international condemnation for brutal attacks on his own people, he tried to influence American opinion in order to reduce pressure from the Obama administration. In hacked emails from his public relations advisor, Ja'Afari, who is also the daughter of the Syrian ambassador to the UN, Ja'Afari offers coaching tips to Assad in preparation for his interview on ABC with Barbara Walters:

After doing a major research on the American Media's coverage on the Syrian issue and the American Society's perspective of what is happening on the Syrian ground, I have concluded some important points that might be helpful for the preparation of the upcoming interview with Barbara Walters. I based my research on online articles written about the Syrian issue, *my personal contacts with the American journalists*, my father and Syrian expatriates in the States. . . [THE] AMERICAN PSYCHE CAN BE EASILY MANIPULATED . . . PREY ON LIBERAL GUILT [emphasis added][50]

International Media

The international media based in Western Europe is also ultra-leftist and outright corrupt, while the Arab/Muslim, Qatari-owned Al Jazeera TV network indoctrinates not only Europe but through direct-satellite feeds to the Middle East, southwest Asia, and North Africa with anti-American and anti-Israel propaganda. Staged events, doctored/photoshopped images, and false reporting are *routine* for the international media, all in a concerted effort to convey the desired leftist storyline. Whether it's the BBC, CNN International, France 2, Al Jazeera, Al Arabia, the Associated Press, Reuters, or *The New York Times*, they can be relied upon to glorify the cultures of those who celebrate cutting the throats of sleeping babies while demonizing those with the most humane values who would hospitalize and save the lives of the very terrorists attempting to butcher them. Up is down, and down is up with the international media. And their influence cannot be understated, as their broadcast reach extends from the tents of the desert to the most luxurious hotel rooms throughout the world. They have great influence over the perceptions of a world that few know the truth about, a world where they demonize the values of virtue and celebrate the depraved.

Entertainment

Many if not most people don't have the time to follow what's going on in the world. They are busy trying to make ends meet. They often get their news and information late at night from comedians and entertainers. Most entertainers are ultra-leftists promoting their ideology through their humor. With high-profile stars such as John Stuart, Stephen Colbert, Bill Mahr, David Letterman, or Jay Leno, the left pretty much has a monopoly on entertainment that "informs" both directly and indirectly through comedy. The cheers of the studio audiences are taken seriously, as if to affirm the host's political judgments as "truth." Most TV viewers don't give much thought to the type of people that somehow find the time, motivation, and direction to be in the studio audiences of these entertainers. And comedians obviously aren't the only entertainers who influence values. For instance, the exceptionally talented leftist cartoonist Seth McFarlane constantly bashes the right through the popular, long-running shows *Family Guy* and *American Dad*.[51] Such colorful propaganda impacts culture and values. Fortunately, *South Park* creators Matt Stone and Trey Parker balance things out with an artistic, albeit vulgar, genius, fairly and accurately attacking all sides of the political debate.[52] They managed to escape the constraints of political correctness by using animated proxies depicting schoolchildren. The little kid said it, not the creative artists. Viewpoints are cleverly expressed under this cover and the distance between animated characters and humans. This is palatable to the public because the sympathetic child characters drive home the message at the conclusion of each episode.

For the most accurate, insightful, and profound—although amusingly vulgar—summation of the left, the right, and geopolitics, Stone's and Parker's movie *Team America: World Police* is unparalleled.[53] The stars of this full-length feature film are compelling humanlike marionettes. But Stone and Parker are the exception in contemporary culture. Astoundingly, leftists not only dominate contemporary culture but have even gone back to substantially scrub, alter, edit, and whitewash for political correctness the original art forms of animated classics such as Disney's *Fantasia*, the Looney Tunes Collection (including Bugs Bunny), Hanna-Barbera's Tom & Jerry, several Warner Brothers' Merrie Melodies characters, Mr. Magoo, and many others. Ultra-leftist CNN founder Ted Turner was a major force behind this "sanitization." Those who own the rights to such properties should do as they please. If they want to compromise the integrity of the artists and the time period, that is their choice. But if they have rendered these creative works inauthentic and dishonest, they probably should not be shown. If they don't want us to know or learn from our history, they might as well burn the original art forms for which they disapprove—as did the Nazis.

Influence over the Uninformed

Most uninformed people are influenced by leftist entertainers, who also have no clue about the world or the true root causes below propagandized patinas. Leftist entertainers know only what the leftist mainstream media websites and what those in their insulated, guilt-ridden cliques tell them, which they then perpetuate—consciously or unconsciously—using their entertainment platform to spout their destructive ideologies and values. Truth is not as important to them as the cosmological comfort they get from the support of their peer groups. This is the nature of sociology and why we too often see celebrities posing for the cameras with clothing or accessories emblazoned with images or symbols of mass murderers. Whether they display images of Che Guevara, Mao, or the scarves of Palestinian terrorists, the insulated elite voice their abject ignorance through the media to influence the values of the masses. Movies and television further influence the values of the masses with storylines and fashions which promote the false message of the left. For example, the movie *Game Change* vilified an attractive conservative woman political candidate whom they believed would challenge their political idol for the White House.[54] The movie *Runaway Jury* is another example.[55] The premise of it said that it's not psychopathic murderers who kill people, it's the intelligent innovator gun companies that provide the protection from such murderers. Even some cable series characters gratuitously wear T-shirts emblazoned with leftist causes such as *NPR*, the taxpayer-funded leftist political radio station.[56] This is only a miniscule sample, but the leftist dominated entertainment industry is loaded with propaganda.

There is generally nothing wrong with excessive indulgence in entertainment. That is our escape from daily tedium. Such fantasies mitigate monotony usually without harm. We should at least be able to experience them vicariously through entertainment, and the free market should determine such content. But when political propaganda is infused every day, it has the cumulative effect of shifting the collective consciousness of the masses leftward, which will decay the cultural *values* required for health and prosperity.

The New Medium

As technology progresses and high-speed Internet connections become more accessible to everyone, TV will eventually merge completely with the Internet. This will continue to loosen the leftist stranglehold on existing news and entertainment outlets, and it should provide more varied ideological influences on values. However, even though the Internet provides broader access to both information providers and consumers, it also serves to reinforce the views of ideologues who already lack perspective. Leftists will seek cosmological comfort by visiting leftist websites, while those on the right will do the same but only on websites on the right, further entrenching each monochromatic view. Ironically, the same perspective lost on the elite leftist mainstream media may also occur with the choices of the Web's various ideological flavors, as each person maintains an addiction to their favorite cosmological comforts. But at least values would not be force-fed, because people might have the freedom to choose. For too long, the biased and now corrupt leftist mainstream media has had control over the "microphone" to influence culture. Fortunately, that is changing, and they no longer have a monopoly in reporting human events. The intelligent innovators made sure of that by equipping cell phones with camera and video capabilities at the ready so that people can record spontaneous events. Now anyone with such a commonplace device may expose truth in contravention of the corrupt mainstream media's agenda by uploading the recorded content to the Internet for proliferation. That is a true game changer.

Social Conditioning of the Goodness Illusion

When fed a steady diet of something all your life, you become it. It's all you know. The leftist-controlled educational institutions and mainstream media have created a culture of politically correct automatons who are so infused with guilt for the sins of their ancestors that it is difficult for them to see clearly. Their sense of fairness and justice is organically impaired by a conditioned prejudice, wherein they do not look to cause and effect, only to whether one is in comfort or discomfort. They do not look to the values underlying that comfort or discomfort. Values are like seeds; some produce prosperity, some produce misery, some produce love, some produce hate. Socialism, Marxism, and political correctness as propagated through education and the media tell us that all seeds are the same. They are not. Sadly, through all the traumas and world wars, humanity has not learned its lessons. Only the protection of life, liberty, and property can generate the conditions for peace and prosperity, with which each person has the ability to develop and contribute their abilities as value to others in exchange for commensurate compensation. We must all be treated equally. But even under conditions of equal opportunity, people can never be equal insofar as achievement. We are not the same. We are not a number. *The next time a leader tells you we are all the same, ask him to step down so you can take his place.* If we are all the same it should make no difference who leads. As repeatedly stated, we are all unique individuals, each with different challenges we must overcome on our individual paths to enlightenment. A small percentage will always be more prosperous than the rest. Not everyone values education. Not everyone values hard work. Not everyone believes in self-reliance. Not everyone believes our rights come from our source of creation. Not everyone believes in freedom. Not everyone abides by the law. This is reality. We must acknowledge truth. But irrational emotion keeps us from enlightenment. Instead of culling the disciplined values of virtue which produce prosperity, the indulgent "values" of envy, theft, and vilification still dominate humanity. The minority of evil and the minority of good are perpetually engaged in a tug of war. However, as science has demonstrated, disorder comes much more easily than the work required of order, so evil often has an advantage. It's much easier to destroy than to build. Similarly, the good minority who built their success through the salient virtues are always scapegoated for the failures of the majority. An evil minority exploits the basest indulgent emotions of the majority to attain and maintain power, all at the expense of freedom and prosperity. History will continue to repeat itself until all cultures and people at least *aspire* to the values of virtue as the ideal. A naturally indulgent humanity will always find it difficult to adhere to such virtue. But this is our test and purpose. We are supposed to be seduced by the comforts money and power provide. Our choices in how we acquire such material comforts determine our grades. And until we graduate, we will repeat our lessons and exams. As in the past, the pride and shame of maintaining indulgent cultural and ethnic values of failure are assuaged by vilifying the successful, elevating an elite rule that trades virtue for self-indulgence. To gain perspective and clarity, we need only review our history, which shows us that values are the key and the litmus test. They create cultures of prosperity and misery.

Most "advanced" contemporary cultures have been socially conditioned through education and the media to believe that institutionalized theft of the most productive and redistribution to the least productive is somehow a virtue that serves the unfortunate by creating a more "equitable distribution of wealth." This is the Goodness Illusion, and those who disagree with such systems are stigmatized as greedy, evil, and racist. However, wanting to control other people's money in addition to your own is a much more accurate description of greed, and coercion of the law-abiding populace cannot be a virtue, nor can the enslavement of the unfortunate with entitlements. Wealth must be created by individuals. After giving an equal percentage of labor in taxes as everyone else to protect life, liberty, and property of the state, only those who earned or lawfully acquired their money should decide what to do with it. A society with those values would be eager to take care of the unfortunate *voluntarily* and on a more personalized basis. Socialism, social democracy, liberal democracy, welfare state, nanny state, open society, and even theocracy are all different *degrees* of the same thing—tyrannical state control over the means of production, distribution of goods and services, *and the central planning of billions of lives by a small class of elites.* No matter how you romanticize them, under such systems *someone has to decide who gets what.* Those who make these decisions become the ruling elite, and even in its mildest form this type of government manifests itself as inequitable crony capitalism. The predominance of such tyrannical systems creates values which incentivize political efforts to gain influence over the planning class[57] instead of the virtues which incentivize contribution of value to others in goods and services in order to acquire power. Such societies are infused with the wrong values to be sufficiently compassionate, productive, or good. Even under the best of intentions of a "benevolent" tyranny, the security of entitlement in goods and services for the masses requires an unsustainable level of entropy or debt while necessarily limiting freedom and prosperity. Both the U.S. and Europe are prime contemporary examples of such "benevolent" tyrannies. Again, sustained prosperity can be maintained only under a system of natural capitalism, whereby life, liberty, and property are protected from those without virtue and the role of government is limited to that single purpose. Since the smaller the government the greater the freedom, not only would each individual have the greatest freedoms and unlimited prosperity potential but the ruling elite would have generally earned their power and status as millionaires and billionaires by virtue of their being the greatest contributors of perceived value to others in goods and services, which elevates living standards for everyone. This would also change the culture to one where no one could be left behind. But this has not been the case in the twentieth century or so far in the twenty-first. Humanity is naturally emotional and indulgent and is easily led astray by the promises of corrupt, power-hungry elites. Elite dictators, theocrats, leftists, progressives, and social "democrats" all believe in coercion, and they consistently employ the same tried and true formula to attain and maintain their own power at the expense of the freedom and prosperity of their subjects. Because coercive rule can never sustain a broad prosperity, the masses must be diverted from understanding the cause of their oppression—their leader's refusal to protect their lives, liberty, and property. People generally do what feels good, especially when they are suffering, and it may feel good for the majority to vote into legislation the systemic theft of the minority, but "you cannot legislate the poor into freedom by legislating the industrious out of it. You don't multiply wealth by dividing it."[58] *Systemic freedom and prosperity are reserved for the virtuous.* Emotion and indulgence keeps the masses susceptible to the formula, which keeps them enslaved. The elite always designate an enemy—internal, external, or both—to exploit envy and/or guilt with a false compassion. This is universal and cross-cultural. The masses are trained to transfer the anger of dissatisfaction from the leaders who oppress them to another enemy. Ironically, that enemy is usually those with virtuous values who have sustained exceptional prosperity as a result. Because the nature of the formula is designed to preserve a coercive elite rule, it is subversive, and it has effectively suppressed the true causes of decline and stagnation—cultural values. The shadow of evil perennially casts a pointed finger upon the light of the world. All you have to do is look at the background and actions of those pointing that finger. They are usually the dictators, the barbaric murderers, the violently corrupt unions, and those who advocate theft in the name of "social justice" while elevating themselves into power and control of the masses. When cultural values fail a society, instead of feeling shame and courage to reevaluate, modify, and move forward, most cultures display an obstinate pride and blindly accept the ruling elite's designated enemy and blame *them* for their failures, the few they can't control; the tiny percentage that is enlightened enough to understand how to leverage humanity's distinguishing gifts of intelligence and property *for the benefit of society*—the intelligent innovators and their institutions.

SECTION III

THE INTELLIGENT INNOVATORS

VS.

THE ELITE CENTRAL PLANNERS

AND

"THE RELIGION OF PEACE"

Chapter 9

THE INTELLIGENT INNOVATORS,

SOVIET/RUSSIA AND CHINA IN BRIEF,

AMERICA, AND EUROPE

The Intelligent Innovators and their Institutions of Several Forms

The intelligent innovators and their institutions are most recognized and stigmatized in the following forms:

- CORPORATIONS: They provide the world's goods and services and earn money/power in return.

- CAPITALISM: Provides the mechanism for intelligent innovation and *cooperative* exchange.

- AMERICA: The only nation-state in history up until a century ago to protect life, liberty, and property by constitution, and as a result became the most innovative and prosperous society in the world.

- JEWS: Collectively represent a mastery of capitalism, prosperity, and contribution of value to the world with overrepresentation and unparalleled achievement at the top of almost every profession of cognition.

- ISRAEL: Represents the Jewish aggregate to the world and is the only true Middle Eastern democratic republic.

Not coincidentally, these are the world's most vilified entities. Although they consist of imperfect humans with failings like everyone else, their unmatched aggregate prosperity as a result of their relatively virtuous values acutely exposes the shortcomings and envy of everyone else, and therefore they are easy targets for transferring the frustrations of the failed cultural values of others. Multi-generational worldwide campaigns of organized indoctrination consistently and effectively perpetuate libels against them all in order to suppress truth in furtherance of attaining and maintaining coercive power at the expense of values, freedom, and a broad prosperity.

Soviet/Russia and China in Brief

The Soviet/Russian and the Chinese elite leaderships of the last century and to the present achieved great power and control over their people at the expense of freedom and prosperity by appealing to the envy and emotion of the masses with the fiction of a classless society called communism. The elemental values of coercion, envy, and tyranny on a grand scale, with the elite central planning of millions of individual lives, could result only in misery, marginalizing nature's most talented and artificially elevating the marginal. Yet current leftists believe that if they mix those same elements/values, the results would be different. I have rarely mentioned communism because it is a fiction not worth more than a short discussion. A classless society is a logical impossibility because someone must hand out the goodies, decide who gets what, and who must do what. *That of course is a separate class in itself.* Moreover, the sociological nature of humanity precludes a classless society. A small elite will always rule, either by cooperative, meritorious contribution of value or by coercion. Communism was just a ruse designed to plunder the property of the intelligent innovators. Thus, the intelligent innovators were denounced as the enemy, imprisoned, and murdered, only to be supplanted by a different small class. Millions upon millions were killed for a new elite order with coercive control over the masses. Capitalism and corporatism were obviously condemned and prohibited. The Chinese called their designated enemy "capitalist roaders" and "class enemies," while the Soviets/Russians called capitalists the "enemy of the people."[1] The leadership of the Soviets (now Russia) and the Chinese socialists eliminated religion and any virtuous values that may have been contained therein so they could create the peoples' allegiance to and dependence upon the almighty State—elite rule by coercion. Lacking virtuous values, those societies failed miserably, causing only hunger, poverty, and death. For subsistence, they had to eventually institute the cooperative exchange of capitalism, albeit state-capitalism, but a broad prosperity could not endure where life, liberty, and property were not protected. Not coincidentally, the one independent Chinese province which America classifies as "a free and open society where human rights are respected, courts are independent, and there is well-established respect for the rule of law,"[2] great prosperity abounds. This is Hong Kong (formerly British-controlled until 1998), a specially protected region of free capitalists with a fair/flat tax, to boot! Ideological values of self-reliance, freedom, and equal/fair taxation of labor yielded their prosperity. However, for mainland contemporary China, as well as for present-day Russia, their systems of governance are no longer about ideology, if they ever really were. They are primarily about power and coercive control, and the intelligent innovators are the greatest threat. Russia has always backed the destruction of freedom and the intelligent innovators of the U.S. and Israel. In the Russian tradition of killing and suppressing the intelligent innovators (the tsars of tsarist Russia blamed and banned Jews as the enemy), Soviet Russia financed, armed, and actively supported Islamic terror against the Jewish aggregate from the moment Israel was founded. Freedom is not on the agenda of values for either Russia or China. Today, Russia's ideological brethren in China aggressively and violently suppresses any freedom movement, while Russia relatively recently seized and imprisoned in a Siberian penal colony its wealthiest citizen—the *capitalist, corporate* billionaire and *Jew* with political aspirations—Mikhail Khodorkovsky.[3] The intelligent innovators have not fared well under such systems, where life, liberty, and property were not protected. And thus, neither could their general populace.

America

It is one of the most fascinating true stories ever told: Indisputable evidence surfaced in 1963 proving that the Great Depression was not a failure of capitalism but was in fact caused by the leftist progressives' most significant central planning institution—the Federal Reserve. If Americans had only been informed about how freedom and the U.S.

Constitution were permanently eviscerated in both setting up the conditions for and the aftermath of the Great Depression, American values and prosperity would abound today. Instead, "educators" incessantly indoctrinated and alienated Americans from their constitutional heritage by using false accolades for elite central planners such as Woodrow Wilson, Franklin Delano Roosevelt, and Lyndon Johnson. Elite planners of the twentieth century forged what the elite planners know today:

"Never let a serious crisis go to waste."[4]

Thus, the 16th Amendment and the progressive income tax developed from the serious crisis of inequitable tariffs, the New Deal from the serious crisis of the Great Depression, and the Great Society from the serious crisis of the JFK assassination. As a result, life, liberty, and property were no longer protected, only diminished with the continued growth of government power. The greatest governing charter of values in world history—the U.S. Constitution—was both amended and circumvented in order to serve the political interests of the elite central planners, and America would never again achieve the potential freedom and prosperity of natural capitalism. Capitalism became the designated enemy for which the elite government planner FDR derided in his inaugural speech (1933) to forever change American values:

> *The rulers of the exchange of mankind's goods have failed, through their own stubbornness and their own incompetence, have admitted their failure, and abdicated. Practices of the unscrupulous money changers stand indicted in the court of public opinion, rejected in the hearts and minds of men. True they have tried, but their efforts have been cast in the pattern of an outworn tradition . . . They know only the rules of a generation of self-seekers. They have no vision, and when there is no vision the people perish. The money changers have fled from their high seats in the temple of our civilization . . . Our greatest primary task is to put people to work . . . It can be accomplished in part by direct recruiting by the Government itself.[5]*

A society of self-reliant, free individuals seeking to provide and acquire goods and services through the establishment of relationships would gradually transform into a nation of supplicants and entitled wards of the state. Americans would no longer simply yield the fruits of their industry and fail upon their mistakes, but would become entitled to the labor of others for their "security" while true freedom and prosperity was held hostage by the elite planners.

The left was rescued from the freedom and prosperity of capitalism's self-reliant Industrial Revolution by the Great Depression, manufactured by their own elite central planning. Contrary to the falsehoods taught in union-controlled K-12 schools and leftist-controlled institutions of "higher education," capitalism did not fail Americans, Americans failed capitalism, relinquishing the virtuous values of the U.S. Constitution which protected it. Although the greatest governing charter in human history protected life, liberty, and property from plunder and limited federal government to only a few specific enumerated powers, with all others reserved to the individual states, it was no impediment to the indulgent appetites of power-hungry elite progressives eager to rule over and enslave the world's only free, self-reliant people. To do this they fundamentally changed the U.S. Constitution and the nature of American cultural values, disregarding the Founding Fathers' prescient warnings. In "Federalist 10," Madison asked, "What are the different classes of legislators but advocates and parties to the causes which they determine? ... The apportionment of taxes on the various descriptions of property is an act which seems to require the most exact impartiality; yet there is, perhaps, no legislative act in which greater opportunity and temptation are given to a predominant party to trample on the rules of justice."[6] Because America's Founding Fathers knew that the majority would indulge upon the property and virtuous earnings of the minority, they specifically made it unconstitutional to tax one person a greater percentage than another just because of his ability to create greater value to others in goods and services for commensurate income:

"ALL DUTIES, IMPOSTS AND EXCISES SHALL BE UNIFORM THROUGH-OUT THE UNITED STATES." —*Article 1, Sec 8, (1)*.[7]

This protection would be further bolstered by the 14th Amendment's "equal protection" of the laws for all United States citizens. As one who created the charter of American civilization and its governance, Thomas Jefferson stated:

"To take from one, because it is thought his own industry and that of his fathers has acquired too much, in order to spare to others, who, or whose fathers, have not exercised equal industry and skill, is to violate arbitrarily the first principle of association, the guarantee to everyone the free exercise of his industry and the fruits acquired by it."[8]

Thus, the Founding Fathers did not even believe in an income tax, as federal revenue was raised through tariffs on imports and consumption. But such tariff rates became excessive and selective as government typically causes when it comes to taxation, for this is their source of power. Such inequitable tariff rates impacted the masses when purchasing for consumption. But instead of *directly* addressing the problem which they caused, such a serious crisis could not simply go to waste. They would use it to fundamentally change the system of American government. Politicians promised to take from certain citizens and give to others in exchange for voting them into power. This would become America's new values: theft and redistribution over virtue and industry. Votes would be bought with money stolen from others through legislation. But before the leftist progressives could take advantage of the crisis and transform the system, the Constitution would have to be changed. This is because the last time a progressive income tax was passed whereby the unrestrained indulgent majority could steal from the minority (1894), the Supreme Court found it to be an outrage. Justice Stephen Field, a seventy-seven-year-old with thirty years on the Court, predicted that taxing one group more than others would *"be but the stepping stone to others, larger and more sweeping, till our political contests will become a war of the poor against the rich."*[9] As James Madison stated in authoring the U.S. Constitution:

"I cannot undertake to lay my finger on that article of the Constitution which granted a right to Congress of expending, on objects of benevolence, the money of their constituents."[10]

Undeterred, the American majority changed the Constitution so they could legalize a personal income tax. The prospect of changing the constitutional values of restraint from plunder of liberty and property would attract a feeding frenzy of the world's most indulgent leftists ready to devour it. And so they did. Forging the mold of future elite progressive central planners, Woodrow Wilson was an academic with a law degree. As a professor and president of an elite educational institution—Princeton University—the academic "knew" what was best for people in how they should spend their money and conduct their lives, and would get the chance to prove it. On November 5, 1912, Wilson was elected president of the United States. Less than three months later, on February 3, 1913, the American majority amended the Constitution to enact the 16th Amendment, giving the politicians in Congress a new power, which they would use to justify new legislation that allowed the government to tax different groups different percentages according to their corruptocratic whims.[11] Even though this is why the Founding Fathers had fled the English monarchy, the U.S. Constitution was amended to give that same power to America's politicians:

> "THE CONGRESS SHALL HAVE POWER TO LAY AND COLLECT TAXES ON INCOMES, FROM WHATEVER SOURCE DERIVED, WITHOUT APPORTIONMENT AMONG THE SEVERAL STATES, AND WITHOUT REGARD TO ANY CENSUS OR ENUMERATION." —16th Amendment[12]

With that in Wilson's pocket, it was time to fundamentally transform America. President Woodrow Wilson summoned and made a special appearance before Congress to persuade them to enact his progressive agenda. The time was right, because this was the first time in eighteen years that both houses were controlled by the leftist Democratic Party (does this sound familiar to 2008 and Obamacare, when the leftist progressives passed legislation compelling health care labor?). Previously known as "the White Man's Party," the Democratic Party advocated slavery, and thus fought against freedom in the Civil War. Leftists are generally indulgent and prefer the labor of others rather than their own, whether it is direct slavery or taking the labor of others for their purposes through taxation. Accordingly, in the twentieth century they revived involuntary servitude in contravention of the 13th Amendment specifically prohibiting it, and of the 14th Amendment requiring equal protection of the laws to all citizens.[13] On October 3, 1913, President Wilson signed into law the Underwood Tariff Act/Revenue Act of 1913.[14] His ostensible goal was tariff reform or the reduction of tariff rates so that goods and services would be more affordable to the populace. But mitigating excessive tariffs wasn't Wilson's primary ambition. It was taking revenue from the most productive and self-reliant to increase his power with their money/labor, dangling it as a gift to the masses who had voted for and supported his political party of plunder. With the anticipated reduction in government revenue from lower tariff rates, a progressive federal income tax was also attached to the tariff bill to become law. This created the first *permanent* progressive or graduated federal income tax in U.S. history. By this new law, progressives and the financially frustrated indulged and advocated theft from the most productive. Disregarding the principle that all men should be treated equal, the legislation compelled certain citizens to labor for others. Since most people had to work so they could eat, they were now required to pay taxes on that labor. Thus, they are coerced by threat of imprisonment to turn over the fruits of their labor to elite government "bag men" who redistribute it to the groups and designees who pay to put them in power. Different tax rates and different exemptions apply to different entities, depending upon who paid how much to lobbyists and government officials. Generations of Americans have been unwittingly conditioned to accept this as if it always was. America suffers today because these are its *present values*. However, the U.S. Constitution previously provided for no such discretion, and in fact was designed to prevent such abuse of power by government:

> *"A wise and frugal government . . . shall restrain men from injuring one another, shall leave them otherwise free to regulate their own pursuits of industry and improvement, and shall not take from the mouth of labor the bread it has earned. This is the sum of good government."*
> —*Thomas Jefferson*[15]

Education controlled by leftists and corrupt public employee unions make sure to suppress or *revise* American history so that the truth does not disturb their thievery and racketeering cartels. Even though society already benefited from the sacrifice, toil, and industry of the intelligent innovators' goods and services, it was not enough, so the fruits of their labor was plundered, too. The responsibility to protect the life, liberty, and property of Americans, which was previously extended *equally to each individual according to their consumption*, was placed upon the most envied and productive, who paid taxes for almost everyone else. But if this was not enough to end economic freedom in America, President Wilson's signing of the Federal Reserve Act of 1913 did it.[16] Heretofore, a few elite men would control the supply of money, and therefore the labor and prosperity of the masses.

The Federal Reserve caused the Great Depression

The Federal Reserve caused the Great Depression by *contracting the money supply by one-third*, as the National Bureau of Economic Research revealed in the most famous economic study, rarely discussed, *A Monetary History of the United States, 1857-1960.*[17] As co-author Milton Friedman stated, "The Great Depression, like most other periods of severe unemployment, was produced by government mismanagement rather than by any inherent instability of the private economy."[18] Prior to the creation of the Federal Reserve ("the Fed"), banks cooperated with one another and pooled their resources to help other banks with liquidity issues so that bank runs would not panic the populace and the banks could stay in business. However, the government usurped that role and responsibility with the creation of the privately owned Federal Reserve, of which the president of the United States names a chairman. Stock markets reflect the emotions of the people, including greed. They peak and crash, but they do not cause great depressions. As long as goods and services are produced and the government does not interfere with commerce, economies can continue to function above depression levels. But a sufficient supply of money must be available to represent the exchange of labor on a nation-state scale, and not too much money or else that would dilute its value to the point where people could not acquire enough to command the labor of goods and services. In either extreme, employment is severely impaired. The purpose and charter of the Federal Reserve is to make sure that the banks have sufficient reserves. *Instead, the Fed made sure they did not.*

After the stock market crash of October 1929, a panic run on the privately owned Bank of the United States in New York took place. Once the Fed had taken on the role of insuring liquidity for American banks, it had an obligation to do so, because the banks now relied on that. All the Fed needed to do to avert the Great Depression was to purchase government securities to expand the money supply in accordance with its specific charter—or at least to buy bonds from the bank's investment portfolio, because the bank was financially sound. All it needed was more vault cash. As proof of their liquidity, upon liquidation, the Bank of the United States in New York was found to have paid their depositors 92.5 cents on every dollar.[19] However, the elite planners of the Fed had not done the job it had usurped from the banks, and as a result, the large, official-sounding but private Bank of the United States in New York went under, and the public panicked. In what Woodrow Wilson had created in his elite wisdom as a "Supreme Court of Finance," the Fed as lender of last resort just stood by and allowed banks in the South and Midwest to fail.[20] To make matters worse, they increased the rate at which banks could borrow money for reserves. Banks were forced to hoard their cash just to pay their panicked depositors, but it was not enough, so many had to call in their commercial loan portfolios, which bankrupted those borrowers, who were already cash-strapped. More panic ensued, and by March of 1933 half of the country's banks had to declare a holiday in order to suspend their obligations to their depositors. To exacerbate matters, the Fed, as the sole agency for relief, acted like typical bureaucrats. Instead of increasing liquidity, *they reduced it* by selling bonds to collect money out of circulation. They also continued to increase the rate at which banks could borrow money from them, which made restoring liquidity even more daunting. In fact, when the British went off the gold standard in 1931, the Fed responded with the greatest *increase* in discount rate history. This further dried up an already depressed economy that was devoid of cash. The money supply decreased so dramatically that the Federal Reserve banks themselves closed. The central planners of the leftist-created "Supreme Court of Finance" exhibited the greatest and grossest negligence and incompetence in American monetary history. They wiped out ten thousand of the twenty-five thousand commercial banks and citizens' deposits and shrunk the money supply by a third, thereby causing the Great Depression.[21] *Such a substantial and dramatic reduction in the money supply could not have occurred without a central agency of a few men with complete power and discretion over it.*

Unfortunately, economists were not aware of what the Fed had done until the National Bureau of Economic Research report was issued more than thirty years later, and by then most people with influence over policy were already invested in Keynesian economics, an even greater increase in government intervention in economic policy. But leftist government would have most likely found or created another serious crisis anyway to implement their progressive agenda. That is what they do. The elite need control of the masses, or else they can't feel so elite. They usually have no real world accomplishments, just "academic." Moreover, central planning was the rage from Europe and the Soviet Union to Maoist China, and American elite central planners would not be left out of the fun. Although the Great Depression was caused by the leftist-created central planning institution known as the Fed, the elite central planners used the serious crisis to further transform the nature and values of America. FDR was elected president in the wake of the Great Depression to administer America's transformation, bringing an onslaught of unprecedented legislation known as the New Deal(s). The deal was new only in that this time the elite central planners completely disregarded the Constitution and the Founding Fathers' specific words. They didn't even bother with an attempt to amend it. Their self-inflicted monetary crisis was their mandate, just as the recent self-inflicted housing and banking crises became the leftist mandate to further fundamentally transform America. In the twentieth and twenty-first centuries, leftists and progressives indulged any desire on the backs of hardworking taxpayers by either ignoring or falsely citing non-existent authority in the Constitution's "General Welfare" and "Interstate Commerce" clauses. The 10th Amendment, which reserved all powers to the states not otherwise enumerated to the federal government, was also dismissed.[22] Such issues cannot rationally be arguable without suppressing the actual words of the people who wrote the U.S. Constitution. Their *specific comments on the specific issues* demonstrate indisputable intent, as there can be no better source than the authors of the U.S. Constitution. And once the elite central planners set the precedent of disregarding reverence of the Founding Fathers and their words, America would not return to its charter. Thus, James Madison would not be heeded in calling it an "absurdity" to use the General Welfare clause as an independent source of power, as he reasoned in Federalist Paper 41:

> *For what purpose could the enumeration of particular powers be inserted, if these and all others were meant to be included in the preceding general power? Nothing is more natural nor common than first to use a general phrase, and then to explain and qualify it by a recital of particulars. But the idea of an enumeration of particulars which neither explain nor qualify the general meaning, and can have no other effect than to confound and mislead, is an absurdity...*[23]

He could not be more lucid, nor could there be any true doubt about the intent of the General Welfare clause, as his following statements prove:

With respect to the words general welfare, I have always regarded them as qualified by the detail of powers connected with them. To take them in a literal and unlimited sense would be a metamorphosis of the Constitution into a character which there is a host of proofs was not contemplated by its creators . . .[24] . . . the powers of the federal government are enumerated; it can only operate in certain cases; it has legislative powers on defined and limited objects, beyond which it cannot extend its jurisdiction . . .[25] the government of the United States is a definite government, confined to specified objects. It is not like the state governments, whose powers are more general. Charity is no part of the legislative duty of the government . . .[26] If Congress can do whatever in their discretion can be done by money, and will promote the general welfare, the government is no longer a limited one possessing enumerated powers, but an indefinite one subject to particular exceptions . . .[27] If Congress can employ money indefinitely to the general welfare, and are the sole and supreme judges of the general welfare, they may take the care of religion into their own hands; they may appoint teachers in every State, county and parish, and pay them out of their public treasury; they may take into their own hands the education of children, establishing in like manner schools throughout the Union; they may assume the provision of the poor; they may undertake the regulation of all roads other than post-roads; in short, every thing, from the highest object of state legislation down to the most minute object of police, would be thrown under the power of Congress. WERE THE POWER OF CONGRESS TO BE ESTABLISHED IN THE LATITUDE CONTENDED FOR, IT WOULD SUBVERT THE VERY FOUNDATIONS, AND TRANSMUTE THE VERY NATURE OF THE LIMITED GOVERNMENT ESTABLISHED BY THE PEOPLE OF AMERICA. [emphasis added][28]

Thus, the man who wrote the Constitution leaves no ambiguity. Nor does co-author Thomas Jefferson:

Congress has not unlimited powers to provide for the general welfare, but only those specifically enumerated . . .[29] THEY ARE NOT TO DO ANYTHING THEY PLEASE TO PROVIDE FOR THE GENERAL WELFARE, but only to lay taxes for that purpose. To consider . . . [Otherwise], would render all the preceding and subsequent enumerations of power completely useless. It would reduce the whole instrument to a single phrase, that of instituting a Congress with power do to whatever would be for the good of the United States; and, AS THEY WOULD BE THE SOLE JUDGES OF THE GOOD OR EVIL, IT WOULD BE ALSO A POWER TO DO WHATEVER EVIL THEY PLEASE . . . CERTAINLY NO SUCH UNIVERSAL POWER WAS MEANT TO BE GIVEN THEM. It was intended to lace them up straitly within the enumerated powers and those without which, as means, these powers could not be carried into effect. [emphasis added][30]

The issue was obviously never in doubt as the leftists and progressives lead us to believe even to this day. No rational, informed human being can deny the law of the land, the bedrock of the civilization the Founding Fathers chartered. It would only be outright defiance and corruption by an elite band of criminals who think they are above the law. The remarkable prescience of our Founding Fathers goes unheeded. As Thomas Jefferson reportedly said in a letter to John Adams in 1816:

"The issue today is the same as it has been throughout all history, whether man shall be allowed to govern himself or be ruled by a small elite."[31]

Americans chose to be ruled by the small elite, trading the virtues protecting liberty and property for a false and impossible security.

Woodrow Wilson opened the door for that small elite with his initial assault on the U.S. Constitution, eliminating the protection of property, liberty, and equal protection under the law, thus enabling the indulgent majority to loot the minority. His establishment of the Federal Reserve enabled the elite central planners to control American money/labor, shrinking the supply of money/labor by one-third and causing the mass suffering of the Great Depression. This kick-started the cycle of serious crises caused by progressive elites who were eager to plan the lives of others. They would use each self-inflicted crises as a rallying call for more progressivism and a political platform for more central planning. However, they could not progress past the laws of nature which the U.S. Constitution codified. But a new generation would continue to try. They were led by Franklin Delano Roosevelt, as he, too, thought he knew better than the Founding Fathers.

FDR and his New Deal(s)

FDR's inaugural speech of 1933 vilifying the intelligent innovators set a new tone for governance, which was hostile to the capitalism and freedom that built the Industrial Revolution and the greatest prosperity in human history, and America would revert to the ubiquitous master/ serf relationship. The constitutionally reserved separation of powers of the legislative, judiciary, and the executive branches, designed to prevent a dictatorship, was also perverted, as FDR usurped and delegated the duties of the legislative branch to the executive branch agencies, which he controlled and directed. No longer would the elected legislators of the House and Senate "toil" in their designated role as lawmakers. That work was outsourced to special interests over the interests of the populace. This process continues today as so eloquently articulated by former House Speaker Nancy Pelosi, "We have to pass the bill so you can find out what is in it."[32] Thus, the statutory nanny state onslaught, which was financed by looting the intelligent innovators and outsourced to special interests, began with the New Deal as the following unprecedented legislation demonstrates (and continues to this day with The Affordable Care Act of 2010/Obamacare):

- The Emergency Banking Act (1933)
- The Economy Act (1933)
- The Federal Securities Act (1933)
- The Tennessee Valley Authority (1933)
- The Civilian Conservation Corps (1933)
- The Federal Emergency Relief Administration (1933)
- The Glass-Steagall Act (1933)
- The Civil Works Administration (1933)
- The Public Works Administration (1933)
- The National Recovery Administration (1933)
- The Agricultural Adjustment Administration (1933)
- The Farm Credit Administration (1933)

- The Federal Housing Administration (1934)
- The Gold Reserve Act (1934)
- The Reciprocal Trade Agreements Act (1934)
- The Works Progress Administration (1935)
- The Public Utilities Holding Company Act (1935)
- The Social Security Act (1935)
- The National Labor Relations Act (1935)
- The Soil Conservation and Domestic Allotment Act (1936)
- The National Housing Act (1937)
- The Farm Security Administration (1937)
- The Fair Labor Standards Act (1938)

This was not America. The judicial branch, designed as a check against such a power grab by a few elite dictators, resisted for a while, issuing more than fifteen hundred federal injunctions to prevent the unconstitutional taking of liberty and property.[33] The Supreme Court held firm at five to four against New Deal legislation until FDR threatened additional legislation which would add more than the constitutionally provided nine justices to the Supreme Court. Such coercive legislation was drafted so that FDR could get his New Deal legislation approved through additional leftist jurists. If the pesky Constitution and the laws got in the way, he believed he could indulgently change them. Why respect the Founding Fathers who provided FDR and his family with the great blessings of liberty and the wealth it yielded them? He could just take over and shut the door behind him. It wouldn't matter how many people died in war to protect freedom and the U.S. Constitution, not even to the judiciary. Cowering under FDR's tyrannical threats to change the constitutional structure of the Supreme Court, one of the justices switched to leftist unconstitutional rule to avoid FDR's court-packing plan, thus the famous but often misunderstood line "a switch in time that saved nine."[34] This plan was defeated in the legislature, but the left turn was a fait accompli with the "switch in time" of Justice Owen Roberts.[35] And once FDR was re-elected for a second term, he claimed it as a mandate to reject any potential judiciary resistance. But he didn't have much. In 1942 the judiciary lost all respect for logic (and themselves) in fear of their master in the executive branch and the elites in Congress. The Constitution enumerates certain powers of the federal government, including authority of the legislative branch (the U.S. Congress) "to regulate commerce with foreign nations, and among the several states, and with the Indian tribes." —Article I, Section 8, Clause 3 And of course any powers that are not enumerated in the Constitution are reserved to the states in accordance with the 10th Amendment. However, to increase their power and have control over the masses, the elite rulers ended economic freedom for good with the absurd indulgence that *not* participating in interstate commerce is in fact a form of interstate commerce, and thus subject to federal control under the Commerce Clause. This was established by the Supreme Court in the case of *Wickard v. Filburn*, 1942, wherein they held that the liberty to grow and eat your own food on your own property is subject to federal control as a form of interstate commerce.[36] The flood gates of intelligent innovation were now controlled by unmerited bureaucrats bought by constituencies who wanted to direct the markets to their advantage. Thus, government controlled the means of production. This defines socialism.* When people lament that capitalism failed America, they should know the actual truth; *socialism failed America.*

Recall that despite the warnings of the Founding Fathers, who prohibited elected officials from deciding whom to tax and how much personal income tax they could collect, an Amendment to the Constitution and legislation under President Woodrow Wilson's reign changed this. Government officials who knew better than the intelligent innovators of goods and services now controlled the cooperative business relationships of Americans. Some people suffered the consequences of their bad business decisions, while those who could influence government officials got bailed out by the labor of those without such privileged relationships. The new order; *subsidies for friends and tax audits for enemies.*[37] Instead of allowing freedom for the natural markets to take their course, the government artificially set minimum prices for farming products. If farmers didn't receive those prices, government coercively took money from other citizens to pay the farmers the difference. Government even paid farmers with taxpayer-looted funds *not to work* in order to keep prices artificially high with a lower crop yield. If a good harvest of oranges fortuitously provided a large supply and low prices, hunger didn't stop the collusion of government and farmers from letting the oranges *rot* so that a reduced supply

---

* Little to no practical distinction exists between control of the means of production and distribution vs. ownership of same. If you own a business but can operate it and distribute its yield only by instruction of others (government), the meaning of *ownership* has little significance. You are really a licensee/employee of the State.

kept prices higher.[38] Government control over the means of production and mandated price controls continue to this day in America. Even a government milk-pricing cartel exists.[39]

Progressives were brilliant at usurping and exploiting power, if not moral and virtuous. Government comes from and influences the morals and virtues of the people. The confluence of genius in the Founding Fathers had proved right all along. They saw the revolutions in other European countries such as France, so they consciously made the American one different. The difference was, as John Adams stated:

> *"Want of honesty; and if the common people in America lose their integrity, they will soon set up tyrants of their own."*[40]

And so they did. This caused the intelligent innovators to become exceedingly cautious. They were justifiably concerned that FDR and Congress would take the fruits of their labor and hand it over to bureaucrats and their cronies so they could buy votes. Strikingly similar to the reign of the Obama administration, businesses held on to their cash then just as they do today, fearing what would happen to it if they put it into the market. And just like today's failed "stimulus," the New Deal was an abject failure. Prosperity could not be funded by the coercion and theft of the very people who could create it—the intelligent innovators. Nevertheless, the imperious FDR tried to do the same thing again in what was called the Second New Deal. But he funded it in the same coercive manner as the first failed New Deal. He continued to slander, punish, and raid the intelligent innovators and their corporate aggregates by employing what was popularly called the "soak-the-rich" tax of 1935 and the undistributed profits tax of 1936.[41] He believed that if the intelligent innovators didn't spend their money, he would just confiscate it and use it for his own purposes. And he did. FDR's Treasury Secretary, Henry Morgenthau, commented on the class-warfare "soak-the-rich" tax: *"It was more or less a campaign document."*[42] Morgenthau was a close friend confidant of FDR and an architect of the failed New Deal(s). This is what he had to say about the efficacy of such unprecedented theft and redistributive spending:

> *"I say after eight years of this Administration we have just as much unemployment as when we started . . . and an enormous debt, to boot!"*

"We have tried spending money. We are spending more than we have ever spent before and IT DOES NOT WORK."[43]

The elite central planners then, were as they are today—utter failures. The cycle of unemployment of the Great Depression caused by their creation of the Fed and their solution to fund an artificial employment with funds confiscated from the toil of the intelligent innovators could not possibly bring prosperity. In fact, after eight years of FDR's attacks upon and theft of the intelligent innovators as a means to end the Great Depression unemployment was even higher throughout 1939 than it was in 1931.[44] FDR had four terms in which to fundamentally transform America into a coercive and plundering society. In this he succeeded. With the most time in office of any other U.S. president to execute such depraved values, FDR only exacerbated and perpetuated America's economic woes. Yet we are taught that he was one of the greatest American presidents. This reflects our transformed values. We laud those who steal from the prosperous and falsely paint them as righteous, as we do with President Obama.

Today's leaders should know the truth, but that is obviously not what it's all about for them. It is a matter of both power over, envy of, and contempt for the intelligent innovators and their different institutions of *merited* power. They cannot control and manipulate them as easily as they do with the masses. But once the masses are led over the gates of liberty and property, they become insatiable animals at the feeding trough. And who is to stop their engorgement on the labor of others? FDR's creation of the central-planning Ponzi scheme known as Social Security is an example. There is no Social Security trust fund.[45] It has been devoured already through plunder. Each new generation must now work for the next. A society with a Ponzi scheme as a primary institution for the elderly does not have sufficiently virtuous values for a sustained prosperity. Individuals in the private sector are prosecuted and imprisoned for such conduct, but it is somehow acceptable for government officials to employ the same depravity. When the patriarchs of a society who are supposed to have achieved wisdom accept this, or otherwise prefer to scam the children and grandchildren to pay for their retirement instead of virtuous saving and investing, the fabric of society has issues of integrity that will lead to collapse.

America Transformed

After FDR, presidents Truman, Eisenhower, and Kennedy*
brought some modicum of sobriety back to America, but because of the
fundamental changes to the system of American governance and values
initiated by Wilson and FDR, government has continued to grow to this
day while individual freedom has shrunk commensurately. Leftists, progressives, and socialists love to proclaim that the post-war years of the
1950s and 1960s were proof that high taxation does not inhibit prosperity, but *they ignore the fact* that practically no one paid the high marginal
rates because of gaping loopholes and generous exemptions for those in
the highest tax brackets (this is why the "Alternative Minimum Tax" was
devised in the 1960s).[46] Intelligent innovation of wartime production to
protect the lives and liberty of Americans, plus the technologies derived
from the war effort and applied to domestic and commercial use, caused
the prosperity of the 1950s and 1960s. Any review of popular magazines
of that time show the explosion in goods and services in the two decades
after World War II. In addition, America was the only significant power
not domestically devastated by the war, so it pretty much had a monopoly
on the world's production and distribution of exports, for which it received
great income. A disciplined labor force of the "Greatest Generation" returning from World War II overseas also helped. And once Kennedy was
elected, his famous statement "Ask not what your country can do for you,
but what you can do for your country" inspired an opportunity for a new
tone of contribution rather than indulgence.[47] But this was not to be. The
values of the entitled adolescent radicals of the 1960s would not permit
such virtue. Although he was a Democrat, JFK recognized how legislation
had manifested a transformation of American values, especially through
the redistributive tax code. As he said:

> *"Our present tax system . . . exerts too heavy a drag on growth . . . It
> reduces the financial incentives for personal effort, investment, and*

---

* However, Kennedy's monumental mistake in executive order 10988 allowing federal
employees to unionize, even against the warnings of ultra-leftist FDR, who considered it
"unthinkable and intolerable," would lead to theft cartels which would greatly corrupt the
political process and break many public budgets. The purpose of unions is to get a greater share of company profits, but since government does not make profits, the purpose
of public employee unions is to indulgently feed at the trough of taxpayer money. They
succeeded to create a special class of public employees with pay and unearned benefits
that their private sector counterparts for whom they work do not receive.

risk-taking . . . The present tax load . . . distorts economic judgments and channels an undue amount of energy into efforts to avoid tax liabilities." (November 20, 1962)[48]

He also said:

"Lower rates of taxation will stimulate economic activity and so raise the levels of personal and corporate income as to yield within a few years an increased—not a reduced—flow of revenues to the federal government." (January 17, 1963)[49]

JFK was also an ardent supporter of civil rights. Meanwhile, his estranged vice president and successor, Lyndon Johnson, did not particularly like black people, to put it mildly. Previous to becoming vice president, he was a U.S. congressman (1937–1949) and U.S. senator (1949–1961) from Texas. As a powerful senator, Johnson ardently resisted civil rights legislation proposed by both President Harry Truman and his successor, President Dwight D. Eisenhower, which was designed to protect blacks in the 1950s, including anti-lynching laws. Senator Johnson fought vigorously against such legislation. However, after the assassination of JFK, Johnson took over the presidency with a mandate to enact JFK's civil rights agenda, but only so that *"I'll have those niggers voting Democratic for the next two hundred years"* (Lyndon B. Johnson to two governors on Air Force One).[50] As a progressive, he didn't let the serious crisis of JFK's assassination go to waste. To increase his own power, Johnson doubled down on FDR's philosophy to greatly expand the welfare state. Anytime politicians have to assign a phrase with an adjective to a large body of intended legislation it generally serves as verbal Vaseline. Thus, once Johnson trotted out the term *the Great Society,* people should have gotten ready for the plundering. The Great Society wasn't so great. After trillions of dollars spent for big government programs to fight poverty, poverty today is essentially at the same level as it was when Johnson's Great Society programs began more than a half century ago.[51] If people thought Johnson treated blacks harshly while he was alive, his legacy has done far worse with an enduring "Great Society" of impoverished dependents. Johnson would have done well to read up on the genius of the Founding Father Ben Franklin, at least when it came to helping the poor:

"I am for doing good to the poor, but I differ in opinion of the means. I think the best way of doing good to the poor, is not making them easy in poverty, but leading or driving them out of it."[52]

Instead Johnson grew dependency, the entitlement state, bureaucracy, regulation, and debt with the following government expansions:

- 1964 Economic Opportunity Act (EOA)
- 1965 Medicare Act
- 1965 Appalachian Regional Development Act
- 1965 Omnibus Housing Act
- 1965 Department of Housing and Urban Development
- 1965 Elementary and Secondary Education Act
- 1965 Higher Education Act
- 1965 National Foundation on the Arts and the Humanities
- 1965 Voting Rights Act
- 1965 Immigration Act
- 1965 Wilderness Preservation Act
- 1965 Water Quality Act
- 1965 Clean Air Act Amendment
- 1966 Truth in Packaging Act
- 1966 National Traffic and Motor Vehicle Safety Act
- 1966 Highway Safety Act
- 1966 Department of Transportation
- 1966 Demonstration Cities and Metropolitan Area Redevelopment Act
- 1967 Corporation for Public Broadcasting
- 1967 Air Quality Act

Government became a colossus in America, intervening in almost every aspect of American life, from housing to healthcare. Liberty and property were taken from many who lived virtuously and given to many who lived in depravity. This was not the limited role of government envisioned by the Founding Fathers of the American experiment, although some saw how corruption could devolve it so. Most government programs supplant personal responsibility and the values of virtue required for a prosperous society. The consequences are artificial housing bubbles, bank failures, and depressions and recessions great and not so great. Even health care became an entitlement or right. Before the government drove up the prices of medical care with Medicare, Medicaid and the trillions in fraud and corrupt tax code carve-outs which they spawned, everyone's health care needs were taken care of, because doctors did well enough to treat the poor for free.[53] But government usurped the role of charity in the private sector, socializing and emasculating American health care freedom while eviscerating the doctor-patient relationship. Once again the elite central planners caused a serious crisis and would not let it go to waste, this time in the most expensive area—health care. After gaining control of the White House in 2008, the most radical elites in American history enacted one of the most unconstitutional government programs ever—coercing Americans into buying a service.[54] But even big-government progressives on the right had already been in on the action. Previous president George W. Bush forced healthy taxpayers— those who watch their weight and eat right—to pay for the medications of those who don't. Nature's intended consequences for bad individual decisions in consumption and expenditure—overindulgence in toxic foods, alcohol, cigarettes without exercise—were shifted to others. Overindulgence should not be condemned—life is not easy and we all seek pleasure when we can get it. However, shifting the consequences to others is immoral and defeats nature's intent for us to learn individually from our mistakes through suffering. But nature cannot be cheated. By design, the collective suffers for its bad policy decisions.

Most people don't realize that the main culprit is once again the Fed, because without it, government couldn't spend so much money on entitlements. The Fed keeps flooding America with trillions of created dollars in exchange for pieces of paper from the U.S. Treasury called American bonds, all to fund colossal government programs while plunging America into an seemingly insurmountable debt that now exceeds 16 trillion dollars. The economy cannot correct itself with such a cancerous pathology of the nation-state body. Many people blame Wall Street, but they are only as good or better at looting the taxpayers than all the other subsidized entities. As long as the government keeps doling out the goodies at the expense of taxpayers' children, grandchildren, and great-grandchildren, Wall Street will vie for its share. In fact, they have more insiders in the current Obama administration to make this happen than anyone else, as evident by the bailouts they received. They are somehow special and more important human beings than the millions of other business owners who did not get bailouts, many of which went out of business.

Not allowing the serious crisis which they caused go to waste, corrupt lawmakers Barney Frank and Christopher Dodd sponsored complex special-interest legislation that was almost a thousand pages long so that monstrous government bureaucracies of incompetents could intrusively control American financial services.[55] Known as Dodd-Frank, this legislation was passed by the leftist-controlled congress and signed into law by President Obama, but was subsequently revealed to be the biggest government overreach (along with Obamacare) since the aftermath of the Great Depression. As is typical of corruptocrats, they granted waivers to their favored companies so that certain Wall Street cronies remained too big to fail, defeating the whole point of the legislation. This is obviously inequitable and immoral to those who virtuously suffer the consequences of their bad decisions. In any event, the industrious and virtuous taxpayers must pay. This consistent pattern is as fascinating as it is disheartening. The two legislators who were central figures in causing the serious crisis (Great Recession) stemming from entitlement to home ownership and the toxic securities they spawned, ultra-leftists Barney Frank and Christopher Dodd were the very ones who coerced everyone else under government control.[56] No bailouts should have been granted in the first place. People have to suffer the consequences of their decisions. The pain would have been great for everyone, but that's the price the populace should pay for government engineered overindulgence in massive entitlements—unearned goods and services. Only the free market should determine such matters. Although the pain of letting the big, corrupt financial institutions fail would be acute, the economy would recover much more quickly than dragging out an inevitable correction which would be felt by subsequent generations that didn't cause it. Moreover, without pain, the populace would be more likely to repeat their mistakes.

After running out of the money from the productive, America now borrows at least forty-two cents for every dollar it spends.[57] No society can sustain itself with such values. The natural outrage of those who play by the rules and live relatively virtuous values is healthy and productive, as is expressed by the popular Tea Party movement. By the standard of truth, they have been unjustly maligned for the temerity to demand adherence to the true virtuous values of the U.S. Constitution—limited government and fiscal responsibility. The immoral and corrupt, led by the leftist mainstream media, have been very effective in retaliating against those calling for responsibility and virtue. Up is down, and down is up

for the depraved. The virtuous are condemned, and the corrupt are cham-
pioned. While the Tea Party is a grassroots movement that expressed
outrage at the moral decadence, the Occupy Wall Street movement was
financed, sponsored, and manufactured by the neo-radical left (Stephen
Lerner and George Soros, et al).[58] And while the Tea Party protests were
always peaceful and lawful, with their assembly areas left clean, they were
called racists and manufactured, as the truly manufactured Occupy Wall
Street movement was rampant with crime, including rape, battery, theft,
and public defecation.[59] Anti-Semitism is characteristically pervasive in
such depraved movements, because the prosperous, intelligent innovators have to be scapegoated for the failures of the indolent and incompetent.[60] Predictably, the Occupy Wall Street protesters left their areas of
protest filled with garbage and infested with rats, reflecting the nature
of their message for those who were articulate enough to express it: the
majority (99%) must loot and lynch the most prosperous minority (1%).
The truth is that the overwhelming majority of millionaires in that one
percent minority in America are self-made,[61] and they make the lives of
the ninety-nine percent better with not only goods and services, but jobs
too. Any system which discriminates against, penalizes, or plunders the
fruits of one's labor and contributions of perceived value to others is inequitable and counterproductive. Nonetheless, the neo-radical left operating in accordance with *PEGIT* (see Chapter 7, "The Biology and Genetics
of Values") believe that the indolent are entitled to the labor of others in
goods and services: It's the corporations that are evil, not we who rape and
rob. Of course they are too profoundly stupid to realize that almost every material possession they have and covet is made by corporations. The
most effective way to disrupt the moronic demonization of corporations
is to ask the individual(s) who lament them:

> "Who made your shirt, your shoes, your socks, your wrist watch,
> your cell phone, your iPod, your guitar, your food, your..."
> —CORPORATIONS

*The intelligent innovators and their institutions must be demonized in order
to deflect the failed values of others.* The Humane Society is a corporation,
as are essentially all the ultra-leftist organizations that promote the demonization of corporations. Corporations are only legal entities, but they
are obviously comprised of individual human beings. Some corporations
consist of virtuous individual people, while others consist of corrupt in-

dividuals—most have both. Consistent with their depraved values, many leftists want legislation that *requires* employees to own the corporations for which they work and to make corporate decisions by majority vote of the employees. Using such logic, Thomas Edison, who failed 9,999 times to invent the light bulb, should have let his employees take equal profit from his unequal and inventive toil, as if they were qualified to make decisions for his ingenious industry. Such leftist values would have caused Edison to quit after his first two failures. Why should he try 9,999 experiments only to turn it all over to those who believe they are qualified and entitled to the fruits and control of his labor and intelligent innovation? The platitudes of leftists show no respect for logic, but are flailing attempts at an alternate universe where risk, sacrifice, and merit have no place. This is the reality of leftist values—they don't include much virtue.

The Divide—Good and Evil

The character of those at the top or the leaders of each corporation usually determine the culture and values of each organization. Interestingly, values and virtue of those funding political movements of the left and right present clear and distinct choices for the public. If values and virtue determine prosperity, examining the values and virtue of the two are instructive. The left constantly rails against "the evil Koch Brothers" for funding causes of freedom on the right. So let's look at what they call "evil." Koch Industries *contributes actual value to millions of people in goods and services, employing fifty thousand people (in the U.S. alone) who earn money to feed their family.*[62] They are compensated commensurately for the tremendous value they create. This is called merited success. For the indolent, lecherous Occupy Wall Street losers and their self-hating Jewish puppet masters of destruction—George Soros, Stephen Lerner, Andy Stern, Bill Ayers, Frances Piven—industry and merited success means "evil," even though all their cherished possessions, including the clothes on their back, are made by successful industrialists. To them in their virulent pathology, plunder is a virtue. They would rather steal the labor of others than contribute value in goods and services. In contrast to the Koch Brothers, who fund causes of virtuous values, the neo-radical left is funded largely by George Soros, who obtained his money primarily through megalomaniacal destruction, manipulating and breaking the currencies and economies of several nation-states to enrich himself. His actions, done only to indulge himself, have destroyed many lives. He didn't create value for those people, and thus his wealth was not earned, because taking billions of dollars of other peoples labor caused them only misery. No matter how Soros tries, fomenting revolutions which take from those who earn and give to those who don't, while clipping huge commissions, cannot discharge his guilt. Demonizing the intelligent innovators who actually create value for others will also fail to discharge the guilt of his immorality. The guilt is telling him to correct his behavior—stop scamming and provide value to others.

So which side represents virtue, the destroyer of nation-state economies (the Soros-backed tyrannical neo-radical left) or those who create economies of value in goods and services (Koch Industries freedom advocates)? Complaints about corrupt Wall Street companies and their big-government bail-out sponsors are bona fide and well placed. But there is also a SIMPLE SOLUTION:

> *"If you take government out of it, the only way Wall Street can make money is by benefitting everyone else . . . you have to cut off the head of the snake. [Government] should not be able to give bail-outs."*[63]

Only an enlightenment of American values of virtue in the revival of reverence and adherence to the genius of the words of the Founding Fathers can yield an optimal freedom and prosperity. America is the last great hope for human freedom and prosperity because the formula is already in its founding charter. It just needs some adjustments such as an amendment prohibiting progressive taxation so that people are treated equally under the law and a balanced budget amendment. American culture must be transformed from one of dependence and depravity to one of self-reliance and virtue. And that may be facilitated through an economy of natural capitalism whereby the role of government is limited solely to the protection of life, liberty, and property. This would emancipate the human animal's distinguishing characteristics of intelligence and innovation for the greatest benefit to all. This is *libertarianism*, and as the ultimate evolution for human society, such freedom will not come anytime soon. But it shall, eventually, manifest.

Europe

Europe is one of humanity's greatest tragedies. Europeans brought Western civilization to the world with a beautiful and passionate diversity of cultures. They stumbled upon the concept of freedom with the Magna Carta, created the best conditions for advancing the arts and sciences with the Renaissance, initiated the Industrial Revolution, and spawned the greatest chartered society in human history with the American experiment. They also brought organized barbarism and mass murder to prolific heights with the Spanish Inquisition, the French Reign of (guillotine) Terror, and the Third Reich. The intelligent innovators of prosperity were deemed the enemy to be eliminated then just as they are now. Values of virtue have never quite been a priority for the European majority, and that hasn't changed to this day. Although they recognize and feel tremendous pain, shame, and guilt for their tumultuous history of violence and war, they have failed to learn their lessons. Instead of distinguishing what they did wrong and what they did right—culling the virtues of their past and discarding the depravity—they manifested a pathology to whitewash their individual cultures into a European Union of political correctness and allegiance to secular indulgence. Understandably, they righteously sought to eliminate the ultra-nationalism and religion which they believed caused centuries of war and human suffering. But it wasn't nationalism and religion that caused their nightmares, it was their *values*.

As with many societies, nationalism and religion have been instruments of great good and great evil for Western Europe. People should want to do great things in the name of their country and by divine providence, too. But instead of adopting the virtuous values of each and eliminating the evils, Europe has generally sanitized both altogether. Overcompensating with a demand for intrastate multiculturalism, Western Europe failed to consider that values compose cultures and that some cultures have values which conflict with the values of others, making intra-state coexistence impossible. Such ill-conceived overcorrection, along with an entitlement society planned by bureaucratic elites, has failed to extirpate their historic tendencies, but only transformed the methodologies. Instead of direct religious extremism, they mass import it from the Islamic world. Instead of herding millions of the most prolific intelligent innovators into the ovens of Auschwitz, Europe organized international committees, courts, NGOs, and corrupt media to libel, demonize, and delegitimize the relatives and progeny of the same six million living in their aggregate historic homeland, all to placate both their imported Islamic citizens who pray daily for another holocaust and their own historic hatred. Those pesky overachievers with relatively virtuous values are the first to get it when people become economically frustrated and envious. And Europe's coming pain as a result of their impossible entitlement culture virtually ensures it. Why should the Europeans blame their economic hardships on a scientifically flawed political system of collectivism/socialism and coexistence with barbarism when they can blame the prosperous intelligent innovators who not only civilized the world, but make the world a better place with the goods and services to which Europe feels entitled?

Europe believes that their adoption of political correctness gives them cover for their sins. But political correctness is just like clouds providing shade from the sunlight of truth. Eventually the truth shines through. In the words of the chancellor of Germany, the prime minister of England, and the president of France:

"Multiculturalism has failed."[64]

Translation: WESTERN JUDEO-CHRISTIAN VALUES AND ISLAMIC VALUES CONFLICT. In its efforts to remediate the horrors of the past, Western Europe has self-sedated, emasculated, and castrated itself.

Collective guilt has turned into either self-hatred, self-absorption, or both, because they will not reproduce—literally. For a society to remain static, without growing or shrinking, it must have an average birthrate of 2.1 babies per female.[65] Europe averages an approximate 1.3.[66] Because Europeans have traded the values of liberty and the responsibility of self-reliance for a false security of entitlements, their prosperity is limited. Wealth is difficult to achieve in Europe under such redistributive conditions. They believed they could trade liberty for security, and of course they got neither. Coercion takes precedence over cooperation. European intelligent innovators cannot fire protected classes of employees once they hire them, so many don't take the chance.[67] European society is overregulated by the elite central planners. This inhibits productivity and growth.

Nevertheless, everyone is entitled to benefits, paid vacations, healthcare, and retirement plans in such societies. Someone has to pay for the able-bodied unproductive and their summers on the Riviera. Since they are limited in income and their values are about entitlements, making babies cuts into their already limited budget and freedom. But without a sufficient productive labor force to support the entitlement state, what would happen to Western Europe? Entropy. Decay represented by colossal debt. And the brilliant solution from the elite central planners? For every non-Muslim child born, approximately eight Muslim children are born into the world.[68] Would importing Muslims support the European entitlement culture? Or would Europe be more likely to see the oft anticipated minaret on top of Paris' Eiffel Tower, from which the faithful are called to prayer five times a day (as this may be somewhat inconsistent with the secular society Western Europe had envisioned, and so many daily prayers might inhibit productivity). Although they accept government entitlements to support their family, Muslims have otherwise generally refused to integrate into European society, as death befell many apostates who did. Consistent with its value system, Western Europe exports its money/labor to Islamic states while importing oil, terror, and large Islamic families on which to lavish entitlements paid for with borrowed capital.

In addition to anointing an elite who go from school to school to learn such brilliant central planning, two fatal deficiencies would signal the demise of Western Europe—virtuous values and families to impart them. Both would be ceded to the most destructive culture on Earth in the literal name of submission—Islam.

Chapter 10

ISLAM
"The Religion of Peace"

Western ignorance of Islam is so profound, especially among leftists and their elite leaders, that Western Civilization wouldn't stand a chance of maintaining its culture without the knowledge and efforts of the valorous enlightened few who are still trying to preserve it. Western elites proclaim themselves to be so multi-cultural and intellectual, but as narcissists they see Islam only through egocentric Western values, as if Muslims were secular or followed the teachings of Jesus. Mohammed and Jesus had starkly different values and lifestyles, and each of them manifested a completely different culture. Jesus was not only a Jew but also a rabbi. He came from the people of the Torah ("instructions"), a value system which enabled them to survive for over four thousand years and prosper more than any other society, even while under perpetual siege. In the words of America's co-Founding Father John Adams:

> *"I will insist the Hebrews have done more to civilize men than any other nation. If I were an atheist, and believed in blind eternal fate, I should still believe that fate had ordained the Jews to be the most essential instrument for civilizing the nations."*[1]

At the opposite pole, Muslims have done more to barbarize men than any other nation. The values of each society can be measured by their level of prosperity and misery. While Jesus professed peace and love and did not advocate violence, Mohammed, six hundred years later, was a self-professed violent warlord of hate. He would surprise unsuspecting caravans and populations in order to conquer, pillage, and loot them of their property, while coercively growing his following. He knew that people would be much more willing to die for an afterlife of bliss in submission to a prophet of God than for a warlord leading a band of pillaging marauders. However, he proposed an even better no-lose situation for those who would follow him. If they didn't die for a blissful afterlife, that meant they had succeeded in battle, indulging in the spoils of the conquered, including their women and children:

> *Those who barter their life in this world for the next should fight in the way of Allah; whether he is killed or victorious, a glorious reward awaits. Qur'an 4th surah.*

> *The Prophet had their men killed, their children and women taken as captives. Safiyah was amongst the captives. She first came in the share of Dihyah but later on she came to belong to the Prophet. Muhammad made her manumission as her "Mahr [wedding gift]." The captives of Khaybar were divided among the Muslims. Then the Messenger began taking the homes and property that were closest to him. Bukhari:V5B59N512*

> *The Prophet conquered Khaybar by force after fighting. Khaybar was something that Allah gave as booty to His Messenger. He took one-fifth of it and divided the remainder among the Muslims. Tabari VIII:130*

> *So Muhammad began seizing their herds and their property bit by bit. He conquered Khaybar home by home. The first stronghold defeated was Naim. Next was Qamus, the community of Abi Huqayq. The Messenger took some of its people captive, including Safiyah the wife of Kinanah, and her two cousins. The Prophet chose Safiyah for himself. Tabari VIII:116/Ishaq:511*

To be fair, Mohammed did show some restraint:

> *The Apostle prohibited four things the morning of the Khaybar raid: carnal intercourse with pregnant women who were captured, mingling his seed with another man's; nor is it lawful for him to take [rape] her until she is in a state of cleanness [not menstruating]; nor can a Muslim eat the flesh of donkeys; nor eat any carnivorous animal; nor sell any booty before it has been duly allotted. Nor is it lawful for a Muslim to ride an animal belonging to the booty with the intention of returning it to the pool when he has worn it out; nor is it lawful for him to wear a garment belonging to the booty of the Muslims with the inten-*

tion of returning it to the pool [of stolen goods] when he has reduced it to rags. Ishaq:512 [2]

In the name of Islam, Mohammed and his armies raped and enslaved the conquered people's women and children before forcing them to submit to his new religion. As for their husbands and fathers, Mohammed made them watch their loved ones being violated just before he relieved them of their head. The prophet of the "religion of peace" personally beheaded over five hundred people. But that was just a venting of stress through barbaric violence, as such coercive values of indulgence in other people's women and material things could cause this.

The prophet of Islam was consistent in imparting indulgently depraved values to domestic matters, as well. At age 53 Mohammed married a six-year-old girl named Aisha. He consummated the marriage when she was nine:

When the Prophet married Aisha, she was very young and not yet ready for consummation. Tabari IX:128

The Prophet wrote the [marriage contract] with Aisha while she was six years old and consummated his marriage with her while she was nine years old and she remained with him for nine years [until he died]. Bukhari:V7B62N88

My mother came to me while I was being swung on a swing between two branches and got me down. My nurse took over and wiped my face with some water and started leading me. When I was at the door she stopped so I could catch my breath. I was brought in while Muhammad was sitting on a bed in our house. My mother made me sit on his lap. The other men and women got up and left. The Prophet consummated his marriage with me in my house when I was nine years old. Tabari IX:131

Muslims most want to emulate and aspire to be like Mohammed. He is considered in Islam as the ideal man.

You have in the Messenger of Allah a beautiful pattern of conduct for anyone to follow. Qur'an 33:21

Along with the Koran, Muslims follow the *hadiths,* which they consider to be reliable reports about how Mohammed lived his life and, along with the "divine" law of Sha'ria, are compiled together in what is known as the Sunnah or "way" of the Prophet. Living the way of Mohammed is living a holy life for Muslims, even though Mohammed was a terrorist and the Koran proudly professes terror as the means for salvation:

> *Allah said, "A prophet must slaughter before collecting captives. A slaughtered enemy is driven from the land. Muhammad, you craved the desires of this world, its goods and the ransom captives would bring. But Allah desires killing them to manifest the religion." Ishaq:327*

> *So the Prophet killed the Qurayza men. He distributed their women, children and property among the Muslims. Bukhari:V5B59N362*

> *Prepare against them whatever arms and cavalry you can muster that you may strike terror in the enemies of Allah, and others besides them not known to you. Whatever you spend in Allah's Cause will be repaid in full, and no wrong will be done to you. Qur'an:8:60*

> *The Prophet cut off the hands and feet of the men belonging to the tribe of Uraina and did not cauterize [their bleeding limbs] till they died. Bukhari:V8B82N795*

> *The infidels should not think that they can get away from us. Prepare against them whatever arms and weaponry you can muster so that you may terrorize them. They are your enemy and Allah's enemy. Qur'an: 8:59*

As you can see by these writings, it is not a coincidence that most of the world's terrorism is committed by Mohammed's followers in the name of Islam. He may be physically dead, but he lives on in the hearts and minds of over a billion people. *They aspire to Mohammed's values.* Such emotionally indulgent values are not conducive to prosperity. They are about hate, terror, destruction, coercion, and falsehoods. Western leftists would do well to pick up a Koran and read it before assisting Mohammed's modern apostles. Whenever Muslims are arrested for acting to advance this ideology, apologists say that these are only the extremists or radicals. But the core and sine qua non of Islam specifies only three options for human beings: 1. SUBMIT to theocracy as a Muslim; 2. PAY a tax as a subservient dhimmi; or 3. DIE. That's it.

> *When the sacred forbidden months for fighting are past, fight and kill the disbelievers wherever you find them, take them captive [enslave them], beleaguer them [torture them], and lie in wait and ambush them using every stratagem of war. But if they relent, [and become Muslims by . . .] performing their devotional obligations and paying the zakat tax, then open the way. Allah is Forgiving, Merciful. Qur'an 9:5*

> *Our Prophet, the Messenger of our Lord, ordered us to fight you till you worship Allah alone or pay us the Jizyah tribute tax in submission. Our Prophet has informed us that our Lord says: "Whoever amongst us is killed as a martyr shall go to Paradise to lead such a luxurious life as he has never seen, and whoever survives shall become your master." Bukhari:V4B53N386*

Those who do not believe this cannot be Muslims. This is why Muslims generally do not assimilate in non-Muslim countries and why they commit "honor killings" of their children and family members who do. This is why the leaders of Germany, Britain, and France all separately proclaimed that "multiculturalism has failed."[3] Islam is not just a religion. It is a political system and ideology which incorporates the barbarism of sharia law.[4] This includes stoning women, hanging homosexuals, amputating and/or mutilating the limbs of children, removing the female pleasure organ so that women cannot enjoy sexual relations, the rape of virgins with stated intent to prevent the virgins from a blissful afterlife, and many more affronts to civilized humanity.[5] This is the "religion of peace" which many Westerners and reality escape artists of the elite leftist mainstream media constantly crow. They feel justified by making such ridiculous statements because the Koran also contains verses about peace and tolerance. But those who cherry pick such verses as proof of a peaceful Islam, do so out of ignorance. The peaceful verses are subsequently followed by verses which require terror upon all who fail to submit to Islam, and thus the Islamic doctrine of *naksh* or "abrogation" controls in accordance with both *Qur'an 2:106 and Qur'an 16:103:*

Whatever Revelation We abrogate or cause to be forgotten, We substitute something better. Qur'an 2:106

When we replace a message with another, and Allah knows best what He reveals, they say, "you have made it up." Qur'an 16:103

Both the penultimate (sura 9) and the very last chapter (sura 5) "written" by Mohammed in the Koran contain the following instructions:

Fight and kill the disbelievers wherever you find them, take them captive, harass them, lie in wait and ambush them using every stratagem of war. Qur'an 9:5

The punishment for those who wage war against Allah and His Messenger and strive after corruption, making mischief in the land [those who refuse to surrender to Islam] is murder, execution, crucifixion, the cutting off of hands and feet on opposite sides, or they should be imprisoned. That is their degradation and disgrace in this world. And a great torment of an awful doom awaits them in the hereafter. Qur'an 5:33

Since any contradiction of verses requires that the earlier verses of peace be abrogated in favor of later verses of violence and murder, it should be clear why terror reigns supreme in Islam without objection by "the majority of peaceful Muslims." Political correctness, denial, ignorance, corruption, and laziness to investigate the values of the massive, billion-member death cult cause the international media and mendacious elite leftists to be complicit in Islamic terrorism, a phenomenon of incidences so voluminous that a separate book would be required to list them all.

House of Islam and House of War

For Muslims, there is only Dar al Islam ("House of Islam") and Dar al Harb ("House of War").[6] Any territory that is not under the control of Islam is considered to be the House of War, for which Jihad is required to bring about a world Uma or Caliphate. Jihad and *Mein Kampf* mean the same thing—"my struggle." And the means of struggle for both are the same: incitement to hatred, propaganda about the intelligent innovators (the Great Satan and/or the Little Satan), coercion, and mass murder. Any means used to indoctrinate others with hatred and falsehoods in order to incite to violence and murder is acceptable. In fact, Islamists most admire and replicate much of the propaganda they learned from their alliance with Hitler and the Nazis during the Third Reich. Hitler and the Grand Mufti of Jerusalem had a close relationship that Islam publicly reveres, as expressed in its indoctrination materials (fig. 12).

Fig. 12: Islamic indoctrination materials of anti-Semitic propaganda, same as the Nazis after their WWII alliance.

The Muslims of Persia were so enamored with Hitler's racist mass-murder doctrine that after thousands of years they changed the name *Persia* to "Aryan" or Iran.[7] Their leaders still publicly vow to fulfill Hitler's goal, but now with nuclear technology to wipe the Jewish state "off the map."[8] An Israeli nuclear reprisal is no deterrent, but is in fact welcomed by Iran's mullahcracy so they can create the chaos required before Shia Islam's twelfth Imam returns (the nephew of Mohammed).[9] No doctrine of Mutually Assured Destruction (MAD) exists to prevent an apocalypse as there was with the societies of the Cold War, even among the Islamic world's majority—Sunni Islam. This is because both Shia and Sunni Muslims welcome death through the mass murder of infidels so they can enter paradise:

> *The Prophet said, "Nobody who enters Paradise likes to go back to the world even if he got everything on the earth, except a Mujahid [Islamic fighter] who wishes to return so that he may be martyred ten*

times because of the dignity he receives." Our Prophet told us about the message of Allah: "Whoever among us is killed will go to Paradise." Umar asked the Prophet, "Is it not true that our men who are killed will go to Paradise and those of the Pagans will go to Hell?" The Prophet said, "Yes." Bukhari:V4B52N72

Allah's Apostle said, "Know that Paradise is under the shade of swords." Bukhari:V4B52N73

Honor in Deceit

The Koran promotes a value system wherein deceit and lying to non-Muslims incurs no dishonor if it is done to advance Islamic control. Such values are inconsistent with enlightenment to virtue, so they cannot produce a prosperous society. Mohammed stated that "War is Deceit," and since all societies that are not under Muslim control are considered to be in the House of War (state of war), they may be deceived in order to bring them into the House of Islam:

Allah's Apostle said, "War is deceit." Bukhari:V4B52N268

Muhammad bin Maslamah said, "O Messenger, we shall have to tell lies." "Say what you like," Muhammad replied. "You are absolved, free to say whatever you must." Ishaq:365 Tabari VII:94

Surely the hypocrites strive to deceive Allah. He shall retaliate by deceiving them. Qur'an 4:142

Allah has already sanctioned for you the dissolution of your vows. Qur'an 66:2

Magic was worked on Allah's Apostle and he was bewitched so that he began to imagine doing things which in fact, he had not done. Bukhari:V7B71N661

Umar said, "Our best Qur'an reciter is Ubai. And in spite of this, we leave out some of his statements because Allah's Apostle himself said, 'Whatever verse or revelation We abrogate or cause to be forgotten We bring a better one.'" Bukhari:V6B60N8

I am the best of plotters. I deceived them with My guile so that I delivered you from them. Ishaq:323

By Muhammad's order we beguiled them. Ishaq:442

Remember how the unbelievers plotted against you (Muhammad). They plotted, and Allah too had arranged a plot; but Allah is the best schemer. Qur'an 8:30

Westerners don't understand that Muslims do not hold truth, vows, or agreements in the same regard as the Judeo-Christian ideal:

Hajjaj said to the Apostle, "I have money scattered among the Meccan merchants, so give me permission to go and get it." Having got Mohammed's permission, he said, "I must tell lies." The Apostle said, "Tell them." Ishaq:519

That she heard Allah's Apostle saying, "He who makes peace between the people by inventing good information or saying good things, is not a liar." Bukhari:V3B49N857

The Prophet said, "If I take an oath and later find something else better than that, then I do what is better and expiate my oath." Bukhari:V7B67N427

Allah and His Messenger dissolve obligations. Qur'an 9:3

Nation-states and peoples that are not Islamic do not realize that they are in the House of War and are to be deceived at least until they convert, become a subservient dhimmi, or die. Muslim loyalty is to the Uma (Islamic world body) in furtherance of a global caliphate.[10] We must remember that Islam dominated much of the world before the Renaissance ("rebirth") of Western values, when Galileo's scientific method set the conditions for intelligent innovations in technology which outclassed the primitive means of Islamic warfare. Since the values of Islam have generally not been conducive to intelligent innovation in scientific technologies, they have been at a technological disadvantage with the West that extends to the military. Strikingly, before Mohammed arrived in the seventh century, Arab civilizations were prolific intelligent innovators. They built the pyramids and made great accomplishments in mathematics among other advances. However, the values of Mohammed changed all that. While intelligent innovation continued with the people he conquered, once his value system set in and transformed them, intelligent innovation all but ceased, except with terrorism. Islam would make few constructive technological gains, having instead to depend on oil located and extracted by American intelligent innovators seeking value and profits. In fact, most modern technologies used by the Islamic world are imported from the infidels, whose value systems are conducive to intelligent innovation.

Taqiyya and Dissimulation

At a technological and military disadvantage, Muslims are sanctioned to use any means necessary to advance Islam in accordance with the Koran and Sunna, including masking their intentions until they gain enough strength to conquer their enemies. Thus they employ any falsehood necessary in order to bring others into the House of Islam. Mainstream Islamic leaders proudly profess their intention of destroying Western life and values so they can re-establish their glory of Islam under a worldwide caliphate. *Manipulating truth as a weapon or strategy to further such intentions is called* taqiyya, *meaning dissimulation.*[11] Incidentally, this is the same way that neo-radical left Alinskyites led by Barack Obama and George Soros view the truth and why they have such an affinity for Islam—power is paramount, and manipulating the truth is a means to achieve it. Such evil is the converse of our purpose, whereby truth as enlightenment to virtue is the goal and power (measured by our treatment of others) is the bait, means, and test. This is also why no matter how many people are murdered and suffer under the coercive tyrannies of Islam, Obama continues to call it a "great religion."[12] In this context, it cannot be too surprising that upon taking office, Barack Hussein Obama's very first international call as president of the United States was to a Palestinian terrorist leader, his first international speech a humiliating American apology to one of the densest Muslim populations in the world (Cairo, Egypt), and his highest priority for the pride of American technological achievement—NASA—was "to find a way to reach out to the Muslim world and engage much more with dominantly Muslim nations to help them feel good about their historic contribution to science . . . and math and engineering."[13] And for the first time in American history, the greatest force of human freedom in world history, for which countless have died, literally bowed subserviently to the values of Mohammed. Recall how President Barack Hussein Obama bowed in submission to an overindulgent Saudi king who finances Wahhabist education and terror in America.[14]

Trojan Horse in the House of War

Through deception, Muslims have infiltrated societies in the House of War with a determined and concerted effort to transform them from within. And they have largely succeeded in the West, most effectively in Europe, but in America as well. Because elite Westerners can't see outside their own value systems, Islam has made tremendous gains, infiltrating the most important aspects of Western civilization, which include the media, the law, and finance. Islam laughs at Western political correctness, appeasement, and weakness. They know that intimidation and violence will silence the cowardly, corrupt Western mainstream media. As Islamists murder their gay population, instruct men in how to beat their women (property), and amputate or mutilate the limbs and sexual organs of children, the corrupt Western mainstream media's mindless groupthink continues to tell the world that Islam is the "religion of peace," while simultaneously promoting Islam's hatred for the only real democracy in the Middle East—Israel. The Western mainstream media is one of the greatest gifts to modern barbarism. They not only provide cover and outright lies touting the peaceful nature of Islamic values, but they duplicitously hide in fear of exposing or even printing any satire of Mohammed or Islam. The mainstream media loves to publish vulgar critiques and satire of Judaism and Christianity because they know Judeo-Christian values will not be remotely as likely to invite a homicidal bomber to their offices. Although free speech may have been a value of Western liberal democracies, it is strikingly absent when speaking of Islam. Islam has successfully intimidated the West into silence, the latter responding as weak parents to unruly children: "Just appease them to prevent a terror tantrum." But this has only emboldened them. The heart of Western civilization has become known as "Londonistan," where the development of civilized jurisprudence, from which America derived its common law, has suddenly yielded to eighty-five sharia courts and libel laws which have effectively prohibited criticism of Islam.[15] In fact, authors and publishers have been successfully sued in Britain as retribution and intimidation for writing and publishing *truths* which exposed Islamic terror-financing. In spite of that, thanks to the great efforts of organizations such as ACT for America, the U.S. Congress and several states have relatively recently passed laws providing protection for American writers and publishers under the U.S. Constitution's 1st Amendment standards.[16] But Islamic efforts to silence those who speak the truth about barbarism continue, as the fifty-seven-member Organization of Islamic States has sponsored proposed UN resolutions banning any international criticism of Islam as prosecutable hate speech.[17] U.S. Secretary of State Hillary Clinton, who has publicly professed her love for the international propaganda arm of Islam—Al Jazeera—was specifically sought out to assist the effort.[18]

Islam has even infiltrated the highest levels of Western intelligence and government. Understanding Western ignorance of Islam and political correctness, the Council on American Islamic Relations (CAIR) has worked closely with U.S. intelligence agencies. But their true agenda was revealed as an unindicted co-conspirator and sponsor of terrorism. CAIR is the American affiliate of the terrorist organizations Hamas and the Muslim Brotherhood.[19] The FBI claimed it has severed its ties with them, but Obama and his appointed Justice Department chief, Eric Holder (who called America "a nation of cowards"),[20] have aggressively pushed back against the scrutiny of Islam in America. They have even appointed a member of the Muslim Brotherhood, Mohamed Elibiary, to the Homeland Security advisory council, providing his organization with security clearance and access to sensitive U.S. security documents.[21] This appointment took place even *after* he was previously reported to have taken sensitive reports from the Texas Department of Public Safety. In an unrelated and stunningly courageous exposé, David Gaubautz, a former U.S. Air Force Office of Special Investigations agent, military counterterrorism specialist, and U.S. State Department-trained Arabic linguist, partnered with his son Chris, who bravely infiltrated CAIR as a recruit and convert to Islam.[22] They obtained over twelve thousand pages of damning confidential CAIR documents and a hundred hours of recorded video. Those CAIR materials revealed what should have been obvious, but for political correctness: CAIR exists to covertly Islamicize America. They have infiltrated not only the FBI but also the CIA, the State Department, local police departments, and even Congress, where they have placed spies on Capitol Hill as congressional staffers. Even President George W. Bush (who led "the war on terror") was fooled early on in his administration. Just after the 911 attacks, standing alongside CAIR officials and other Muslim groups at the Islamic Center of Washington, Bush stated, "It is my honor to be meeting with leaders who feel just the same way as I do. They're outraged, they're sad. They love America just as much as I do."[23] Almost a decade later, on October 15, 2009, four Congressmen from Bush's own political party held a press conference to announce CAIR's infiltration. Rep. Paul Brown (R-GA) said:

> "[CAIR] is connected to or supports terrorists [and] is running influence operations or planting spies in key national security-related offices."[24]

But CAIR was soon gratified to hear the United States chairman of the House Judiciary Committee at the time, John Conyers, an ultra-leftist, sell out his country and soul for votes in heavily Muslim populated Michigan:

> "Numerous Muslim-American interns have served the House ably and they deserve our appreciation and respect, not attacks on their character or patriotism."[25]

Had Conyers and Bush read the Koran or Sunna or noticed that no meaningful "moderate Islam" outcry against terrorism exists, they would know that Islam is incompatible with the U.S. Constitution and that deceit or taqiyya is part of Islamic doctrine. In a simple illustration of taqiyya in America, CAIR Director Dr. Bassem Khafagi intentionally promoted the fiction of "moderate Islam," but in Egypt he stated the actual truth in his own words:

> *"Moderate Islam is a violation of Islamic law."*[26]

The CAIR director also stated that:

> *". . . the U.S. constitutes a criminal element in this world."*[27]

> *If anyone contradicts or opposes the Messenger after guidance has been conveyed to him, and follows a path other than the way, We shall burn him in Hell! Qur'an 4:115*

With an extensive criminal history of his own, that same Dr. Bassem Khafagi was announced by the Egyptian Muslim Brotherhood as its candidate for president of Egypt in the wake of the so-called "Arab

Spring" of 2011. This is the same Muslim Brotherhood which produced Al Qaida terrorist chief Ayman al-Zawahiri and the same organization which assassinated Anwar Sadat in 1981 for making peace with "the little Satan," as if nearly fifteen hundred years of barbaric values would suddenly yield to an "Arab Spring." As the American front group of the Muslim Brotherhood and Hamas terrorist organizations, CAIR's exposed documents revealed seditious intent. And even after several high-level CAIR officials were convicted of terrorism-related charges, the Western media still welcomes and promotes CAIR and its officials on television and cable news programs, characterizing them as law-abiding, legitimate representatives of "moderate Islam." This American brainwashing is not only dangerous but seditious. The Western media even ignores that CAIR is largely funded by extremist Wahhabists of Saudi Arabia, the same death cult that brought us the 911 terrorists and who continue to indoctrinate Western children through Islamic deceit in school textbooks. The West needs to wake up. It is amazing that even after a prominent journalist from *60 Minutes* is gang-raped and almost murdered by teeming little Mohammeds in front of thousands of jubilant Muslims in Egypt's Taharir Square, the Western media and the Obama administration continued to tout the Arab rebellion as the "Arab Spring," implying a blossoming transformation of peace.[28] Yet their first "diplomatic" proclamation was their intent to end their peace treaty with their neighbor Israel. The values of Islam can produce only dark winter.

Unfortunately, as a result of collective guilt and demographics, it is too late for much of the West, specifically Europe. They will almost certainly become subservient dhimmis in their own land, if they aren't already. The most common baby name for boys in all of Britain is Mohammed, and it is also the most popular baby name in several other major European cities.[29] France has over 750 "no-go zones" that even police do not enter, as they are separate Muslim enclaves of sharia law.[30] The majority of the population of Belgium, also known as "Belgistan," is expected to be Muslim in less than fifteen years, and Islamists have already flooded Parliament demanding sharia law, stopping debate with shouting and threats.[31] Since the European birth rates remain low and the Muslim birth rate continues to be exceptionally high, Muslims see the inevitable outcome. They are already flexing their muscles by imposing sharia on non-Muslims. Even female European sunbathers have been physically attacked for exposing their skin.[32] In their ignorance and political correctness, twentieth and twenty-first century Europeans did not foresee the prospect of becoming the property of Islamic men. This is the fatal conceit of Western elite liberalism. Although Mohammed was illiterate, he was much smarter than they are, and he would laugh at their tolerance of an intolerant barbarism that contradicts everything elites profess to love and protect.

> Surely the hypocrites strive to deceive Allah. He shall retaliate by deceiving them. Qur'an 4:142

Fortunately, aside from America's vociferous minority of politically correct and self-absorbed/self-loathing leftists, most Americans are different than Europeans. They do not surrender so easily. In addition to their ability to piece together the worldwide pattern from even a small sampling—New York bombing in 1993, New York 9-11, Fort Hood massacre by a Muslim soldier practicing taqiyya, Madrid's train bombings, London's Tube bombings, Beslan's three hundred murdered school children, LAX murders, Bali's massacre—Americans reproduce at an average which exceeds the 2.1 babies per woman required for population growth.[33] And once fully informed of the truth of Islam through the technologically transformed new media, they will eventually ignore the pathology of the corrupt (and soon to be irrelevant) mainstream media groupthink and leftist apologists to defend Western values.

The Middle Eastern House of War

Islamic use of taqiyya is not limited to the West. It occurs everywhere that's not under Islamic control—the House of War. Lebanon is the perfect Middle Eastern microcosm to illustrate how Islam operates as a minority within nation-states to transform the values of, and eventually become, the majority. Israel, however, the only other non-Muslim majority in the Middle East, has resisted and remains the last Middle Eastern protectorate of Western Judeo-Christian values.

The Lebanon Microcosm

As a Christian majority derived from Phoenician merchants, the Lebanese state enjoyed Western values and freedoms and thus had a great tolerance of their Muslim minority. Even without the benefit of vast oil resources, Lebanon was the most prosperous nation in the Arab world, as the majority maintained the Western/Christian values conducive to prosperity. They revered education and welcomed foreigners seeking education in their prestigious universities. Their coastal city of Beirut was considered to be a cosmopolitan "French Riviera of the Middle East," as movie stars and other celebrities enjoyed the openness of predominantly Western values with an Arabic flavor. Oil sheiks came there to enjoy openly what they could not in their own Islamic monarchies. Failing to consider the impact of a culture with radically different values, Lebanon had an open-border policy. Living among the majority of Christians, Lebanese men generally had one wife in the Western tradition of "Till death do us part" and created a nuclear family to which they imparted similar values. In contrast, the Muslim minority had much different values. Muslim men generally indulge themselves in several women simultaneously as multiple wives and had many children. In accordance with Islamic values, Muslim men can dump the wives they are finished with by simply stating, *"I divorce you, I divorce you, I divorce you."*[34] Then they could quickly move on to indulge themselves with other women and have additional children. This significantly impacted Lebanese demography. But another demographic influence loomed that derived from a destructive value of Arab culture common to both Lebanese Christians and Muslims—the daily indoctrination of hate. *Christian tolerance of the intolerant Muslims in Lebanon and their shared Arab intolerance of Jews eventually led to the demise of the Christian majority and the Western way of life in Lebanon.* The commonality of Arab Jew hatred resulted in an unprovoked military attack on the neighboring nascent Jewish state and the temporary welcome of Israel's Muslim population, who expected to quickly return from Lebanon to a destroyed Israel of Jewish blood and treasure.

Brief Background of Today's Middle Eastern Nation-States—How They Got There

Because the Middle East is critical to world stability and is the subject of frequent Western debate (mostly filled with propaganda and Islamic taqiyya), a basic understanding of the early twentieth century history of the Middle East, which largely determined today's geopolitics, warrants a brief but critical digression so that informed ideological opinions may hereafter be drawn. Most of the world remains woefully ignorant of the true history of the region.

NONE OF THE INDEPENDENT STATES OF TODAY'S MIDDLE EAST EXIST-
ED UNTIL AFTER WORLD WAR I. BEFORE THEN MOSTLY SCATTERED
ISLAMIC TRIBES HAD LIVED THERE FOR APPROXIMATELY FOUR HUN-
DRED YEARS. THE NEW STATES FORMED WERE EGYPT (1922), IRAQ
(1932), SAUDI ARABIA (1932), LEBANON (1943), JORDAN (1946),
SYRIA (1948), AND ISRAEL (1948).

Because of the Islamic deception of taqiyya and the perpetual assistance of the corrupt international media, most of the world does not
know that most of today's independent Middle Eastern states did not exist in the four hundred years prior to the early 1920s. Since we know of
ancient civilizations such as Egypt and Israel, we assume that because
those names appear today, the ones which the Muslims and international
media don't deny have somehow always been there, and by association,
the other Middle Eastern states as well. However, until the early twentieth
century, the Middle East was a tribal region of different ethnicities but
mostly Arab Muslim tribes under the control of the Turkish Ottoman
Empire; an Islamic caliph which lost power to the West's technological
advances. The Turks tried to catch up with the West through secularization and an alliance with Germany in World War I. But after their defeat
in the Great War, the Turkish Ottoman Empire collapsed, and the region
came under British and French control. The British and French carved
up the region into different states. For the first time in over four hundred years, the Arabs were free of Turkish rule and both would get independent states: Turkey (1923), Egypt (1922), Iraq (1932), and Saudi Arabia
(1932). As for the backwater wasteland region known as Palestine, the
British would not only administrate the area, but would formally cede it to
the Jews on November 2, 1917 with "His Majesty's Government" approval
of the Balfour Declaration:

> His Majesty's Government view with favor the establishment in Pal-
> estine of a national home for the Jewish people, and will use their best
> endeavors to facilitate the achievement of this object, it being clearly
> understood that nothing shall be done which shall prejudice the civil
> and religious rights of existing non-Jewish communities in Palestine, or
> the rights and political status enjoyed by Jews in any other country.[35]

This was ratified as a League of Nations Mandate on July 24, 1922:

Whereas the Principal Allied Powers have also agreed that the Mandatory should be responsible for putting into effect the declaration originally made on November 2nd 1917, by the Government of His Britannic Majesty, and adopted by said powers, in favour of the establishment in Palestine of a national home for the Jewish people . . . Whereas recognition has thereby been given to the historical connection of the Jewish people with Palestine and to the grounds for reconstituting their national home in that country. . . .[36]

The area which now spans all of Jordan, Israel, Judea, Samaria, and Gaza, was thereby ceded back to the Jews after millennia of exile as a "reconstituted" Jewish state (map 1). But political winds would cause the British to renege on its promise and switch their support to an Arab alliance. In a dramatic reversal, Britain gave eighty percent of Palestine as a kingdom in honor of Arab tribal chieftain Abdullah—a direct descendant of Mohammed (through his daughter Fatima and Mohammed's first cousin Ali bin Abi Talib, the fourth caliph of Islam).[37] Although Abdullah was from Mecca in today's Saudi Arabia, in 1921 the British imported him to be ruler of most of Palestine, retitling him and the region as Emir of Transjordan (map 2).

Transjordan became the independent state of Jordan in 1946, when the British left the region. The British then, as they do today, fervently attempted to appease the Arabs of Islam. In the 1930s, American companies discovered the world's greatest known oil reserves in the Middle East, and the British knew it was under Islamic control. To appease the Muslims, they did all they could to prevent an independent state for the Jews of the Middle East, even barring entry into the region of European Jews attempting to escape Hitler's inferno. And also just as today, such appeasement of Islam did nothing to create Muslim loyalty to the British. As Hitler attacked the British in the blitzkrieg Nazi bombing of London, the Arabs of Islam quickly forgot that the British not only had freed them from the Turkish Ottoman rule but had given them kingdoms and had fought for them fervently to prevent a Jewish state.

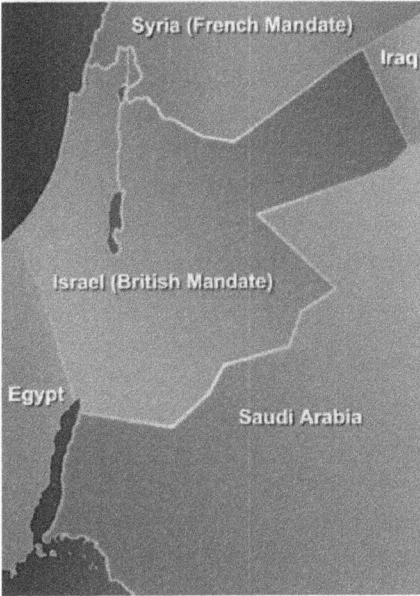

Map 1: League of Nations mandate map; Palestine including Jordan, originally supposed to be Israel.

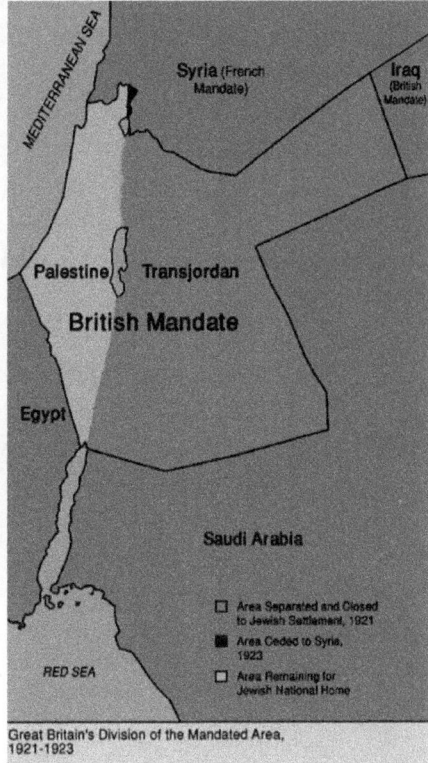

Great Britain's Division of the Mandated Area, 1921-1923

Map 2: In a dramatic reversal of League of Nations Mandate, Britain would give 80% of Palestine as a Kingdom in honor of Arab tribal chieftain Abdullah—a direct descendant of Mohammed.

The appeal of the Nazi imperative of exterminating the Jews (as Mohammed preferred) caused the Islamists to take Hitler's side against Britain, because the Islamic value of hate superseded the value of loyalty:

> The Prophet said, "If I take an oath and later find something else better than that, then I do what is better and expiate my oath." Bukhari:V7B67N427

Stretched thin militarily and sapped by World War II, the British Empire was near its end. The one hundred thousand British troops still in

Palestine had their hands full fighting to appease "Islamic sensibilities" in preventing the Jews from entering their own holy land after escape from Europe's extermination camps. The highly organized Jewish underground in Palestine, consisting of the Irgun, the Lehi, and the Hagana, would not abide. They mounted an effective campaign which included blowing up critical British military installations.[38] When the British hung members of the Jewish underground, the Jews retaliated by capturing and hanging two British soldiers. This shocked many in Britain and influenced public opinion, which demanded that their troops be brought home.[39]

As for the tiny twenty percent of Palestine remaining after Britain gave the rest (present day Jordan) to the Arab Muslims, the exhausted British army eventually turned it over to the Arabist U.N. Even though Lebanon, Jordan, and Syria had become new independent Arab and Muslim states in 1943, 1946, and 1948, respectively, U.N. Resolution 181 authorized another one to be called Palestine.[40] This would comprise half of the remaining twenty percent of the area, and was to be gerrymandered through the other half, which U.N. Resolution 181 authorized as a Jewish state—Israel (map 3).[41]

Thus, the U.N. gave the Jews only ten percent of the area legally authorized for them by both the British Balfour Declaration (1917) and League of Nations Mandate (1922), and made sure that an Arab Muslim state (Palestine) was gerrymandered through it. As most geopolitical and military experts advised, the U.N. believed this would insure the destruction of any Jewish state by the surrounding Muslim states, as it was less than the size of the Bahamas (map 4).[42] However, for the world body, authorizing a Jewish sovereign state would at least provide the appearance of conscience, albeit a feigned one, for their complicity and contributions to the recent Holocaust.

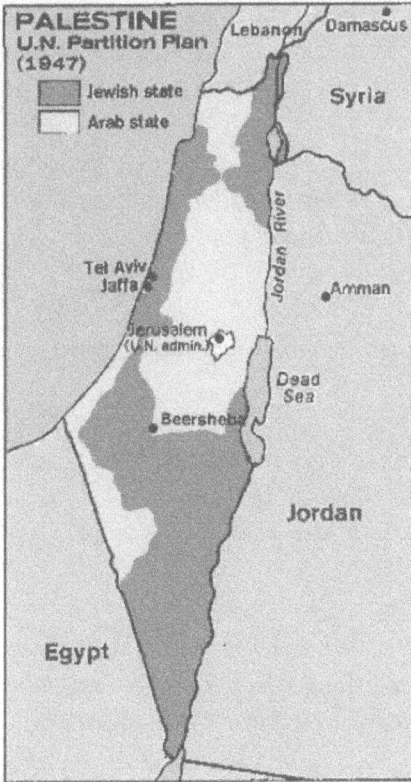

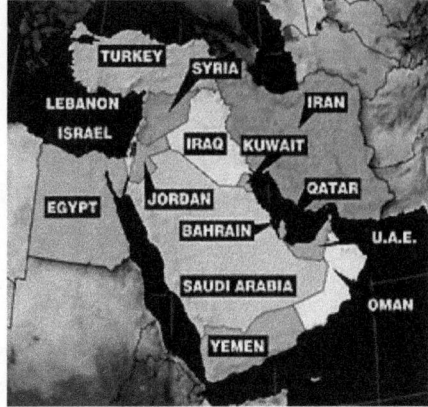

Map 4: Israel in relation to the surrounding Muslim countries.

Map 3: After giving most of the area designated for the Jews to Islam, even half of the remaining 20% would be reconfigured as an additional Arab/Muslim state of Palestine gerrymandered through the Jewish homeland.

The Muslims Won't Have It

After four hundred years of Arab statelessness, the newly created Arab states could not have any greater legitimacy than a re-established Jewish nation-state. A Jewish presence in the area dates back to Abraham and Jesus, so it's reasonable to assume that the Muslims did not design or construct the Western Wall of the Jewish Temple Mount in Jerusalem below the Aqsa Mosque. What's more, the Koran talks about Mohammed's constant interactions with Jews, and it wasn't by telephone to another continent. Just as it was back then, and even though the newly created Arab states surrounding the Jewish state were more than five hundred times its size, a sovereign Jewish state that protected all religions was unacceptable to the Arabs and Muslims.

Curses were pronounced on the unbelievers, the Children of Israel who rejected Islam, by the tongues of David and of Jesus because they disobeyed and rebelled. Qur'an 5:78

The bestial transformation occurred when Allah turned Jews into apes, despised. Ishaq:250

Allah's Apsotle said, "You Muslims will fight the Jews till some of them hide behind stones. The stones will betray them saying, 'O Abdullah (slave of Allah)! There is a Jew hiding behind me; so kill him'" Bukhari:V4B52N176

Allah's Apsotle said, "The Hour will not be established until you fight with the Jews, and the stone behind which a Jew will be hiding will say, 'O Muslim! There is a Jew hiding behind me, so kill him.'" Bukhari:V4B52N177

If military conquest of territory makes right and legitimacy over law (U.N. Resolution 181), the Muslims soon attempted to prove it—until they lost.* Therefore, all the Arabs and Muslims rejected U.N. Resolution

---

* Then they would then switch hats and claim to be displaced victims. At that time, the narrative fiction of a dispossessed "Palestinian People" or land would not be contemplated for at least twenty years because they had overwhelming military power surrounding the tiny Jewish state and believed it would be an easy slaughter. But once they realized they could not win militarily, they would turn to what they were best at, Islamic deception or taqiyya. They would effectively create the fiction of a "Palestinian People" dispossessed of their homeland. And it was an easy sell because most of the world is ignorant of the history of the region. They didn't know the truth: Palestinia was the Roman pronunciation for the Aegean sea people known as the Phillistines, an ancient foe of the Jewish people who have long since disappeared. When the Romans conquered Judea, they wanted to sever all Jewish attachment to the land, so they spitefully called it "Palestinia." When Muslims conquered the area, the Roman name disappeared from the land itself for centuries, until the British took control of the area in the twentieth century. *"Only for political and tactical reasons do we speak today about the existence of a Palestinian people, since Arab national interests demand that we posit the existence of a distinct Palestinian people to oppose Zionism."* —PLO executive committee member Zahir Muhsein, March 31, 1977, interview in the Dutch newspaper *Trouw*.

181. In line with Islamic tradition and values, the five Arab and Muslim armies from Lebanon, Syria, Iraq, Jordan, and Egypt planned to destroy and plunder the Jewish state in the spirit of Mohammed:

> We shall rouse Our (Muslim) slaves to shame and ravage you (Jews), disfiguring your faces. They will enter the Temple as before and destroy, laying to waste all that they conquer. Qur'an 17:7

To make way for Mohammed's twentieth-century warriors, Lebanon's open borders received as many as 180,000 Muslims fleeing Palestine in 1947 and 1948.[43] They were warned in advance not to get in harm's way during the Jewish slaughter and to expect a swift return to collect their share of pillaged booty.

On May 15, 1948, the day after the Israeli Declaration of Independence, five Muslim armies simultaneously attacked Israel from all directions—air, sea, and land. Unlike the nascent Jewish state, Lebanon, Syria, Iraq, Jordan, and Egypt had well equipped air forces, tanks, and the latest Soviet armaments. But Mohammed would have been ashamed, as the Jews beguiled them even without tanks, initial air power, or an adequate supply of weapons. The Jews feigned strength and held out until they could assemble sufficient ragtag forces and scrap equipment to beat back the Islamic invaders. After fleeing the ovens of Europe and enduring twenty months of five invading Muslim armies, the State of Israel was victorious, and it remains as a permanent open sore for Islam.

> "Israel is a serious wound in the Arab [Islamic] world body, and we cannot endure the pain of this wound forever. We don't have the patience to see Israel occupying part of Palestine for long. We Arabs total fifty million [in 1954. Today they total over three hundred million.] Why don't we sacrifice ten million of our number and live in pride and self-respect?" —King Saud of Saudi Arabia, 1954[44]

Lebanon had to keep all the other Muslims expecting a return to a destroyed Israel of Jewish booty, at least until the next attempt. Meanwhile, Lebanon set them up in refugee camps, where they bred many children of Islam. Lebanon's Christian majority was reaping what they sowed, and even more trouble was on the horizon with another influx of Muslims.

Verily,

> *The Holy Prophet (peace be unto him) said, "No one should pray the afternoon prayer until they are in the territory of the Qurayza because warfare against the Jews is incumbent upon Muslims." Tabari VIII:29*

Channeling Mohammed directly, on June 7, 1967, Jordan's King Hussein broadcast to his modern Muslim army:

> *"Kill the Jews wherever you find them. Kill them with your arms, with your hands, with your nails and teeth."*[45]

This happened only a week after Iraqi President Aref stated on May 31, 1967:

> *"Our goal is clear: to wipe Israel off the map."*[46]

In June of 1967, after years of terrorist raids on Israel, attempting to cut off their water supply and vengefully stockpiling a huge quantity of modern weaponry far exceeding Israel's arsenal, Egypt, Syria, and Iraq amassed hundreds of thousands of troops along Israel's border to make another go at a Muslim plunder, and would be joined later by Jordan in the Muslim effort to destroy the Jews.[47] Once again the Muslims of the Palestinian region and Israel fled to Lebanon, this time certain that they would soon return to pick up the spoils of dead Jews, as the Muslim armies had overwhelming firepower. But the Jews had the advantage of intelligence, with spies among the leaders of the invading new nation-states.[48] Israel quickly wiped out Egypt's air force while it was still on the ground. The war ended in six days, and Mohammed's disciples were again humiliated. This time Israel captured the Muslim launch areas of the attack: the Golan Heights from Syria, the West Bank (Judea and Samaria) and East Jerusalem from Jordan, and the Gaza Strip and Sinai Peninsula from Egypt, tripling Israeli territory. To mitigate their disappointment, Muslims massacred and expelled the families of Jews who had lived among Arab and Muslim populations for centuries. Hundreds of thousands of Jews residing in the newly formed Arab and Muslim nation-states were not only killed or expelled as refugees, but their property and businesses were stolen, as well. This is wholly consistent with the ways of Mohammed and Islamic values.

Meanwhile, Lebanon was becoming transformed. In addition to the masses of Muslims flooding into Lebanon (and Jordan) from Israel and the Palestinian areas, the Lebanese also had to deal with Yasser Arafat and his merry band of PLO ("Palestine Liberation Organization") terrorists of Mohammed's tradition. Arafat first tried to set up shop in Jordan, but after attempting a coup to topple the government there, King Hussein had the PLO and many civilians massacred, sending the survivors fleeing for their life. However, no Arab or Muslim country would take them in. Only multicultural Westernized Lebanon welcomed the region's most prolific terrorists, and thus Arafat and the PLO established its terrorist headquarters there. Before long, Lebanon's Christian majority became the minority.[49] Their way of life didn't just end, it ended badly. Portending Europe, leftist Lebanese Christians advocated a greater Islamic presence in government for the new "Palestinian People" and their "religion of peace." Consistent with Mohammed's values, the Islamists soon gained the upper hand and turned on and mass murdered the leftist fools who promoted "the religion of peace" in government.[50] A civil war broke out, and the Christians learned all about the unrestrained barbaric values that would soon beat them into submission. The Muslims turned Lebanon into a zone of terror, committing atrocities such as ripping Christian babies limb from limb in front of their parents.[51] Lebanon's tolerance for the intolerant ended its predominantly Western values and prosperity. They had welcomed Muslims in a naïve multicultural endeavor but ultimately suffered the brutality of the values of Mohammed as taught to Muslims for almost fifteen hundred years. Islam infiltrated the Lebanese government and tipped the scales demographically so that barbaric values of violence, terror, and deceit became dominant in Lebanese culture. Once the Muslims established their dominance in Lebanon, both Syria and the Islamic Republic of Iran established terror bases there, and the Iranian-trained holy warriors of Hezbollah drove a once flourishing and prosperous Lebanese people from the House of War into the House of Islam.

The Protectorate of Western Values

Despite all the bloodshed, Israel still stood in the House of War as the last Middle Eastern protectorate of the infidel Western values.

Consequently, in 1973, while the Jews were praying on their most holy day—Yom Kippur—Syria and Egypt made a stunning surprise attack on Israel.[52] Israel suffered heavy casualties, but they regrouped, calling up their civilian reserve military. They stopped the Islamic invaders, counterattacked, and eventually surrounded the Egyptian forces. Syria and Egypt pleaded for international help to end the war so they could live to fight another day for Islam.

Israel remains the only protectorate of Western values in the Middle East. It is the only liberal democracy in the region where the values of freedom to worship are protected for Christians, Jews, and even Muslims. Women and gays are treated with equality, and the legal system has no death penalty—not even for terrorists. *Muslims have the right to vote and hold political office. These are Western values. Interestingly, Israeli Arabs prefer to live under Israeli values of order than under the wanton street murders, violence, and torture of Mohammed's values.* Israeli/Jewish values are about invention, freedom, dignity, education, love, and celebration of life. This is the opposite of Islamic values—destruction, oppression, humiliation, ignorance, hate, and glorification of death. It shouldn't be hard to figure out which set of values results in the intelligent innovations necessary for a prosperous nation-state. Even after expending more per capita than any country on Earth for its protection against the incessant terrorist attacks by its immediate Islamic neighbors, Israel's one hundred billion-dollar plus economy is bigger than all of their economies combined, and it has the highest average living standards in the entire Middle East.[53] But both Jews and Christians and the values of prosperity which they protect would not be safe in the land where both King David and Jesus lived if Islam had its way:

> *Curses were pronounced on the unbelievers, the Children of Israel who rejected Islam, by the tongues of David and of Jesus because they disobeyed and rebelled. Qur'an 5:78*

> *Allah's Apostle said, "Plague is a means of torture sent on the Israelis." Bukhari:V4B56N679*

> *O believers, do not hold Jews and Christians as your allies. They are allies of one another; and anyone who makes them his friends is one of them. Qur'an 5:51*

As for those who deny Islam . . . they shall be the faggots for the Fire of Hell. Qur'an 2:10

They are surely Infidels who say Christ, the Messiah is God. Qur'an 5:72

Fight and kill the disbelievers wherever you find them, take them captive, harass them, lie in wait and ambush them using every stratagem of war. Qur'an 9:5

Allah made the Jews leave their homes by terrorizing them so that you killed some and made many captive. And He made you inherit their lands, their homes, and their wealth. He gave you a country you had not traversed before. Qur'an 33:26

The Jews said, "We will never abandon the Torah or exchange it for the Qur'an." Asad said, "Since you reject this proposal of mine, then kill your children and your wives and go out to Muhammad and his Companions as men who brandish swords, leaving behind no impediments to worry you. If you die, you shall have left nothing behind; if you win you shall find other women and children." The Jews replied, "Why would we kill these poor ones? What would be the good of living after them?" Ishaq:462/Tabari VIII:30

The Jews were made to come down, and Allah's Messenger imprisoned them. Then the Prophet went out into the marketplace of Medina [it is still its marketplace today], and he had trenches dug in it. He sent for the Jewish men and had them beheaded in those trenches. They were brought out to him in batches. They numbered 800 to 900 boys and men. Tabari VIII:35/Ishaq:464

The Messenger of Allah commanded that all of the Jewish men and boys who had reached puberty should be beheaded. Then the Prophet divided the wealth, wives, and children of the Banu Qurayza Jews among the Muslims. Tabari VIII:38

Jihad is holy fighting in Allah's Cause with full force of numbers and weaponry. It is given the utmost importance in Islam and is one of its pillars. By Jihad, Islam is established, Allah's Word is made su-

perior [which means that only Allah has the right to be worshiped],
and Islam is propagated. By abandoning Jihad, Islam is destroyed and
Muslims fall into an inferior position; their honor is lost, their lands
are stolen, their rule and authority vanish. Jihad is an obligatory duty
in Islam on every Muslim. He who tries to escape from this duty, dies
with one of the qualities of a hypocrite. Qur'an 2:190

After all Islamic military efforts of several combined armies failed
to destroy the tiny Jewish protectorate of Western values in 1947, 1967,
and 1973, even with Soviet technology, munitions, and support, Muslims
finally realized they did not have the military intelligence. They therefore
turned to what they were good at, the tried and true method of Islam—
taqiyya. And there was no better master of it than the father of modern
terrorism to lead the way. PLO chief and Nobel Peace Prize winner Yasser
Arafat used taqiyya prolifically—and admitted to it—in order to gain international legitimacy while constructing a Trojan Horse to destroy from
within the Middle East's only free democracy of Judeo-Christian values.
Thus, the Oslo Accords of 1993, hosted by U.S. President Bill Clinton.[54]
Only a few months after he feigned interest in a peace agreement, and
unaware that he was being recorded, Arafat told the truth to a group of
Muslims assembled in a Johannesburg mosque:

> *"This agreement, I am not considering it more than the agreement*
> *which had been signed between* OUR PROPHET MUHAMMAD *and*
> *Quraysh." [emphasis added][55]*

He concluded by inciting the worshippers *"to come and to fight*
and to start the jihad to liberate Jerusalem."[56] Arafat was referring to a ten-
year peace agreement that Mohammed signed with the pagan Arabian
tribe Quraysh.[57] Knowing that Quraysh was lulled into peaceful mode,
at the end of the very first year of the agreement, Mohammed surprise-
attacked Quraysh in order to conquer Mecca. Consistent with the values
of Mohammed, in the same month that Arafat signed the Oslo accords on
the White House lawn, he made several statements to the Arab media in
September of 1993 referring to conformance with his 1974 Plan of Phases
for Israel's destruction.[58]

Allah and His Messenger dissolve obligations. Qur'an 9:3

> *Allah has already sanctioned for you the dissolution of your vows.*
> *Qur'an 66:2*

These are Islamic values. Arafat was so effective at taqiyya that he actually got the Israeli government to hand-deliver weapons and train the PLO terrorist group. After thousands of years of persecution and international pressure, Jews and their nation-state of Israel developed the delusional pathology that appeasement of their assailants would give them some control of their fate and stop the hate and terror.[59] Like Westerners, they ignored Islamic values at their peril. After Arafat was legitimized in meetings with President Clinton and the Israeli Prime Minister, the father of modern terrorism was offered by Israel and guaranteed by the United States almost everything which he had publicly requested. Ridiculing appeasement as weakness, and without even making a counteroffer, Arafat revealed his true intent: to destroy the Jews and the Jewish state, as the PLO charter required. He used the weapons handed to him by Israel, along with suicide-homicide bombers and rockets to target infants, schoolchildren, women, and elderly civilians. Once the Israeli government woke up, the values of education, intelligent innovation, and love for life beat back the values of ignorance, hate, and destruction in the latest terrorist onslaught. This Muslim attempt to terrorize the Jews in accordance with the Koran was fulfilled, but just as the previous attempts had failed to do, it did not destroy the Jewish state. They learned, however, the Israelis' greatest vulnerability in what Jews valued most. As Arafat stated to Israeli interlocutors in 1996:

> "Are you Israelis capable of sustaining five hundred fatalities? We can readily sacrifice thirty thousand martyrs, or more. And let there be no doubt that we know what your main weakness is: [sensitivity to] *human life.*"[60]

Muslims understand the effectiveness of taqiyya and terror on those who believe in the sanctity of life. The yearning for peace and civility was a value to be exploited for their barbaric advantage. Islam had the key. Killing babies, teenagers, women, and the elderly in pizza parlors and at Passover dinners didn't faze the corrupt international media, because those killed were of a prosperous demographic or "comforted" (see Chapter 8 "Education and Media"). In fact, even though Mohammed himself would call it terror, the international media were so perverse as to

dub PLO terrorists "freedom fighters." Not only did taqiyya yield a legitimized permanent terror base in Israel, it also enabled Islam to conscript
a mercenary army of corrupt media around the world. This was much
more effective than all their suicide-homicide bombers and army inva-
sions combined. Thus, taqiyya was unleashed on an unprecedented scale.
Collaborating with the international media, Western educational institutions, vociferous radicals, useful idiots, and those coveting the sea of oil
under their feet, Islam delegitimized the Jewish state with unprecedented
and outrageous libels that most of the world believes to this day.

The Importance of the Canary

The Jews and their aggregate Israel are important because they
are the world's proverbial canary in the coal mine—as they go, so trends
the rest of the world. The modern state of Israel has been fighting Islamic
terror since its inception, and the West would have been wise to heed their
warning of what was to come. As a fraction of one percent of the world's
population, they have been anything but negligible. They have received
unparalleled persecution because their values of virtue relative to others
have yielded unparalleled success. As it is with any other culture of human beings, there are good and bad Jews—the virtuous and the corrupt.
Because of the biological and genetic impact of their learned values of
virtue stemming from the Five Books of Moses (Torah), which they have
practiced for millennia, Jews generally inherit exceptional abstract thinking ability or intelligence.[61] Corrupt Jews use such ability to achieve exceptional evil, and virtuous Jews use it to achieve exceptional good. Whether
it is Karl Marx, Saul Alinsky, George Soros, Bernie Madoff on one pole
or Von Neumann, Levi Strauss, Jonas Salk, and Albert Einstein on the
other, Jews are significantly overrepresented proportionally to the world
population on top of both polls. Although most Jews end up on the right
poll when it comes to the arts and sciences, when it comes to important
politics, many if not most Jews gravitate to the wrong poll. Since charity
and helping others are a core requirement of their learned values—

Do not stand idly by as your neighbor bleeds

—they naturally promote the institutionalization of these values within
political systems.[62] However, as with other Western cultures, most Jews
maintain a fundamentally flawed misunderstanding of charity when ad-

vocating its integration into political systems. The Five Books of Moses in the Torah instructs belief in the individual and individual charity and assistance, not the apparatus of State coercion, which is impersonal and only perpetuates dependence.

As eminent capitalists, even non-self-hating Jews in free countries of the twentieth and twenty-first centuries have demonstrated this misunderstanding through their fondness for socialism, as evident in "pre-Netanyahu Israel"* and the Democratic Party in America.† *These Jews have failed to recognize the most critical nuance*: Charity is an *individual moral* obligation, not a *State-coerced* obligation. There is little virtue in charity if it is coerced, as this is a form of servitude which creates an oppressor and oppressed relationship. Coercion and cooperation are diametrically opposed values; the former leads to misery while the latter leads to prosperity.

Intelligent Innovators—the Enemy

But when it comes to intelligent innovation, the virtuous values imparted from their instructions were understood (Torah). Consumption and practiced expenditure of such values have benefited humanity in science, medicine, law, business, and entertainment. As previously noted, along with the highest ratio of university degrees to the population in the world, Israel has more engineers and scientists and produces more scientific papers per capita than any other nation-state in the world.[63] Israel(i's) developed the cell phone, voice mail, and even instant messaging (purchased by AOL).[64] Israel's booming high-tech economy is today's epicenter of intelligent innovations, contributing dramatically increased value to the world through exports *invented* in Israel—from flash drives to drip irrigation. At the same time, no culture has been more maligned. Exceptional achievement causes envy, hatred, and libel from those with failed values. Instead of examining the causes of failure—values—it is indulgent to conjure excuses such as a global Jewish conspiracy, as if billions of people suffer because a few million prosper in free markets. Jews did not

---

* As Israeli minister of finance from 2003 to 2005, Benjamin Netanyahu rescued Israel from economic calamity. He advocated and instituted free-market financial reforms that included low taxes and reduced government spending. Both have transformed Israel and elevated it to its greatest period of prosperity, because the government has freed its citizens to achieve unprecedented intelligent innovations, over which Netanyahu currently presides as prime minister.

† Most American Jews identify and vote with the Democratic Party.

conspire to bring the world $E=mc^2$, the computer architecture (for which virtually every electronic computer ever built is rooted), the first device to allow paraplegics to walk, Hollywood, Las Vegas, Google, or Facebook. Values determine prosperity. Their aggregate State of Israel had few natural resources and little manpower, but the values of intelligent innovation and turning adversity into advantage produced a much greater (and charitable) prosperity than did the oil-rich and highly populated Islamic world around them.[65] Because of Islam's humiliating contrast in lifestyle and their cosmological security constructed around the values of their prophet Mohammed, Muslims cannot recognize the true causes of their misery—the *values* of Mohammed.

With leaders who oppress them and overindulge in the vast wealth created by their oil industry, why wouldn't the people revolt?* To maintain power, the leadership must deflect their citizens' anger and frustration onto an enemy. The best enemy to designate is one which evokes great emotion. Prosperity evokes the powerful emotion of envy in those who are needy. Thus, the world's top two intelligent innovators—America and Israel—became the Great Satan and the Little Satan. This is exactly the deal that the Saudi dictators made with the Islamic clergy in order to preserve their own power. The Islamic clergy were all too happy to fill the restive population with hate toward the Western infidels instead of the rulers and the values that are the true oppressors. Therefore, the Islamists instilled the most virulent Wahhabist hatred in their oppressed peoples, providing both fuel and direction for them to vent their anger toward the external enemy. This produced the 911 terrorists, thousands of mass murderers, and millions of jihadists just waiting for the call to kill. And the Muslim leaders laughed amongst themselves as Americans financed the export of Islamic culture into American textbooks, educational institutions, the media, government agencies, prisons, and mosques through the purchase of the oil located below Saudi palaces. But Saudi Arabia isn't the only country to blame for spreading such virulent hate, as this reflects the values of Islam and the Muslim world.

---

* However, some oil-rich governments of Islamic culture placate their citizens with largesse from the proceeds of oil, keeping them dependent and complacent rather than self-reliant and productive.[66]

The Values of Hate

Life is cheap in the Muslim world. The agreed-upon exchange rate in the Middle East is hundreds of Muslim terrorists in Israeli jails for one kidnapped Jew. That is how every trade works out between them. *The value of each Muslim is actually tied to their values.* One Israeli will likely innovate something which contributes to world prosperity, while that person's Islamic counterpart will probably be strapped into a vest rigged with explosive devices that will be detonated for mass destruction in a public market, on an airplane, or at a private wedding. So why is life so cheap in Islam? It all comes down to their values. From the moment a baby is born in the Muslim world they are indoctrinated with hate every day at home, in school, and through their media outlets.

Fig. 13: Picture of Islamist (Hamas) baby with suicide-homicide belt (Picture: IDF)

The hatred is produced as a weapon; the greatest honor and glory for Muslim children is to indulge that hatred by sacrificing their life in exchange for an afterlife of bliss. Even small children are dressed in paramilitary garb, complete with weapons and suicide-homicide belts, to pose for endearing family photos (fig. 13). The Hitler Youth which they were modeled after look like Boy Scouts and Girl Scouts in comparison. As an actual statement broadcasted to their youth by their own television stations, Muslim children are *"created to be fertilizer for the land of Palestine, to saturate the land with their blood."*[67]

Fig. 14-19: Islamic youth in paramilitary garb and suicide-homicide belts, and Muslim grandmothers inciting killing. (Source: "iranpoliticsclub.net")

And the Persian Shia Muslims of Iran treat their children no differently from those of the Arab Sunni Muslims of Palestine. During the Iran-Iraq war (1980-1988), Islamic values produced a most efficient technology to clear the Iraqi-laid minefields—children. Iran imported five hundred thousand small plastic keys from Taiwan, and before each mission a key would be hung from each child's neck to be used as their key to the gates of paradise. To prevent the escape of those who lost their nerve, children were roped together in groups before they were sent to clear the minefields:

> They went into the mine fields. Their eyes saw nothing. Their ears heard nothing. And then, a few moments later, one saw clouds of dust. When the dust had settled again, there was nothing more to be seen of them. Somewhere, widely scattered in the landscape, there lay scraps of burnt flesh and pieces of bone.[68]

But Muslims are not completely without compassion for their children, and Islamic technology is always advancing. Hence,

> Before entering the mine fields, the children [now] wrap themselves in blankets and they roll on the ground, so that their body parts stay together after the explosion of the mines and one can carry them to the graves.[69]

Are all cultures really as equal as Western elites teach? Only the values of hate can inspire a society to celebrate and pass out candy when three thousand civilian men, women, and children are incinerated, crushed, or forced to jump to their death at New York's World Trade Center, while the families of the victims continued to contribute billions of dollars in aid to those who perpetuate such hate. To paraphrase one of the first democratically elected female world leaders in history, peace will come when Muslims learn to love their children more than they hate others.[70] Because hate and terror are integral values of the warlord Mohammed and the Koran, there can be no peace as long as either are part of Islam. No society can prosper when hate exceeds love.

CONCLUSION

The Unified Field

As each culture clearly demonstrates, the values we consume and expend determine prosperity or misery. Values belong to no culture, but to humanity. Just as any person can idealize and select particular ingredients to prepare a specific meal of health or toxicity, any society can idealize and select particular values to produce a specific culture of prosperity or misery. The consequences of such choices are intended to impact us experientially on our path to enlightenment of virtue.

- VIRTUE: Truth, Industry, Moderation, Self-Reliance, Education, Contribution, Intelligent Innovation, Hope, Faith, Love, Charity, Respect, Cooperation, and Protection of Life, Liberty, and Property = PROSPERITY

- DEPRAVITY: Relativism, Indolence, Overindulgence, Dependence, Ignorance, Entitlement, Complacency, Despair, Doubt, Hate, Greed, Envy, Coercion, Glorification of Death, Tyranny, and Collectivism = MISERY

The various cultures and societies derive from permutations of these universally accessible values. The evidence is clear; toxic information or values produce toxic cultures of misery and suffering, while healthy information or values produce healthy cultures of prosperity and happiness.

Inextricable Singularity

And hereon there can be no legitimate claim of any difference between the social and physical sciences with regard to the application of truth and scientific methodology for health and prosperity, as the following demonstrates logically irrefutable proof of *the inextricable singularity* to forever unify the fields of physics, biology, sociology, anthropology, and economics. No one can legitimately dispute the laws of physics governing open systems. Since everything is decaying in accordance with the second law of energy or entropy, we know that open systems must consume, convert, channel and expend energy to survive. But critically, most people and cultures generally fail to recognize that *information modulates energy, couples with energy, and is a catalyst of life and death,* depending upon the type of information transmitted and consumed; if you didn't know what was fatal and what was of value you could not survive. So how do we know what is fatal and what is of value? Information! Information not only affects us sociologically, economically, biologically, and genetically, but physiologically too. When we receive a life altering letter, email, or phone call informing us of catastrophic or great news, our body manifests very different physiological reactions. Depending upon the information, we might throw up in horror or cry with joy. The information modulates our energy and its manifestations. And the information transmitted is either true or false, one or the other, and this can and does make all the difference for life and death, happiness and suffering.

Information is consumed in many ways, and as mentioned previously, these include transmission by our primary caretakers, government, education and the media, the observation of cause and effect, or even reading the pages of a book such as the Torah, the New Testament, the Book of Mormon, the Koran, etc. Once the information is consumed, it is converted to meaning as it is channeled through the organs of our brain, coupled with our energy, and expended by the method which we act on it—what we do with the information or how we apply it. This is why information or knowledge is only *potential* power.[1] Just as specific values entered into a computer yield the same specific results through conversion, channeling and modulation of energy expenditure, the same is true of specific information processed by the computer we call the brain. Specific information about how we are to conduct ourselves is fundamentally comprised of specific elemental values or quanta, which when consumed, is converted to meaning, and coupled and channeled with our energy to modulate energy expenditure.

If we enter the universal numerical values of one plus three into a working calculator, it will always equal four, regardless of the culture or nationality of the person entering them, as mathematics is a universal constant or language of the universe. Human beings and their aggregate societies generally have choice about the universally available informational values they enter into their system nation-states, and must make decisions on which to choose. Such information and its transmission, consumption, conversion, channeling and coupling with energy, and its modulation of energy expenditure within physical open systems BRIDGES

AND UNIFIES THE SOCIAL AND PHYSICAL SCIENCES, comprising the socio-logical values which manifest culturally to produce physical nation-state economies, thus defining the UNIFIED FIELD of the physical and social; physics, biology, sociology, anthropology, and economics. In other words, the operation of open systems exchanging energy and matter by informa-tion modulation, specifically the energy and information transmitted and consumed by the *physical* open system and its conversion, channeling and expenditure as *sociological* values *unify the physical and social sciences,* logically requiring one *truth* to produce optimum health and prosperity of the open system.

The truth is that we accelerate/increase the decay/entropy of open systems by overindulgence, e.g., government overconsumption in taxation and overspending/expenditures on entitlements, and resist it through moderation and restraint, with virtue as the ultimate antidote. These are expressed by our cultural values—information and energy—and positions along the political spectrum. To resist entropy most effec-tively for prosperity, our cultural values must be conducive to the virtue of intelligent innovation, because although productivity is the fuel of pros-perity, intelligent innovation is the elixir which determines the octane. Such conditions are maximally achieved only when the life, liberty, and property of each individual are protected and due process and equal treat-ment is afforded to all. These are the responsibilities of virtue which true freedom requires. Under these protections, both freedom and incentive are maximized so that people naturally gravitate toward their interests, talents, and passions to create the greatest value in goods and services to others for commensurate compensation without fear of plunder by oth-ers, maximizing GDP to most effectively resist entropy for the ultimate prosperity. This is natural capitalism.

NOTES

Introduction

1. Moses Maimonides, *The Guide for the Perplexed*, 1190 A.D.
2. Deloitte Touche Tohmatsu Limited, 2012.
3. Lawrence O'Donnell, *Morning Joe*, MSNBC, November 5, 2010; Ed Shultz, *The Ed Shultz Show*, March 23, 2010; Rachel Maddow; *The Rachel Maddow Show*, December 9, 2011.
4. *Newsweek*, February 9, 2009.
5. Ronald Reagan, Liberty State Park, Jersey City, New Jersey, September 1, 1980.

Chapter 1

1. Jaime E. Settle, Christopher T. Dawes, Nicholas A. Christakis and James H. Fowler, "Political Orientations Are Correlated with Brain Structure in Young Adults," 2011; Ryota Kanai, Tom Feilden, Colin Firth, and Geraint Rees, "Friendships Moderate an Association between a Dopamine Gene Variant and Political Ideology," 2009. [the word "right" on the left side of the monitor or the word "left" on the right side of the monitor "to detect and signal the occurrence of conflicts in information processing."]
2. "Islam's War on Muslim Mothers, Daughters, Sisters," Atlasshrugs2000.typepad.com, July 10, 2010.
3. Werner Heisenberg,"*Ueber den anschaulichen Inhalt der quantentheoretischen Kinematik und Mechanik*" [original paper on Uncertainty Principle], 1927.
4. Agustin Blazquez with the collaboration of Jaums Sutton, *Political Correctness: The Scourge of Our Times*, April, 8, 2002.
5. Ibid.
6. Ibid.
7. Ibid.
8. Saul Alinsky (1909-1972).
9. Saul Alinsky, *Rules for Radicals*, 1971; NEA.org.
10. Richard Poe, "The Chicago Connection: Hillary, Obama and the Cult of Alinsky," The Turrish Weekly, March 2, 2008.
11. Id.
12. Alinsky, *Rules for Radicals*, 1971, pp.10-11.

13. Id at *Prologue xv.*
14. Karl Polanyi, *The Great Transformation: the Political and Economic Origins of Our Time, 1944.*
15. Napoleon Hill, *Think and Grow Rich,* 1937.
16. Arthur Shopenhauer, *On the Will to Nature,* 1836.
17. George Gilder, *The Israel Test,* 2009.

Chapter 2

1. A.R. Radcliffe-Brown, *The Andaman Islanders,* 1965; Richard R. Wilk and Lisa C. Cliggett, *Economies and Cultures, Foundations of Economic Anthropology,* 2007.
2. CBS News, "How Celebs Make a Living After Death," June 20, 2010.
3. Alexandr Solzhenitsyn, *The Gulag Archipelago,* 1973.

Chapter 3

1. *"Max Planck – Biography,"* Nobelprize.org, May 20, 2012.
2. Adam Smith, *An Inquiry into the Nature and Causes of the Wealth of Nations,* 1776.
3. Id at Book 1, chapter 5.
4. Karl Marx and Friedrich Engels, *The Communist Manifesto,* 1848.
5. Arjun Appadurai, *The Social Life of Things: Commodities in Cultural Perspective, 1986.*
6. George Gilder, *Silicon Israel,* City Journal Summer 2009.
7. Fox News, February 1, 2010.
8. Fox News, *The O'Reilly Factor,* March 2010.
9. Elena Kagan, U.S. Supreme Court, Oral Arguments on Health Care Mandate, *Department of Health and Human Services v. Florida (11-398),* March 28, 2012.
10. Alexander Hamilton, Federalist 21, *Other Defects of the Present Confederation,* Independent Journal, December 12, 1787.
11. Michael F. Sproul, *Backed Money, Fiat Money, and the Real Bills Doctrine,* Working Paper 789, Department of Economics, University of California, Los Angeles, Bunche 2263, March 14, 1999.
12. Danika, "Productivity and GDP of Nations," Danika's Thoughts on Globalization, WordPress.com, November 7, 2006.
13. Milton Friedman & Anna Jacobson Schwartz, *A Monetary History of the United States, 1857-1960,* 1963.
14. Milton Friedman, *Capitalism and Freedom* 2002 (1962), p. 50.

Chapter 4

1. Albert Einstein, from the soundtrack of the film, *Atomic Physics*, J. Arthur Rank Organization, Ltd., 1948.
2. Peter Tyson, "The Legacy of E=mc²," NOVA, pbs.org, October 11, 2005.
3. Eugene Wesley Roddenberry, *Star Trek*, 1964. Desilu Productions, 1966-67, Paramount Television, 1967-69.
4. Arthur Eddington, a British astronomer, coined the term "Thermodynamic Arrow of Time" in 1927.
5. Hew Price, *The Thermodynamic Arrow: Puzzles and Pseudo-Puzzles*, Cornel University Library, February 6, 2004.
6. Ibid.
7. Jeff Tollaksen, "Back to the Future," *Discovery* magazine, April or May 2010.
8. Jeffrey Long, M.D., *Evidence of the Afterlife*, 2011.
9. Charles B. Thaxton, et. al., "The Mystery of Life's Origin," 7-15, *Thermodynamics of Livings Systems*, 1992.
10. Michael Tanner, How We Spend Nearly a Trillion a Year Fighting Poverty—and Fail. Policy Analysis, 694,The CATO Institute, April 11, 2012.
11. Arthur Laffer, *The Laffer Curve, Past, Present, and Future,* 2004. Coined by Jude Wanniski of the Wall Street Journal in 1974 after a meeting between economist Arthur Laffer, Wanniski, Dick Cheney, and Donald Rumsfeld, and Grace-Marie Arnett. In the meeting, Laffer was arguing against Gerald Ford's tax increase, and he reportedly sketched the curve on a napkin to illustrate the concept.

Chapter 5

1. Napoleon Hill, *Think and Grow Rich,* 1937; James Allen, *As a Man Thinketh,*1902.
2. Napoleon Hill, *Think and Grow Rich,* 1937.

Chapter 6

1. Alinsky, *Rules for Radicals,* 1971, pps.127-134.
2. Deloitte Touche Tohmatsu Limited, 2012.
3. President Obama in Quincy, Illinois, April 28, 2010.
4. George Soros, *The Age of Fallibility: The Consequences of the War on Terror,* 2006, Prologue.
5. Soros, "Why Obama Has to Get Egypt Right," *The Washington Post,*

February 3, 2011.

6. Senator Barack Obama, in Toledo, Ohio, October 13, 2008, "I think when you spread the wealth around, it's good for everybody."

7. Soros interviewed by Steve Kroft on CBS News's *60 Minutes*, November 5, 2006.

8. Soros, "America Needs Stimulus Not Virtue," *Financial Times*, October 4, 2010.

9. Margaret Thatcher, British prime minister, interview by Llew Gardner on *This Week*, Thames Television, February 5, 1976.

10. Benjamin Franklin, Pennsylvania Assembly: Reply to the Governor, November 11, 1755. —*The Papers of Benjamin Franklin,* ed. Leonard W. Labaree, vol. 6, p. 242 (1963). "Those who would give up essential Liberty, to purchase a little temporary Safety, deserve neither Liberty nor Safety."

11. Adolph Hitler, *Mein Kampf,* 1925.

12. George Gilder, *The Israel Test,* 2009, p. 66.

13. James Cameron, *Avatar,* 20th Century Fox, 2009.

14. Milton Friedman, "From Cradle to Grave," *Free to Choose* (television series), vol. 4, 1980.

Chapter 7

1. Peter Roff, "Pelosi's Imperial Speakership: Gulfstream Jets for Her Congressional Air Force," *U.S. News & World Report,* August 6, 2009.

2. Steve Kroft, "Insiders," CBS News's *60 Minutes,* November 13, 2011. Pelosi participates in largest IPO (VISA 2008) just as legislation that would hurt the company was moving through her chamber (the House). It never made it to the House floor.

3. Derek Thompson, "Report: Washington, D.C., Is Now the Richest U.S. City," *The Atlantic,* October 19, 2011.

4. Benjamin Franklin, Constitutional Convention of 1787, when queried as he left Independence Hall on the final day of deliberation, quoted in the notes of Dr. James McHenry, one of Maryland's delegates to the Convention, *The Records of the Federal Convention of 1787,* ed. Max Farrand, vol. 3, appendix A, p. 85 (1911, reprinted 1934). "A lady asked Dr. Franklin, Well, Doctor, what have we got, a republic or a monarchy?" A republic, replied Franklin, if you can keep it."

5. Steve Kroft, "Insiders," CBS News's *60 Minutes,* November 13, 2011.

6. Ibid.

7. Dennis Cauchon, "Federal Pay Ahead of Private Industry," *USA To-*

day, March 8, 2010.

8. Lord Acton, letter to Mandell Creighton, April 5, 1887. —Acton, *Essays on Freedom and Power*, ed. Gertrude Himmelfarb, 1972, pp. 335–36. "Power tends to corrupt and absolute power corrupts absolutely."

9. Deloitte Touche Tohmatsu Limited, 2012; "Facts About Israel and the U.S.," America-Israel Friendship League, http://www.aifl.org/html/web/resource_facts.html, 2012.

10. NASDAQ, 2012.

11. Jaime E. Settle, Christopher T. Dawes, Nicholas A. Christakis and James H. Fowler, "Political Orientations Are Correlated with Brain Structure in Young Adults," 2011; Ryota Kanai, Tom Feilden, Colin Firth, and Geraint Rees, "Friendships Moderate an Association between a Dopamine Gene Variant and Political Ideology," 2009. [the word "right" on the left side of the monitor or the word "left' on the right side of the monitor   "to detect and signal the occurrence of conflicts in information processing."]

12. Ibid.

13. Charles Darwin, *Origin of Species*, 1859.

14. Barack Obama, *Dreams from My Father*, 1995; Barack Obama, *The Audacity of Hope*, 2006.

15. David Maraniss, *Barack Obama:The Story*, June 19, 2012.

16. Dinesh D'Souza, *The Roots of Obama's Rage*, 2010.

17. Brian Ross, "Obama's Pastor: God Damn America, U.S. to Blame for 9/11," ABC News, March 13, 2008.

18. Alinsky, *Rules for Radicals*, 1971.

19. Michael Crowley, "Obama's Risky Fight Against the Chamber of Commerce," *Time* magazine, October 14, 2010; Aaron Blake, "Obama's 'You Didn't Build That' Problem," *The Washington Post*, July 18, 2012.

20. Senator Barack Obama, in Toledo, Ohio, October 13, 2008, "I think when you spread the wealth around, it's good for everybody."

21. Ben Franklin, Founding Father of United States of America (1706-1790).

22. Underwood Tariff Act/Revenue Act, 1913.

23. David Kocieniewski, "G.E.'s Strategies Let It Avoid Taxes Altogether," *The New York Times*, March 24, 2011.

24. James A. Watkins, "Public Employee Labor Unions," Hubpages.com, 2012.

25. Ibid.

26. Ibid.

27. Paul Connor, "Labor Unions Primary Recipients of Obamacare Waivers," TheDailyCaller.com, January 6, 2012.

28. MediaTrackers.com, June 2011.

29. Star Parker, *Uncle Sam's Plantation: How Big Government Enslaves America's Poor and What We Can Do About It*, 2003.

30. Rick Moran, "Rep. Waters: 'Tea Party can go straight to hell,'" *American Thinker*, August 22, 2011.

31. Alicia M. Cohn, "Democratic Rep. Waters calls GOP leadership 'demons,'" TheHill.com, February 15, 2012.

32. Michelle Malkin, "Maxine Waters: Swamp Queen," MicheleMalkin.com, April 27, 2011.

33. George Soros, *The Alchemy of Finance*, 1987.

34. Wilfred McClay, "The Moral Economy of Guilt," FirstThings.com, May 2011, pps 1, 6.

35. Id at p 8.

36. Barack Obama's address to his supporters in St. Paul, Minnesota, after clinching the nomination as the Democratic Party candidate for President of the United States on June 3, 2008.

37. Illustration: Showing famous leftist George Bernard Shaw's London School of Economics' stained glass mural of Fabian Socialist's hammering a heated globe to their "heart's desire."

38. David Rockefeller, chairman of the board of the Chase Manhattan Bank in 1973, "From a China Traveler," *The New York Times*, August 10, 1973.

39. Frederic Bastiat, *The Law*, 1850.

40. Vladimir Ilyich Lenin (1870–1924), Russian Marxist.

Chapter 8

1. John Perazzo, "In the Tank: A Statistical Analysis of Media Bias," FrontPageMagazine.com, October 31, 2008; Seymour Martin Lipset, "The Sources of Political Correctness On American Campuses," The Hoover Institution, 1992.

2. Joel Klein, "The Failure of American Schools," *The Atlantic*, June 2011.

3. NEA.org

4. Michael Graham, "Schools Confusing Effort with Results," *The Boston Herald*, July 20, 2010.

5. Jim Vicevich, "School Kids Taught to Sing Praise to Obama," Radioviceonline.com, September 24, 2009.

6. Adolph Hitler, Germany (1889-1945).

7. Woody Allen, *Annie Hall*, 1977.
8. Seymour Martin Lipset, "The Sources of Political Correctness On American Campuses," The Hoover Institution, 1992.
9. Dan Aykroyd, *Ghostbusters*, Columbia Pictures, 1984.
10. CBS New York, "Report: Group of Columbia University Students to Dine with Iranian President," September 13, 2011; Raja Abdulrahim, "Protest at UC Irvine Against Israeli Official Still Reverberates," *Los Angeles Times*, 2010.
11. Ayn Rand, *The Virtue of Selfishness*, 1964.
12. Ibid.
13. Herman Cain, "Stupid People Are Ruining America", Youtube.com, February 11, 2011.
14. YouTube.com
15. YouTube.com
16. Finley Peter Dunne (1867-1936).
17. W. M. L. Finlay, "Pathologizing Dissent: Identity Politics, Zionism and the 'Self-Hating Jew,'" *British Journal of Social Psychology*, June 2005, Vol. 44 No. 2.
18. Bernard Goldberg, *The O'Reilly Factor*, Fox News, June 19, 2010.
19. Don Wade, *Wade and Roma Show*, 890 WLS, Chicago, IL, September 15, 2009.
20. Kevin Ferris, "Put AG Holder on the Stand; Black Panther Case Dismissal Suggests Justice isn't Blind," *The Columbia Daily Tribune*, July 11, 2010.
21. Bob Schieffer, *Face the Nation*, CBS News, July 11, 2010.
22. Howard Kurtz, *Reliable Sources*, CNN, July 18, 2010.
23. Ibid.
24. David A. Graham, "The New Black Panther Party Is the New ACORN," *Newsweek*, July 14, 2010.
25. Chris Matthews, MSNBC's Potomac Democratic Party Primary Coverage, March 27, 2008; Chris Matthews, *The Tonight Show with Jay Leno*, July 21, 2008.
26. Matthew Sheffield, "AP President Dean Singleton Slobbers Over Obama in Gushing Speech," NewsBusters.com, April 3, 2012.
27. Anita Dunn, Obama administration communications director, speaking at the Washington National Cathedral for the graduation ceremony of St. Andrews Episcopal School students, June 5, 2009.
28. Ron Bloom, Obama administration manufacturing czar, speaking at the Sixth Annual Distressed Investing Forum at the Union League

Club in New York. Feb 27-28, 2008.

29. Van Jones, Obama administration green jobs czar, keynote speaker at the Power Shift 2009 Youth Conference, February 27, 2009.

30. Mark Lloyd, Obama administration diversity czar for the FCC, speaking at the National Conference for Media Reform, June 10, 2008.

31. Bob Woodward and Carl Bernstein, *The Washington Post* [Watergate], 1972.

32. Ballotpedia.org, 2012.

33. NBC News.com, "After 'Shellacking,' Obama Laments Disconnect with Voters; President Vows to Work with GOP, but Stands Firm on Health Care, Tax Cuts," November 3, 2010.

34. Dan Gainor, "Why Don't We Hear About Soros' Ties to Over 30 Major News Organizations?" Foxnews.com, May11, 2011.

35. mrc.org

36. Dan Gainor, "Soros-Funded Lefty Media Reach More Than 300 Million Every Month," mrc.org, May 25, 2011.

37. Dan Gainor, "Soros Spends Over $48 Million Funding Media Organizations," mrc.org, May 18, 2011.

38. Molly Stark, "January 2011 Ratings: Fox News on Top for 9 Years; Beats MSNBC, CNN Combined," Mediabistro.com, February 1, 2011.

39. Doug Ross, "Unprecedented: White House Tries to Ban Fox from Press Pool," Directorblue.com, October 22, 2009.

40. FoxNews.com, "White House Urges Other Networks to Disregard Fox News," October 19, 2009.

41. Doug Ross, "Unprecedented: White House Tries to Ban Fox from Press Pool," Directorblue.com, October 22, 2009.

42. Tony Romm, "White House officials on Fox News: 'It's not a news organization,'" TheHill.com, October 18, 2009.

43. DiscovertheNetworks.org, "Organizations Funded Directly by George Soros and his Open Society Institute," October 2011.

44. Ben Smith, "Media Matters' war against Fox," Politico.com, March 26, 2011.

45. TheDailyCaller.com, "Inside Media Matters: Sources, Memos Reveal Erratic Behavior, Close Coordination with White House and News Organizations," February 12, 2012.

46. Ibid.

47. Ibid.

48. Jonathan Strong, "Documents Show Media Plotting to Kill Stories about Rev. Jeremiah Wright," TheDailyCaller.com, July 20, 2010.

49. Ibid.

50. Liberty Chick, "'Anonymous' Leaks Assad Emails; ABC Interview Tips Exposed: 'American Psyche Easily Manipulated; Prey on Liberal Guilt,'" BigJournalism.com, February 2012.

51. Seth McFarlane, *Family Guy* and *American Dad*, Fox, 2012.

52. Matt Stone and Trey Parker, *South Park*, Comedy Central, 2012.

53. Matt Stone and Trey Parker, *Team America: World Police*, Paramount Pictures, 2004.

54. Jay Roach, *Game Change*, HBO, 2012.

55. Gary Fleder, *Runaway Jury*, 20th Century Fox, 2003.

56. Tom Kapinos, *Californication*, Showtime, 2012.

57. Friedrich Hayek, *The Road to Serfdom*, 1944.

58. Adrian Rodgers, *God's Way to Health and Wisdom [sermon series]*, 1984.

Chapter 9

1. Lin Biao, *Report to the Ninth National Congress of the Communist Party of China*, Foreign Languages Press, 1969.

2. www.state.gov, U.S. Department of State, 2012.

3. Masha Gessen, "The Wrath of Putin," *Vanity Fair*, April 2012.

4. Rahm Emanuel, *The Wall Street Journal* CEO Council in Washington, D.C., November 19, 2008.

5. Franklin D. Roosevelt, Inaugural Address, March 4, 1933, as published in Samuel Rosenman, ed., *The Public Papers of Franklin D. Roosevelt, Volume Two: The Year of Crisis*, 1933 (New York: Random House, 1938), 11–16.

6. Burton W. Folsom, Jr., "The Progressive Income Tax in U.S. History, The Root of Much Evil," *The Freeman*, Volume 53 Issue 5, The Foundation for Economic Education, May 2003.

7. The U.S. Constitution, *Article 1, Sec 8, (1)*.

8. Thomas Jefferson, letter to Joseph Milligan, April 6, 1816.

9. U.S. Supreme Court Justice Stephen Field, *Pollock v. Farmers' Loan & Trust Company*, 1895.

10. James Madison, 4 Annals of Congress 179, 1794.

11. 16th Amendment, The U.S. Constitution, passed by Congress on July 2, 1909, ratified February 3, 1913.

12. Ibid.

13. In relevant part, "Neither slavery nor involuntary servitude, except as punishment for crime whereof the party shall have been duly convicted, shall exist within the United States, or any place subject to

their jurisdiction." 13th Amendment, The U.S. Constitution, passed by Congress January 31, 1865, Ratified December 6, 1865; In relevant part, "All persons born or naturalized in the United States, and subject to the jurisdiction thereof, are citizens of the United States and the State wherein they reside. No State shall make or enforce any law which shall abridge the privileges or immunities of citizens of the United States; nor shall any State deprive any person of life, liberty, or property without due process of law; nor deny to any person within its jurisdiction the equal protection of the laws." 14th Amendment, The U.S. Constitution, passed by Congress January 13, 1866, ratified July 9, 1868.

14. The United States Revenue Act of 1913, October 3, 1913, ch. 16, 38 Stat. 114.

15. Thomas Jefferson, First Inaugural Address, March 4, 1801.

16. The Federal Reserve Act, December 23, 1913, 12 U.S.C. ch.3, ch. 6, 38 Stat. 251.

17. Milton Friedman and Anna Jacobson Schwartz, *A Monetary History of the United States, 1857-1960*, 1971.

18. Milton Friedman, *Capitalism and Freedom*, 1962.

19. Lawrence M. Stratton and Paul Craig Roberts, "The Fed's 'Depression' and the Birth of the New Deal," Hoover Institution, Stanford University, August 1, 2001.

20. Ibid.

21. Ibid.

22. "The powers not delegated to the United States by the Constitution, nor prohibited by it to the states, are reserved to the states respectively, or to the people." 10th Amendment, U.S. Constitution, 1791.

23. James Madison, *The Federalist No. 41*, Independent Journal, January 19, 1788.

24. James Madison, Letter to James Robertson, April 20, 1831.

25. James Madison, Speech on Ratification of Federal Constitution, June 6, 1788.

26. James Madison, speech, House of Representatives, during the debate "On the Memorial of the Relief Committee of Baltimore, for the Relief of St. Domingo Refugees," January 10, 1794.

27. James Madison, letter to Edmund Pendleton, January 21, 1792.

28. James Madison, addressing the House of Representatives, referring to a bill to subsidize cod fisherman introduced in the first year of the new Congress, February 7, 1792.

29. Thomas Jefferson, letter to Albert Gallatin, 1817.

30. Thomas Jefferson, letter to George Washington on the constitutionality of the Bank of the United States, 1791.

31. "Democracy in America, Overinterpreting," *The Economist*, April 6, 2011.

32. Nancy Pelosi, Speaker of the House, remarks at the 2010 Legislative Conference for National Association of Counties, Washington, D.C., March 9, 2010.

33. Lawrence M. Stratton and Paul Craig Roberts, "The Fed's 'Depression' and the Birth of the New Deal," Hoover Institution, Stanford University, August 1, 2001.

34. Philadelphia Reflections, "Owen Roberts: A Switch in Time," 2012. http://www.philadelphia-reflections.com/blog/599.htm.

35. Ibid.

36. Ibid.

37. Burton W. Folsom, Jr., "The Progressive Income Tax in U.S. History, The Root of Much Evil," *The Freeman*, Volume 53 Issue 5, The Foundation for Economic Education, May 2003.

38. Michael McMenamin, "Tedious Fraud: Reagan Farm Policy and the Politics of Agricultural Marketing Orders," CATO Institute, December 6, 1983.

39. Chris Edwards, "Milk Madness," *Tax & Budget Bulletin*, No. 47, CATO Institute, July 2007.

40. John Adams, letter to John Jay, London, September 23, 1787.

41. Merill Matthews Jr., "Obama: Campaigning Like It's 1936," Forbes.com, October 28, 2011.

42. Ibid.

43. Morgenthau Diary, May 9, 1939, Franklin Roosevelt Presidential Library.

44. Burton W. Folsom, Jr., *New Deal or Raw Deal?* 2008.

45. Steve R. Smith, "There is No Social Security Trust Fund," *The Augusta Chronicle*, October 2, 2011.

46. R. Jason Griffin, "The Individual Alternative Minimum Tax: Is it Touching People that it Shouldn't Be?" *Houston Business and Tax Law Journal*, 2004.

47. President John F. Kennedy, Inaugural Address, January 20, 1961.

48. President John F. Kennedy, president's news conference, November 20, 1962.

49. President John F. Kennedy, address to Congress, January 17, 1963.

50. Ronald Kessler, *Inside the White House*, 1996.
51. Jerome Korsi and Kenneth Blackwell, "Democrats' War on Poverty Has Failed," HumanEvents.com, September 6, 2006.
52. Benjamin Franklin, "On the Price of Corn and Management of the Poor," 1766.
53. Jacob Hornberger, "Let's Admit Enacting Medicare Was a Mistake," CampaignforLiberty.com, June 9, 2011; Ron Paul, during a CNN debate in Jacksonville, Fla., Jan. 26, 2012.
54. Affordable Care Act ("Obamacare), 2010.
55. The Dodd–Frank Wall Street Reform and Consumer Protection Act (Pub.L. 111-203, H.R. 4173), July 21, 2010.
56. Eric Golub, "Occupy Wall Street, Jon Corzine, and Other Failed Human Beings," *The Washington Times*, November 8, 2011; "No Worries for Dodd and Frank," FreeRepublic.com, December 8, 2011.
57. Stephen Dinan, "Govt. Sets Record Deficit in February," *The Washington Times*, March 8, 2012; Peter Suderman, "Congratulations, America, You're in Debt up to Your Eyeballs! U.S. Sets Monthly Budget Deficit Record," Reason.com, March 8, 2012.
58. Tiffany Gabbay, "Who Is Behind the 'US Day of Rage' to 'Occupy' Wall Street this September 17th?" TheBlaze.com, August 19, 2011; AskMarion.wordpress.com, "Fraud Exposed: 'Occupied Wall Street Journal' (Full-Color, Free Newspaper) Written by an Anarchist, Anti-Capitalism Group Funded by George Soros, the Tides Foundation, Code Pink and Michael Moore, Protestors Being Paid and...," October 11, 2011; Matt Kibbe, "Occupy Wall Street Is Certainly No Tea Party," Forbes.com, October 19, 2011.
59. Jim Treacher, TheDailyCaller.com, November 16, 2011.
60. Jennifer Rubin, "Occupy Wall Street: Does Anyone Care about the Anti-Semitism?" *The Washington Post*, October 17, 2011.
61. Michael Tanner, "The Real '1 percent,' Beyond the Class-War Myths," *New York Post*, November 7, 2011.
62. Matthew Continetti, "The Paranoid Style in Liberal Politics," *The Weekly Standard*, April 4, 2011.
63. Peter Schiff at Occupy Wall Street Protest in New York, Youtube.com, October 28, 2011.
64. Sabine Siebold, "Merkel Says German Multiculturalism Has Failed," Reuters, October 16, 2010; "British PM: Multiculturalism Has Failed," Europe on MSNBC.com, February 26, 2011; "Nicolas Sarkozy Joins David Cameron and Angela Merkel View that Multiculturalism Has

Failed," *The Daily Mail*, February 11, 2011.

65. Mark Steyn, *America Alone*, 2006.

66. Ibid.

67. Arcticstartup.com, "This Is Why I Don't Give You A Job," January 9, 2012.

68. Brie Hoffman, "Muslim World: How Muslims Will Take Over the World via Population Growth," brie-hoffman.hubpages.com, 2010.

Chapter 10

1. John Adams, in a letter to F. A. Vanderkemp, February 16, 1809, as quoted in *The Roots of American Order* by Russel Kirk, 1974.

2. Craig Winn, prophetofdoom.net, 2003. Most of the Islamic scripture contained herein was derived from the great meticulous work of Craig Winn in his "Prophet of Doom" (prophetofdoom.net), whose words best describe their true authenticity: The documented references [herein] in Prophet of Doom were derived from English translations of ancient Islamic manuscripts. While hundreds of scholars and researchers have written about Muhammad, his god Allah, and his religion Islam, only five sources can be considered prime, authentic, and to the extent possible, unbiased. All other writings present a cleric's or scholar's opinion, one drawn directly or indirectly from the original sources. So rather than study someone's interpretation of Muhammad, Allah, and Islam, read what Islam's lone prophet had to say about himself, his god, and his religion. If Muhammad got Islam wrong, no one has it right. And without Muhammad, there would be no Qur'an and no Islam. Allah would be completely unknown. The Sirat Rasul Allah was written by Ibn *Ishaq* in 750 A.D. It was edited and abridged by Ibn Hisham in 830 and translated by Alfred Guillaume under the title, *The Life of Muhammad* in 1955 by Oxford Press. Referred to as the Sira, or Biography, Ishaq's Hadith Collection consists of oral reports from Muhammad and his companions. It provides the only written account of Muhammad's life and the formation of Islam composed within two centuries of the prophet's death. There is no earlier or more accurate source. The History of al-*Tabari*, called the Ta'rikh, was written by Abu Muhammad bin al-Tabari between 870 and 920 A.D. His monumental work was translated and published in 1987 through 1997 by the State University of New York Press. I quote from volumes I, II, VI, VII, VIII, and IX. Tabari's History consists entirely of Islamic Hadith. It is

arranged chronologically. Tabari is Islam's oldest uncensored source. Al-Bukhari's Hadith, titled: *Sahih Al-Bukhari: The True Traditions*, was collected by Imam Bukhari in 850 A.D. I have used its original nomenclature because the only printed English translation (publisher: Maktaba, Dar-us-Salam, translator: Muhammad Khan) was abridged and erroneously numbered. Muslim was a student of Bukhari. His Hadith Collection was translated into English and is available online. Most Muslims consider their Hadith to be inspired scripture. They are arranged by topic. I have blended five *Qur'an* translations together to convey its message as clearly as possible: Ahmed Ali, Pikthal, Noble by Muhsin Khan, Yusuf Ali, and Shakir. The oldest Qur'an fragments date to 725 A.D., a century after they were recited. The Qur'an lacks organization and context, so it must be read in conjunction with the chronological Hadith Collections of Ishaq and Tabari.

3. Sabine Siebold, "Merkel Says German Multiculturalism Has Failed," Reuters, October 16, 2010; "British PM: Multiculturalism Has Failed," Europe on MSNBC.com, February 26, 2011; "Nicolas Sarkozy Joins David Cameron and Angela Merkel View that Multiculturalism Has Failed," *The Daily Mail*, February 11, 2011.

4. James Arlandson, "Top Ten Reasons Why Sharia is Bad for All Societies," *American Thinker*, April 13, 2005.

5. *Reliance of the Traveller*, Revised Edition, Amana Publications, 1997; answering-islam.org "Islamic Law on Female Circumcision," 2012; Raphael Shore and Alex Traiman, *Iranium*, the movie, 2010.

6. Gregory Davis, *Religion of Peace? Islam's War Against the World*, 2006.

7. Pejman Akbarzadeh, "Iran or Persia? Farsi or Persian?" Iran-Heritage.org, 2003.

8. Nazila Fathi, "Wipe Israel 'Off the Map' Iranian Says," *The New York Times*, October 27, 2005.

9. Interview with noted scholar Bernard Lewis in the movie *Iranium*. Raphael Shore and Alex Traiman, *Iranium*, the movie, 2010.

10. Gregory Davis, *Religion of Peace? Islam's War Against the World*, 2006.

11. Ali Sina, *Understanding Muhammad, a Psychobiography*, 2008.

12. NBC Chicago, "Obama Celebrates Ramadan, Calls Islam 'Great Religion,'" September 1, 2009.

13. Tom Baldwin, "President Obama's First Call 'was to President Abbas,'" Freerepublic.com, January 22, 2009; Mark Whittington, "Obama's Cairo Speech to Muslims; an Analysis" Yahoo.com, June 4, 2009;

"Obama's Speech in Cairo," *The Wall Street Journal*, June 4, 2009; Mona Charin, "NASA's Muslim Outreach," Real Clear Politics, July 7, 2010.

14. Clarice Feldman, "Obama Bows Down to Saudi King," *American Thinker*, April 2, 2009.

15. Steve Doughty, "Britain has 85 Sharia Courts: The Astonishing Spread of the Islamic Justice Behind Closed Doors," *The Daily Mail*, June 29, 2009; Rachel Ehrenfeld, "The Speech Act and the Islamic Agenda," American Center for Democracy, September 13, 2010.

16. Brigitte Gabriel, ACT! for America, 2012; Aylana Meisel, "Congress Unites to Pass Bill Protecting American Authors and Publishers," The Cutting Edge News.com, August 2, 2010.

17. Soeren Kern, "Caliphate Conference" Seeks to Islamize Europe, U.S.," Gatestone Institute, International Policy Council, February 21, 2012.

18. Rusty Weiss, "Hillary Clinton Claims Al-Jazeera Puts American Media to Shame," NewsBusters.com, March 2, 2011; Editor-in-Chief, "Islamic Governments Push for Speech Curbs in the U.S.," *The Illinois Conservative Examiner*, January 5, 2012.

19. Pamela Geller, "Obama Signs Bill Prohibiting Cooperation with Unindicted Co-Conspirators, Hamas-tied CAIR and ISNA," Atlas Shrugs2000.typepad.com, November 22, 2011.

20. "Holder Calls U.S. 'Nation of Cowards' on Race Matters," Associated Press, February 18, 2009.

21. Tiffany Gabbay, "Want to Know Just How Close the Muslim Brotherhood is to the Obama Admin?" The Blaze.com, April 26, 2012.

22. P. David Gaubatz, *Muslim Mafia: Inside the Secret Underworld that's Conspiring to Islamize America*, 2009.

23. Ibid.

24. U.S. Rep. Paul Brown (R-GA), October 15, 2009.

25. U.S. Rep. John Conyers (D-MI), chairman of the House Judiciary Committee, October 15, 2009.

26. Alan Kornman, "The Unholy Trinity: CAIR- Bassem Khafegi – The Muslim Brotherhood," FamilySecurityMatters.org, April 9, 2012.

27. Ibid.

28. Pamela Geller, "Lara Logan's Vicious, Violent Gang-Rape, Media's Silence=Sanction," Atlas Shrugs2000.typepad.com, February 9, 2011.

29. Richard Allen Greene, "Mohammed Tops List of English Baby Names," CNN World, October 28, 2010; Bruno Waterfield, "Mohammed is Most Popular Boy's Name in Four Biggest Dutch Cities," *The*

Telegraph, August 13, 2009.

30. Claire Reitz, "No-Go Zones for Non-Muslims Multiplying All Over Europe," Technorati.com, September 20, 2011.

31. Dale Hurd, "Belgistan? Sharia Showdown Looms in Brussels," CBN News, March 17, 2012.

32. Claire Reitz, "No-Go Zones for Non-Muslims Multiplying All Over Europe," Technorati.com, September 20, 2011; Dale Hurd, "Belgistan? Sharia Showdown Looms in Brussels," CBN News, March 17, 2012; Steven Erlanger, "Amid Rise of Multiculturalism, Dutch Confront Their Questions of Identity," *The New York Times,* August 13, 2011; John Hooper, "Sun, Sea and Sharia on Women-Only Italian Beach," *The Guardian,* August 3, 2006.

33. Wayne Kopping and Raphael Shore, *Obsession,* the movie, 2005; Mark Steyn, *America Alone,* 2006; Brie Hoffman, *Muslim World: How Muslims Will Take over the World via Population Growth,* brie-hoffman.hubpages.com, 2010.

34. Brigitte Gabrielle, *Because They Hate,* 2006.

35. Balfour Declaration, November 2, 1917.

36. League of Nations mandate, Mandate for Palestine, July 24, 1922.

37. www.kinghussein.gov.

38. Benjamin Netanyahu, *A Place Among Nations,* 1993.

39. Ibid.

40. United Nations General Assembly Resolution 181, November 29, 1947.

41. Ibid.

42. Benjamin Netanyahu, *A Place Among Nations,* 1993.

43. Brigitte Gabrielle, *Because They Hate,* 2006.

44. Benjamin Netanyahu, *A Place Among Nations,* 1993.

45. Id at p79.

46. Id at p132.

47. Id.

48. Id.

49. Brigitte Gabrielle, *Because They Hate,* 2006.

50. Ibid.

51. Ibid.

52. The Yom-Kippur War, 1973.

53. "Modern Israeli inventions," Inreview.com, March 21, 2006.

54. Israeli Prime Minister Yitzhak Rabin, U.S. President Bill Clinton, and PLO Chairman Yasser Arafat signed the Oslo Accords in Washington, D.C., on the White House lawn, September 13, 1993.

55. David Meir-Levi Bio, "Toxic Taqiyya," FrontPagemag.com, January 13, 2012.

56. Ibid.

57. Ibid.

58. Kenneth Levin, *The Oslo Syndrome, Delusions of a People Under Siege,* 2005.

59. Ibid.

60. Ephraim Karsh, *Arafat's War,* 2003.

61. Richard Hernnstein and Charles Murray, *The Bell Curve: Intelligence and Class Structure in American Life,* 1994.

62. Leviticus 19:16.

63. Dan Senor and Saul Singer, *Start-Up Nation,* 2009.

64. "Modern Israeli inventions," Inreview.com, March 21, 2006.

65. Raphael Shore and Wayne Kopping, *Israel Inside,* the movie, 2011.

66. Dan Senor and Saul Singer, *Start-Up Nation,* 2009.

67. PA TV, January 24, 2012.

68. Matthias Küntzel, *Ahmadinejad's World,* Cited in Baham Nirumand, Krieg, Krieg, bis zum Sieg, in: Anja Malanowski und Marianne Stern, Iran-Irak. Bis die Gottlosen vernichtet sind', Reinbek (Rowohlt) 1987, p. 95-6, July, 30, 2006.

69. Ibid.

70. Golda Meir, 1957.

Conclusion

1. Napoleon Hill, *Think and Grow Rich,* 1937.

www.ingramcontent.com/pod-product-compliance
Lightning Source LLC
Chambersburg PA
CBHW031946090426

42739CB00006B/111